D1165547

AMERICANS FIRST

Americans First

Chinese Americans and the Second World War

K. SCOTT WONG

HARVARD UNIVERSITY PRESS
Cambridge, Massachusetts
London, England
2005

Printed in the United States of America

Library of Congress Cataloging-in-Publication Data

Wong, Kevin Scott.
Americans first : Chinese Americans and the Second World War / K. Scott Wong.
p. cm.
Includes bibliographical references and index.
ISBN 0-674-01671-8
1. Chinese Americans—Social conditions—20th century. 2. Chinese Americans—Ethnic identity. 3. Chinese Americans—Cultural assimilation. 4. United States. Army Air Forces. Air Service Group, 14th. 5. World War, 1939–1945—Participation, Chinese American. 6. World War, 1939–1945—United States. 7. World War, 1939–1945—Social aspects. 8. United States—Ethnic relations. I. Title.

E184.C5W65 2005
940.54′089′951073—dc22 2004059790

For Carrie and Sarah
with love and gratitude

Contents

Others [Caucasian veterans] always look back, like the war was the best thing. We always look ahead because we had been through the grind of prejudice. Now there is hope and opportunity that there wasn't before.

—Harry Lim, a veteran of the 407th Air Service Squadron

AMERICANS FIRST

Introduction

Soon after my parents married in 1943 in Philadelphia's Chinatown, they left for Camp Breckinridge, Kentucky, where my father, Henry Wong, was stationed as a second lieutenant in the army air force, one of the more than twelve thousand Chinese Americans who served in the U.S. armed forces during the Second World War. He soon received his orders for overseas duty and spent the rest of the war in the Third Air Cargo Resupply Squadron under the umbrella of the Fourteenth Air Force, flying in a C-46 airdropping supplies to American and Chinese troops in southwest China. When he departed for China, my mother, Mary (née Lee), returned to Philadelphia and lived with her in-laws. My parents' first child was born during this period, and my father would not meet his firstborn son for seventeen months.

Before the war, my parents were among a small number of American-born Chinese in their community. My paternal grandparents were unusual for their time. Wong Wah Ding, a native of China, was married to Emma, an immigrant from Czechoslovakia. They lived in Philadelphia Chinatown, and my grandfather, a merchant and herbalist, was considered its unofficial mayor for much of the 1940s and 1950s. They raised their only child in an English-speaking household as it was the common language between them. My mother, in contrast, spent her early years in Salem, New Jersey, living atop the family laundry with her parents and six siblings, speaking mostly Chinese until she entered school. After her father, Kew Lee, passed away, her mother, Anne Lee, moved the family to Philadelphia and raised the children in Chinatown as a single mother. It was there that my parents met as teenagers and later married.

My grandparents belonged to the Chinese immigrant generation that suffered the pain and difficulties of exclusion policies. Families had been separated, relegating many men to lives akin to bachelorhood as immigration laws prohibited their wives from joining them. Thousands of "paper sons" had entered the country under assumed identities to find work and a means of survival. Despite the barriers and hardships, these immigrants gradually gave birth to a generation of Chinese American children that came of age as the United States was entering the Second World War.

In the years leading up to U.S. involvement in the war, many first- and second-generation Chinese Americans struggled to find acceptance in the wider society. Those with college degrees had difficulty finding jobs outside the Chinatown economy, and some even looked to China for possible employment. However, most American-born Chinese realized that their futures would unfold in the United States. While many received some kind of instruction in the Chinese language and spoke Chinese to their parents and peers, this generation was primarily English-speaking and American in outlook, having been educated in American schools. These Chinese Americans, while acknowledging their heritage and their familial ties to China, sought to carve out a legitimate position in American society and to be accepted as equals of all other Americans.

For Asian Americans, the generational conflicts common to many immigrant groups were exacerbated by U.S. immigration and citizenship policies. Immigrants from Asia were ineligible for citizenship by law. As their American-born children sought acceptance in the broader society, the worldviews of parents and children often diverged. Many parents were unsure whether their futures would lie in America or in Asia, and the children, though citizens, were often unable to safeguard their own rights in the land of their birth. These conflicts were most obvious for Japanese Americans during the war in which Japan was an enemy. They were forced into concentration camps despite the fact that two-thirds of them were American citizens by birth. Because of their internment and the attending issues concerning citizenship, racism, and the magnitude of the national crisis, the wartime experience of Japanese Americans has dominated the study of the impact of the war on Asian American communities. Most research on the war has focused on the hardships of internment and/or the military heroics of the Japanese American 442nd Regimental Combat Team and 100th Battalion. This almost exclusive focus on one group has narrowed the subsequent memory of the war to a bipolar discourse of injustice and achievement, ignoring the complex experiences of other groups of Asian Americans during this period of American social transformation.[1]

Until recently, the Chinese Americans born in the 1910s and 1920s have not received the same sustained scholarly interest as earlier and later cohorts.[2] Many researchers have focused on uncovering the racist past of Asian American history and championing resistance to oppression. The generation born in the 1920s, many of whom by the late 1960s were well established in the American middle class, have been seen by some scholars as assimilationists and therefore as less relevant or less heroic than earlier railroad workers or later-born internees. It is as though scholars of Chinese America had created their own version of the famous observation by Marcus Lee Hansen: "What the son wishes to forget the grandson wishes to remember." In the case of Chinese American studies, the grandchildren have tended to valorize their grandfathers and grandmothers while dismissing their fathers and mothers. But, as the historian David Yoo has argued, this tendency "has meant that many scholars have missed the opportunity to explore how identity formation developed in the lives of second-generation immigrants."[3] This book is an attempt to explore just that: the identity formation of Chinese Americans, particularly the second generation, as it developed and changed in the unique circumstances of the Second World War.

A perusal of books on the war and the years immediately after yields few references to Chinese American military personnel, defense industry workers, relief efforts, or even the repeal of the Chinese Exclusion Acts. And yet Chinese Americans contributed to all aspects of the war effort and suffered and benefited as much as anyone from the deprivations and changes wrought by the war. One slogan on a recruiting poster for the Women's Army Corps could easily apply to Chinese Americans as well: "I'M IN THIS WAR TOO!"

Although I speak Mandarin Chinese (not of great use when trying to interview Cantonese speakers) and can read Chinese, I decided to conduct the interviews for this book in English and to consult mostly English-language sources. The second generation was most comfortable speaking English and received most of its information from the English-language press, not from Chinese-language newspapers. Furthermore, this cohort produced a large body of written sources. They were consciously reflective on the social changes they were experiencing. Now, fifty years later, they are eager to share their thoughts on their lives as second-generation Chinese Americans. In writing about these men and women I have attempted to place their voices at center stage. The story they tell is one of struggle and success: of the ways they supported the U.S. war effort while also aiding China; of the different racial cultures of Hawai'i and the mainland United States; of the soldiers and officers who served in the U.S. military, including the all–Chinese American 14th Air Service Group and 987th Signal Company; of racial segregation and ethnic pride; of American nationalism and Chinese American patriotism.

I

Chinese America before the War

When the United States entered the Second World War in late 1941, Chinese immigrants had been present in the country for nearly a hundred years. However, because of restrictive immigration legislation, anti-Chinese sentiment, residential and occupational segregation, and language and cultural barriers, Chinese Americans remained marginalized in U.S. society. Long considered "perpetually foreign" and inassimilable, many Chinese Americans, in the mid-twentieth century, lived in segregated urban communities, often isolated from mainstream American life.

Although there is evidence that the first Chinese to arrive in the United States landed on the East Coast as a result of Sino-American trade in the eighteenth century, Chinese began entering the country in appreciable numbers soon after gold was discovered in California in 1848. The immigrants were drawn to America because of declining fortunes in China caused by internal disorder, overpopulation, poverty, and Western imperialism, along with the prospect of riches in California's Mother Lode or better wages in America's agricultural sector, small businesses, light manufacturing, or railroad construction. Not long after their arrival in California, however, the Chinese became targets for white Americans' racial antagonisms and economic insecurities. They found themselves restricted by law from intermarrying with whites, forbidden to engage in certain occupations or live in certain areas, denied the opportunity to become citizens and the right to testify for or against whites in courts of law, and subject to fines and fees not levied against other immigrants or racial groups. They were also victims of frequent and large-scale physical violence and intimidation. As a result, they tended to live in close proximity to one another as much for mutual protection as for cultural familiarity.[1]

Chinese American urban communities, better known as Chinatowns, had long been under siege, and San Francisco Chinatown, historically the major settlement of Chinese in the United States, was a key site of the anti-Chinese movement. In 1876 San Francisco hosted federal hearings on Chinese immigration. By that time there was a history of anti-Chinese activity in the city, especially in the form of organizations such as the Workingmen's Party led by Denis Kearney. Kearney's shout at the end of his sandlot speeches—"The Chinese Must Go!"—became the slogan of the anti-Chinese movement. Many viewed Chinatown as an immoral, vice-infested district and the Chinese as mysterious people who could never become "true Americans." One witness at the federal hearings on immigration had this to say about the Chinese community in San Francisco: "An indigestible mass in the community, distinct in language, pagan in religion, inferior in mental and moral qualities, and all peculiarities, is an undesirable element in a republic, but becomes especially so if political power is placed in its hands."[2] The term "Chinatown" was often used in a demeaning manner to elicit images of filth, mystery, crime, disease, and moral depravity. These images became almost generic descriptions for any Chinese immigrant or Chinese American community, giving the impression that all "Chinatowns" were alike. Chinese immigrants often referred to their communities as *tang-ren-jie* (streets of the men of Tang) and more recently as *Hua-bi* (Chinese district), but "Chinatown" became the term most commonly used by Chinese Americans as well as the general public.

The first Chinese Exclusion Act, passed in 1882, prohibited the immigration of Chinese laborers for ten years and declared that Chinese immigrants were ineligible for citizenship. This was the first U.S. immigration law that specifically barred a group of people on the basis of race and class. Those Chinese allowed to enter the United States were of the so-called exempt classes, which included merchants, teachers, students, diplomats, and tourists. Over the next twenty-two years, the original exclusion legislation was repeatedly extended and strengthened. Measures passed in 1888, 1892, 1894, 1902, and 1904 expanded the definition of laborers and narrowed the definition of merchants. These acts dramatically reduced the number of Chinese entering the country.[3]

The exclusionary laws created a strong motivation for illegal immigration, and one feature of U.S. law facilitated it. American-born children of immigrants were U.S. citizens, and children born to a U.S. citizen, whether born in America or not, were also citizens. Thus if Chinese Americans who were citizens could prove that they had children in China, the children would be able to join the parents in America. This led to the development of what came to be called "paper sons": the practice of claiming fictional offspring. After the 1906 earthquake, which destroyed the immigration records in San Francisco, this ploy became especially common. The "parents" would have someone draw up false papers documenting the lives and identities of these children, and the papers would be sold to people in China who could pass for the children. The purchaser would memorize his "paper life" and then attempt to enter the United States posing as the child of a citizen.

Many Americans believed that most Chinese who arrived in the country were entering illegally as such paper sons. San Francisco continued to be the major port of disembarkation for immigrants from China, and the Angel Island Immigration Station, situated in San Francisco Bay and in operation from 1910 to 1940, was the first American site where many Chinese encountered extreme hostility. Thousands were detained at Angel Island, sometimes for over a year, before they were allowed to immigrate. The validity of each would-be immigrant's story was determined by a series of tedious interviews involving verification by witnesses. These interviews were the reason for the long detentions on Angel Island. In spite of these rigors, the majority of those seeking entry into the United States were eventually admitted: in some years the rate was as high as 97 percent. Many who were admitted, after their terrifying experience on Angel Island, immediately sought refuge in San Francisco Chinatown or another U.S. Chinatown.[4]

Negative imagery, language and cultural differences, the fear of illegal immigration, and hostile racism kept many prewar Chinese Americans confined to Chinatown, unable to find jobs or homes elsewhere, and therefore distant from the broader American experience. For this reason, in the 1930s and early 1940s, the residents of Chinatown, especially merchants and members of the political elite, worked hard to transform Chinatown from its old image of a mysterious ethnic enclave into a tourist-friendly attraction with an economy based on restaurants and curio shops.[5]

Social Boundaries

San Francisco Chinatown was the cultural heartland of Chinese America. It was the national headquarters of the Chinese Consolidated Benevolent Association (also known as the CCBA or the Chinese Six Companies), an organization that oversaw relations between Chinese fraternal associations and often fought for civil rights causes on behalf of the Chinese in America. The community supported a number of daily and weekly publications, in both Chinese and English, and was generally regarded as the premier Chinese American community in the nation, followed by that in New York.[6] Despite the rigors of the Chinese exclusion acts and the long-term detentions on Angel Island, a steady stream of Chinese immigrants continued to bring new life into San Francisco. By the Second World War, a distinctively Chinese American culture had developed in San Francisco, a culture that was shaped by the residents' relationship to China and its role in the politics of Asia, their often hostile relationship with white America, and the coming of age of a second generation of American-born Chinese who were struggling to define their place in society.

As a result of various exclusion laws and cultural deterrents, far fewer Chinese women than men immigrated. Chinese women, if single, did not venture overseas alone, and if married, were expected to stay in China and care for their in-laws. Furthermore, since many male emigrants assumed they would return to the home village with the financial fruits of their labors, their wives endured long separations in anticipation of their return. With the passage of anti-miscegenation laws in California and other western states that specifically prohibited intermarriage between Chinese and whites, many men could not find mates, and the development of Chinese American families was severely stunted.

It was not until the mid-1930s that Chinese America finally achieved a sizable adult second generation.[7] These men and women, American-born and thus U.S. citizens, often found themselves caught between their loyalty to and identification with Chinese culture and tradition and their desire to be fully accepted in American society. Because of the difficulty in finding jobs outside Chinatown, many Chinese Americans came to believe that their futures would be more secure in China than in America. It was not uncommon for families to send their children, especially sons, to China for part of their education so that they could perfect their use of the Chinese language, learn Chinese culture, cultivate professional contacts, and perhaps meet a future spouse. This was true not only in larger Chinese American communities such as San Francisco but across the country, including Hawai'i. For example, William Seam Wong and Joseph Yuu of Boston Chinatown went to China to receive a Chinese education. Wong, born in 1920, traveled to China with his mother in 1931 and stayed until the Japanese tightened their hold on that country in 1937. Yuu went to China with his family in 1927 and returned to the United States in 1935. Wong and Yuu, who had been born in the United States and were thus American citizens, had no trouble leaving and reentering the country.[8]

But for many of the second generation, especially those old enough to be worried about careers, the choice between remaining in America and trying their luck in China was fraught with conflict and ambivalence. The tension between the desire to claim a place in America and the feeling that one could have a more promising future in China found expression in a now-famous essay contest of 1936 sponsored by the Ging Hawk Club of New York. The essay topic was "Does My Future Lie in China or America?" The first- and second-place essays appeared in the *Chinese Digest,* a Chinese American periodical published in San Francisco under the editorship of Thomas Chinn. The winner, Robert Dunn from Somerville, Massachusetts, a student at Harvard University, placed his future in America, maintaining that one could serve China "by building up a good impression of the Chinese among Americans, by spreading good-will and clearing up misunderstandings, by interesting the Americans in the Chinese thru personal contacts and otherwise, and, if necessary, by contributing generously to the financing of worthy enterprises in China." He stated that he preferred American social values, asserting that his Chinese relatives "pour contempt upon religion, especially upon Christianity, and fail to see the preciousness and value of the individual life. This culture and attitude is contrary to mine, and I fear that I shall be unhappy in the process of yielding to it." He concluded that "[I] owe America as much allegiance as I do China; that it is possible to serve China while living in America; that remunerative employment, though scarce, is not impossible to obtain in either China or America; and [that] I would avoid the unhappiness and social estrangement due to conflicting cultures by staying in America."[9]

The second-place winner took the opposite position. Kaye Hong, a resident of San Francisco, focused much of his essay on the restrictions placed on Chinese Americans by American racism. He lamented: "I have learned to acknowledge that the better jobs are not available to me and that the advancement of my career is consequently limited in this fair land." Hong rejected the rhetoric on which many Chinese in America relied, which stressed the past accomplishments of Chinese civilization: "The ridicule heaped upon the Chinese race has long fermented in my soul. I have concluded that we, the younger generation, have nothing to be proud of except the time-worn accomplishments of our ancient ancestors, that we have been living in the shadow of these glories, hoping that these arts and literature of the past will justify our present. Sad but true, they do not. To live under such illusions is to lead the life of a parasite."[10] Returning to China, Hong proposed, would allow him to serve China by aiding in its modernization, for only a modern China would garner the respect of the world. This sentiment had been prevalent among Chinese since they began immigrating to the United States. Many believed that a stronger Chinese government would be able to improve the position and treatment of Chinese in America. Unfortunately, this was not necessarily the case.

Dunn's essay drew a heated response from some readers of the *Chinese Digest*. Members of the Chinese Students' Club at Stanford University replied with a scathing letter that informed Dunn: "Your fallacies in reasoning, your ignorance of China's needs, your misconceptions of Chinese culture and civilization, your biased viewpoint, all reveal how poorly qualified you were to correctly evaluate the factors involved in this great problem that confronts the second-generation Chinese in America." They called Dunn's position "pathetic and misleading." Pointing out that their group consisted of both Chinese-born and American-born students, they chided Dunn for his characterization of China as backward and for seeing "our problem through the eyes of an unsympathetic American who has never lived in China. You judge China by American standards—political, economic, and moral." They then revealed their class and regional biases by stating: "We have reason to believe that your contacts have been restricted to Cantonese, who are by no means representative of the whole of China's people. Because some of these contacts have conflicted with your American sensibilities, you have associated the Chinese with unpleasant things." Since the majority of the Chinese in the United States at that time were Cantonese of the urban working and merchant classes, in implying that the Cantonese were the Chinese from whom Dunn felt alienated, the Stanford students were actually attempting to distance themselves from the Cantonese and from the culture that had developed in American Chinatowns. This letter, written by university students who probably came from more affluent backgrounds than most residents of Chinatown, speaks to conflicts within the Chinese American population. Class tensions and regionalism, factors that had separated Chinese in China, manifested themselves in America as well.[11]

The Stanford students did bring up an issue that was important to many Chinese Americans in the prewar years. Dunn had written in his essay: "It is evident, then, that employment is hard to get anywhere; in America, perhaps because of the color line; in China because jobs are scarce. The color line, however, does not entirely prevent the American-born Chinese from getting jobs." The students very pointedly countered:

> Our observation has shown us that such belief is fantastically erroneous. Given two college students of equal ability and training, one a Chinese and the other an American, can you unblushingly lead us to believe that the Chinese has an equal chance against American competition? What fanciful illusions of equality were you dreaming about when you tell us that "the color line, however, does not entirely prevent the American-born Chinese from getting jobs." If not the "color line"—the racial prejudice—what is keeping Chinese out of American industries and governmental offices? Surely not the lack of ability.

The belief that racism was preventing Chinese Americans from advancing in society would find expression time and again, especially among those of the second generation.[12]

The two essays by Dunn and Hong and the responses capture some of the cultural tension faced by the second generation. Unable to find meaningful employment outside Chinatowns, some looked to China for economic opportunity plus a chance to serve China. Others were more optimistic about their chances in America and acknowledged a distance from Chinese culture. In truth, most Chinese Americans in the 1930s chose to cast their lot with America. Born and educated in the United States, they were swept up in a Chinese American existence and tried their best to find good jobs and lead productive, if restricted, lives. As the political situation in China became increasingly unstable, traveling to China and finding work there became less feasible. In fact, Robert Dunn, whose essay indicated that he would stay in America, went to China before the war and worked there for a number of years, in the Chinese civil service and later for the Chinese delegation to the United Nations. After returning to the United States he worked in the Asian division of the Library of Congress until his retirement. While in China he began using his full name: Robert Dunn Wu. Kaye Hong, in contrast, despite his criticisms, remained in the United States and did not go to China until it opened to tourism in the 1980s.[13]

While working in China, Wu began writing a column for the *Chinese News,* a paper founded by Thomas Chinn after his *Chinese Digest* folded.[14] Wu's first article was entitled "Robert Dunn Wu Writes from Chungking." The editorial note introduced him as the first-prize winner of the essay contest, explained that he had gone to Hong Kong and was now living in Chungking (Chongqing) working for the Chinese ministry of affairs. Wu wrote: "The urge to set foot on Free China soil had kidnapped me. I could not resist." This article focused mainly on the hardships of living in war-torn Chongqing and the difficulties of making ends meet in a declining economy. In later issues Wu appeared regularly, writing a column called "Chungking Chatter." In these columns the editorial note claimed that "his writings besides being informative are indicative of the philosophy of China's millions." By this point Wu had come to identify with the Chinese among whom he lived. In spite of frequent bombings by the Japanese, he declared: "With food in our stomachs, we can carry on this war indefinitely." Life in China during the war brought Wu's Chinese patriotism to the fore, and he conveyed it to Chinese Americans through his columns, arousing their sympathies and awareness of China's plight.[15]

Another young man who went to China during this period was John Jan. Described as "a former Sacramento boy who received his B.S. degree in mining engineering at the University of California in 1933," Jan arrived in China in the autumn of 1940 and found work with the Chinese Industrial Cooperative as a mining engineer. He wrote:

> Boy, am I glad I came back! . . . The people I work with and have met are all tops. Here, at least, the attitude toward *Wah kius* [American-born Chinese] is not as have been described. This is a new generation! Fellows from 16 to 30 years old. All honest and willing and able to do the right thing. Among them are graduates of Sun Yat-sen University, wounded ex-soldiers, and just young fellows who see eye to eye with us. I've been welcomed sincerely by them. It has helped their morale to see that there are *Wah kius* who also love China enough to go back and work for it—who can bring them the news that the other *Wah kius* are all for China . . . My salary to start with is low but I can live on it. And by my work I'm helping lick the Japs.[16]

Wu's column and Jan's letter indicate that there were indeed a number of Chinese Americans who found a meaningful existence and work in China, despite some ambivalence and tension concerning their prospects and how they might be received by the Chinese. China was besieged by Japan and those with patriotic feelings saw their time in China as aiding the country while reinforcing their ties to the land of their parents.

In the same year as the Ging Hawk Club essay contest, 1936, Grace W. Wang, a speaker for the New York–based Chinese Women's Association, delivered a speech on the state of second-generation Chinese Americans. She echoed many of the concerns about racism raised by the students from Stanford University. She began by stressing that Chinese Americans were not very different from other Americans, pointing out that "the notorious movie character, Dr. Fu Manchu, is indeed a rare specimen among my countrymen, if ever there was any such creature." Wang went on to describe realities of Chinese American life—the common scene in American public schools, where Chinese American children would pledge allegiance to the flag, study history and geography, "determined to absorb the knowledge that would one day make them responsible citizens of their adopted land." However, she noted, many of these children would not be able to continue their education after grammar school because they would be needed in their parents' stores, restaurants, and laundries. Some would be able to finish high school, but only a few would even consider going to college, and these would be considered the "cream of Second Generation Chinese."[17]

Even with a college degree, Wang argued, a Chinese American faced limited possibilities. Chinatowns could support only a small number of professionals, and smaller Chinese American communities, such as the one in Boston, could support even fewer than those in San Francisco or New York. Thus a Chinese

American would be forced to seek employment outside the community, and Wang saw little chance for success. "The minute that the Chinese college graduate leaves his racial group to seek a position elsewhere marks his introduction into a world of professional rivalry, racial antagonism, petty jealousy and social maneuvering." She then offered a scenario that today would be termed an example of the "glass ceiling" which is often constructed by race, gender biases, and nepotism:

> He goes perchance into a well-established organization, believing that he is on his way to success. He works harder than most of his American colleagues and he tries to be more accurate, more painstaking, more industrious. He attracts the attention of one or two men on the staff. They notice his standard of production and plan to promote him. But circumstances intervene. The Vice-president has a son just out of college whom he would like to place. As a result, the Chinese, who has been promised advancement, is shoved aside and forgotten.[18]

To lend credence to her argument, Wang offered five cases in which similar developments unfolded: a draftsman passed over for promotion for nine years though he had more education than those promoted; an MIT-trained engineer who could only find work as a salesman for a Jewish meatpacking concern, taking orders from Chinese restaurants and stores; a Master of Arts recipient who could not purchase a home on Long Island because of his skin color; another college graduate who could only find work as a clerk in a Chinatown bazaar; and a graduate of medical school who had trouble finding an internship because of the racial attitudes of the patients. Wang pointed out that Chinese American women fared as poorly as men in the public sphere. "There is one Chinese girl reporter in the West, one movie star in Hollywood, a few successful private secretaries, one public school teacher, one restaurant manager, a few banking clerks, one magazine and feature writer, several well known club leaders and church workers, that's about all."[19]

Wang wondered if the prize was worth the struggle. She concluded her speech with a pessimism that appears to have been present among many of the second generation: "With thousands of fair-haired, blue-eyed collegians at his elbows looking for jobs, and thousands of others looking for a raise, ready to take his place the moment he slips, is there any chance for a person with a darker complexion to succeed in an Anglo-Saxon country? . . . It is often said that people are all born free and equal and that one day we shall all become part of one universal brotherhood, having equal rights and opportunity. Will that day of Utopia ever arrive? On this last question, most of my American-born Chinese friends entertain grave doubts."[20]

Five years later, in 1941, these sentiments remained. William Hoy, a columnist for the *California Chinese Press,* explored "the second-generation problem" with reference to a speech by a college student, Maxine Chinn, which was printed in the same issue. Hoy wrote: "Throughout the past two decades articulate members among the American-born Chinese have occasionally raised their voices in protest, in anger, and in rebellion against the unendurable social and economic conditions of which they are helpless victims." He made it clear that even with the impediments to social mobility faced by the second generation, which he saw as racism, and the notion that Chinese Americans were foreigners, their future was not in China but in the United States. He continued:

> Growing up in an era of social ferment in America and the cutting loose of old cultural ties with a civilization of which

> they have little or no knowledge, the second generation found themselves alienated from the older generation of their own people by lack of understanding, and yet not accepted by the Americans of other racial stocks, particularly those of Anglo-Saxon strains. The thesis of these occasional outbursts usually follow the same general pattern of thinking: that being born, reared and educated in this land we are Americans in name and in fact: that we belong to this country and not to China; but that we are treated nevertheless as foreigners still.[21]

Maxine Chinn, a student at Oregon State College, had delivered the speech at a forensics competition at which the topic was "We Who Are Without a Country." After referring to Philip Nolan, the protagonist of Edward Everett Hale's story "The Man Without a Country," she declared: "Born of Oriental parents, but reared in an American environment, and educated in the American way, while at the same time retaining many of our Oriental characteristics and culture, our position, indeed, is a difficult one. We are neither wholly American or completely Oriental, but a coalition of the two. East is East, and West is West, but in us the twain have met." Seeing Chinese American youth as "without a country," Chinn reflected a change in attitude from those who sought their salvation in "returning" to China. Instead, she saw going to China as potentially disillusioning. "Because of our Occidental ways, if we return to China, we are looked upon as foreigners. There we are handicapped, since we neither speak real Chinese nor know modern Chinese culture . . . Then, too, our roots are here in America. We know no other home, so have no desire to transplant ourselves to an entirely new and different environment." But their acceptance in America was also unlikely:

> In the United States, likewise, we are regarded as foreigners; because of the color of our skin we bear a double yoke. Because our parents and grandparents were ground into the depths of degradation by fear and intolerance, many of the younger Chinese have grown up fearing the white man, and allow themselves to be beaten into feeling inferior—so much so, that the majority of them cringe and creep back further into the black depths of Chinatown, afraid to come out and prove [they] can be a desirable element of American society.[22]

An important consequence of this retreat into Chinatown was the relatively low numbers of Chinese Americans pursuing higher education. According to Chinn, only 210 Chinese Americans (out of almost 14,000) in the cities of San Francisco, Portland, and Seattle were enrolled in college. She pointed out that these low numbers did not reflect a lack of ambition, but rather a realization that a college education would not guarantee gainful employment. Instead, Chinese Americans were "doomed to Chinatown . . . [with its] crowded conditions, rooms with insufficient light, little electricity, ancient plumbing, and utter lack of proper sanitary facilities."

Chinn did not blame this situation on Chinese American community or culture, but placed the onus on white Americans to see Chinese Americans as their equals:

> Our primary thought is to cut loose the bonds that hold us to the mode of living that has characterized our people for generations; to have the chance to demonstrate that we are capable of taking our place along with you in the classrooms and prove that we can be as good citizens as you. But what chance have we when no matter in which

> direction we turn we are stymied by prejudice and intolerance? There is no turning for us except to go back to Chinatown and become the little yellow people who roll the dice, deal the cards, mark the lottery tickets, serve the chow mien and noodles, occasionally do the laundry, and continue kowtowing to the Americans!

At the end of her speech Chinn called for a shared effort by whites and Chinese Americans to broaden their idea of what it meant to be an American. "We do not want nor expect you to take us to your hearts as members of your own family or your own social set. We want only to be accepted as Americans and to be able to enjoy the privileges of Americans. We do not want to be an outside group looking in." Chinn's speech revealed the sentiments of many Chinese Americans. They were not satisfied with the restricted lives within Chinatown, but they did not see China as a viable alternative nor were they seeking a false security in full-scale assimilation into white American society. They simply wanted to be considered as "American" as anyone else, which required expansion of the concept of "American" to include nonwhite minorities.

Hemmed in by racial antagonism, many second-generation Chinese Americans felt alienated from much of American society. They often referred to themselves as "Chinese" and to whites as "Americans," even though they too were American citizens. They were made to feel "less American" than whites and were therefore less certain as to where to place their loyalty. As they continued to seek their place in American society, however, they steadily developed a consciousness that acknowledged their Chinese heritage and the culture of their parents, but that would come to full flower as "Chinese American."[23]

Chinese Americans were not alone in recognizing their limited opportunities. In April 1941 the *Chinese News* reprinted an article from the *Christian Science Monitor* entitled "Crisis in Chinatown," by Nate R. White. White wrote: "The heart of Chinatown is frustrated, perplexed, discontented, restless. It represents a melting pot which has in the American slang of saying things, 'let the people down.'" White offered an explanation for this situation:

> The problem is simply this: the Chinese are not preferred. Even though they hold a Master's degree or a Doctor's degree from our best universities, they are not wanted. Even though they can wear a Phi Beta Kappa key with pride, there is still no place for them. Even though the Nation is crying for skilled workers; even though the California aircraft industry has combed the San Francisco market for skilled and semi-skilled workers, university-trained Chinese are passed by. Instead of applying their talents for which they have been trained, they are washing dishes, carrying trays, ironing shirts, cutting meat, drying fish, selling herbs. There are today 400 to 500 skilled and semi-skilled Chinese in California without jobs.

White realized that while some Chinese Americans sought their fortunes in China, most did not choose that alternative: "Third and fourth-generation Chinese boys and girls do not want to go back to China. They are Americans. They love America. Their roots are here."[24]

Although sympathetic to Chinese Americans, White warned that high unemployment among their youth could have detrimental social effects. The earlier generation had "endured hardship, racial persecution, social degradation, without complaint outwardly, without uprising, without inefficiency . . . Those early Chinese were reared in the old-China tradition of perseverance." However, the "second, third, and fourth generations in America are raised in the typically American tradition of better standards, better accomplishments, better education, better jobs. Their patience, while at present restrained by their mood of discouragement and frustration, may break." He saw the real danger of this situation in the possibility that Chinese Americans might pose a problem similar to that of African Americans: "The seriousness of the matter must not be underrated. It is as serious in California, where there are thousands of Chinese, as in the Negro question in some sections of the country." But he quickly drew a distinction between the two "problems": "The Chinese problem is one primarily affecting large cities, especially San Francisco. The Negro problem in the Southern States is, in the main, one of agriculture. There are differences in tastes and standards." In the end, White redeemed the Chinese because of their family values: "It is a tribute, a deep and sincere tribute, to the Chinese character that despite all these things, all these discouraging factors in their American homeland, Chinese family life still holds together."[25] This perception of Chinese American familial bonds would play a role during the Second World War in changing the image of Chinese Americans, an image that would crystallize nearly three decades later when Asian Americans would be seen as the "model minority."

The Chinese American Periodical Press

The *Chinese Digest,* in which the Ging Hawk essays and letters and Grace Wang's speech were published, was the first newspaper published in English that was specifically directed toward American-born Chinese. Although there were a number of Chinese-language newspapers available, most American-born Chinese did not read or write Chinese well enough to be able to read them. According to Dorothy Eng of Oakland, "Our generation couldn't read or write Chinese." They spoke English among themselves, as it "was faster thinking in English. By the time you could figure the Chinese, the person had left." Mary Wong of Philadelphia echoed this position: "Our parents spoke Chinese and we would usually answer them in Chinese, or the parents of our friends. But among ourselves, my brothers and sisters, and friends, we only spoke English to each other." Thus the *Chinese Digest* filled an important need.[26]

Founded in San Francisco in 1935 by Thomas Chinn and Chingwah Lee, the *Digest* was published as a weekly, and later a monthly, until 1939, then published irregularly until it folded in 1940. Thomas Chinn, born in Oregon in 1909 to immigrant parents who moved to San Francisco Chinatown in 1919, was committed to the idea that Chinese Americans should leave their ethnic enclaves and adapt more readily to American society. He came to believe that a publication in English devoted to second-generation Chinese American concerns would facilitate that transition. At the same time, he believed that a knowledge of Chinese history and culture would benefit the second generation. With these goals in mind, Chinn sought financial backing for his newspaper.[27]

Initial financing came from Chinn's friend Chingwah Lee. Lee, eight years Chinn's senior, was also American-born and an advocate of Chinese American acculturation. Lee was well known in the community for his knowledge of Chinese culture and had begun serving as a technical consultant to Hollywood for films requiring Chinese art objects. When the film version of Pearl S. Buck's novel *The Good Earth* went into production, Lee was called upon to recruit Chinese actors. Eventually he landed a significant on-screen part for himself as well. He then used the money from his work on the film to fund the paper, with Chinn as editor and Lee and William Hoy as associate editors. It seems ironically fitting that *The Good Earth*—a film later criticized for being one of many that used Caucasian actors to play major Chinese characters—was the funding source for the first newspaper aimed at second-generation Chinese Americans.[28]

In March 1937 the *Chinese Digest* ran a special issue in tribute to the community's involvement in the production of *The Good Earth*. There was a feature article on the actors, and much of the advertising in the issue was dedicated to them. Among the actors profiled were Roland Liu, described as a "typical second generation Chinese—a good athlete, a high school graduate, the personification of health and pep"; Caroline Chew, a graduate of Mills College and the daughter of Ng Poon Chew, the publisher of *Chung Sai Yat Po,* a major Chinese-language newspaper; and Chingwah Lee, a "zoologist, ethnologist, ceramic art authority and one-time social worker." But more important than the pride the community felt toward its members who acted in the movie was the belief that the film of "Pearl S. Buck's story of Man and the Soil [would], like the novel, do an immeasurable amount of good in eliciting western understanding of and sympathy for China and the Chinese."[29]

That belief was not unreasonable, as many Americans came to "know" China, the Chinese, and, by extension, Chinese Americans through the writing of Pearl S. Buck, who "created" the Chinese people for a generation of Americans. *The Good Earth,* published in 1931, "transformed the blurred subhumans into particular human beings for whom a great and moving sympathy was evoked by a momentary sharing in the universal experiences of mating, parenthood, suffering, devotion, weakness, aspiration. The Chinese girl in the story, O-lan, bride, mother, and grandmother, and the man, Wang, dogged, strong, weak, and sometimes sinning, are certainly the first such individuals in all literature about China with whom literally millions of Americans were able to identify warmly."[30] Many of the second generation, caught between Chinese and American cultural norms and the images generated by the often hostile media, welcomed the production of *The Good Earth* because it portrayed its Chinese characters with a sense of humanity that had been lacking in previous representations. The editors of the *Chinese Digest* recognized this and promoted the movie to encourage Chinese Americans to take pride in their heritage.

During its five-year run, the *Chinese Digest* tried to bridge the gap between the second generation's ties to the culture of their parents and Chinatown and their own attempts to enter the American mainstream. In its inaugural issue an editorial clearly stated the mission of the paper. It began: "The Chinese Digest is not just a hobby or a business—it is all that with a full-sized battle thrown in. We are fighting on five fronts." These "five fronts" are significant to an understanding of the issues confronting the second generation, as they reveal close ties to China but an overriding concern for their welfare in America. The first front was "Killing a Celestial," the Celestial being one of the popular representations of the Chinese. This battle exemplified the desire for self-representation and for the destruction of that stereotype as well as the determination to claim a place in America:

> There are no people in America more misunderstood than the Chinese. From the time of "Sand-lot Kearny" to the present, the Chinese is pictured as a sleepy Celestial enveloped in the mists of opium fumes or a halo of Oriental philosophy, but never as a human being. The pulp magazines and Hollywood have served to keep this illusion alive. The

> *Chinese Digest* is fighting this Celestial bogey and substitutes a normal being who drives automobiles, shops for the latest gadgets, and speaks good English.[31]

The second front was "The Truth Is Our Battle Cry"—meaning that the paper wanted to present more accurate accounts of Japanese aggression in Asia than those appearing in mainstream American papers. The third, "Bridging the Pacific," referred to the desire to foster an appreciation for Chinese history and culture among Chinese Americans. The fourth, "Inter-Trench Communication," was a call for closer ties among Chinese American communities: "Chinese in Boston or Portland have natural ties and common interests. Adverse legislation in one is adverse to all." This last statement refers to the restrictive and discriminatory legislation plaguing Chinatowns, of which Chinese Americans were well aware. The final front, "The War on Neglect," was a call for more economic opportunities for Chinese Americans: "At present Chinatowns everywhere are filled to the bursting point with well trained young men and women eager to find a chance to make their way in the world." This initial editorial, which would be echoed by later articles lamenting the limited opportunities afforded Chinese Americans, showed a conscious effort on the part of the editors to articulate the concerns of their generation and to educate, unify, and mobilize the community.

The editors of the *Chinese Digest* viewed themselves as spokespersons for the community and sought to provoke Chinese Americans to stand up for their equal rights, take pride in their heritage, and serve the community. An editorial of November 1935 warned against a group of "Eastern capitalists" who were said to be interested in constructing a "Little China" in a corner of Chinatown as a tourist attraction for the 1939 San

Francisco Golden Gate International Exposition: "We must make haste to inform our city officials that we do not contemplate having outsiders represent us. These easterner adventurers cannot adequately portray our customs, habits, and culture. Their one aim would be to extract money from tourists at our expense. At best they will arrive at a Hollywood version of long-fingered Mandarins chasing sing-song girls across a chop suey joint. We are tired of comedies."[32]

Although many may have wanted opportunities to leave its confines, second-generation Chinese Americans viewed Chinatown as their cultural base and took pride in it. Realizing the importance of self-representation and control of their own community, the editors called for an end to Japanese American business activity in the area: "The Japanese have already taken the southern half of Chinatown—our best bazaar section—and we are reminded what harm is being done our bazaars when cheap imitations and flimsy curios flood Grant Ave . . . We must post up a warning sign: Keep Chinatown Chinese." And in another editorial they referred to that part of Chinatown as "another Manchukuo" in reference to the Japanese occupation of Manchuria.[33] The editors thus sought to protect their community from being stereotyped and exploited by those who had little connection to or concern for its residents and cultural integrity.[34]

In appearance, the *Chinese Digest* was an interesting blend of Chinese and Western motifs. Its title was printed in "Oriental bamboo lettering," flanked by the Chinese characters *Hua Mei zhoukan,* meaning "Chinese American Weekly." There were two pictures in the upper section of the cover page, one on each side of the title. On the left was a drawing of a Chinese junk and on the right a modern steamship, signifying a Chinese role in the progress of modernization as well as changes in the mode of transportation that brought Chinese immigrants to America.

Below the title, also in "bamboo lettering," was a list of the topics the paper addressed: comment, social, sports, news, culture, and literature. The cover pages changed over time. At first they were simple, with the title and the accompanying characters and pictures occupying the top portion of the page with the text of the feature article below. By the second year, covers featured photographs of Chinese or Chinese American art and architecture, Chinese philosophers or statesmen, and local (San Francisco Chinatown) scenes or people. In keeping with the trend among magazines to enhance their marketability with eye-catching covers, toward the end of the paper's existence the covers featured attractive Chinese American women in stylish Chinese clothes. By this time the pictures of the boats and the list of topics had disappeared, but the title remained in "bamboo lettering" along with the Chinese characters. The covers became increasingly professional and artistic, but there was always an obvious, commercialized blend of Chinese and Western aesthetics.

Inside the magazine, the *Chinese Digest* usually carried news of events in China, especially concerning Japanese aggression. There were also feature articles on traditional Chinese history and art. The majority of the paper, however, was devoted to articles about San Francisco Chinatown, news of other Chinese American communities, Chinese American sports events, fashion tips, and some advertisements for Chinese-owned stores or stores with Chinese American employees. Moore's, a men's clothing store located on the edge of Chinatown, regularly took out ads in the *Digest,* always mentioning that it employed Edward Leong, its "Chinese representative." Advertisements for fashionable clothes, milk, sports equipment, and beauty shops all speak to an increasingly affluent and Americanized audience. As one resident of San Francisco Chinatown recalled: "By the time I was in high school, the big thing, if you had money, was to have a car . . . Then a girl. You would have to dress fairly well, not in dress-up clothing but in sports clothing. My father wouldn't give us any money for working in the store, but we did get an allowance, and I'd use that to try to get the right clothes. Of course, athletics was very important. I guess you could just call us all-American types."[35] In this sense, second-generation Chinese Americans were very much like their counterparts of other racial and ethnic groups. Regardless of the degree of attachment to Chinese culture, many exhibited a strong identification with mainstream American youth culture.

In the autumn of 1940, soon after the *Chinese Digest* folded, William Hoy and a fellow journalist, Charles Leong, founded another periodical, the *California Chinese Press* (later shortened to the *Chinese Press*). This would become the most professional of the English-language Chinese American newspapers. While the *Digest* had been printed on coated paper in a magazine format, the *Press* was the first of these papers to be printed on newsprint. The circulation was also much larger. According to Karl Lo and Him Mark Lai, the circulation of the *Digest* never reached a thousand, but the *Chinese Press* enjoyed a national readership.[36] In the opening editorial Hoy made it clear that the new paper would also be geared toward second-generation concerns: "Over sixty per cent of the 30,000 Chinese [in California] are those of the second or younger generation, the generation that speaks, reads and writes predominantly in the English language. The language of the California Chinese today is the language of their fellow Americans, and therefore their voice should also be in English." Hoy declared that his paper would serve to unite and inform the Chinese American community about their shared interests and to "help them establish and develop good will and friendship among fellow Americans of other racial origins." His next two paragraphs, however, set the new paper apart from its predecessors, the *Chinese Digest* and the short-lived *Chinese News:*

> The California Chinese today are predominantly Americans, either through the privilege of birth or by derivative citizenship. As Americans of Chinese descent their future is the future of America, and their social and political ideals are those of American democracy. As they become rapidly Americanized there is an urgent need for a newspaper to act as a voice for this large group. The California Chinese Press hopes to become this voice.
>
> The California Chinese also look across the Pacific Ocean, seeking opportunities to help China in her present plight and to plan for the reconstruction of a greater China to come. The American people have always been the staunchest helpers of China. And the California Chinese, bound by the ties of race to the people of that Republic across the Pacific, can do no less than to bend their every effort in helping China emerge victorious from her present war with Japan, and later aid her in the gigantic task of reconstruction.[37]

There is a very important difference in language between this editorial and earlier writings in Chinese American periodicals. Although the *Chinese Digest* had been geared toward the second generation as well, it had expressed a sense of conflict between the desire to honor Chinese tradition and the wish to adopt American cultural mores. This first editorial in the *California Chinese Press* makes a very clear statement that this group of second-generation Chinese Americans saw their lives as wedded to America. Without rejecting China or Chinese culture, the editors embraced the United States as the land where their futures would unfold. Even though they referred to themselves as "California Chinese," they also called themselves "Americans," thereby claiming a place in American society. For them China was now "that Republic across the Pacific" rather than the "motherland." By the late 1930s and early 1940s, Chinese immigrants and their offspring had come to the point of strong identification with American society and culture.

War Comes to Chinatown

For China itself and for Chinese Americans, the Second World War was not confined to the years 1941–1945, but began when Japan made its first incursions into Manchuria and Inner Mongolia. News of the dire situation in China filled Chinese American publications. In September 1931 the Japanese attacked the Manchurian city of Mukden, and by the end of the year they were in complete control of Manchuria. Throughout the 1930s the Japanese army put increasing pressure on China and came to occupy more and more Chinese territory. By 1937 Japanese aggression in China was unbridled, as epitomized by the brutal "Rape of Nanjing." In fact, in most Chinese histories of the war, the period 1931–1945 is referred to as the War of Resistance (and Japanese often call it the Fifteen-Year War, or at times the Great East Asian War), because for most of the period the rest of the world was not involved in the Sino-Japanese conflict. The investigation of the Mukden Incident by the weak and ineffective League of Nations deepened Chinese feelings of isolation.

Many Chinese Americans felt doubly assaulted, abandoned by the international community in the struggle against Japan and victimized by racial discrimination in America. Chinese Americans felt besieged on a number of fronts. The war in China was

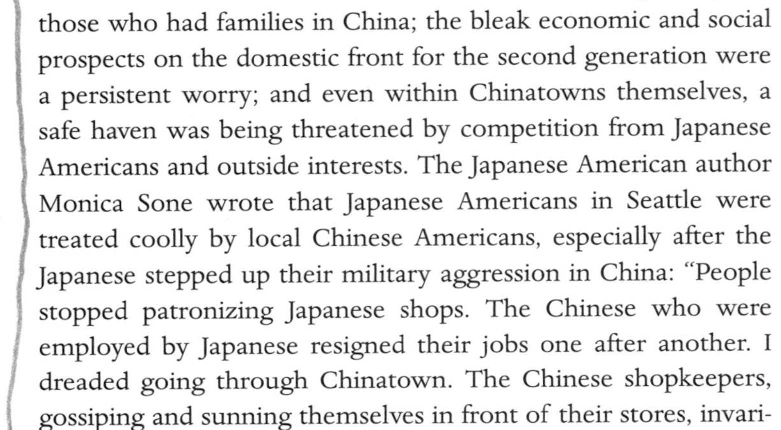

a constant concern on the international front, especially for those who had families in China; the bleak economic and social prospects on the domestic front for the second generation were a persistent worry; and even within Chinatowns themselves, a safe haven was being threatened by competition from Japanese Americans and outside interests. The Japanese American author Monica Sone wrote that Japanese Americans in Seattle were treated coolly by local Chinese Americans, especially after the Japanese stepped up their military aggression in China: "People stopped patronizing Japanese shops. The Chinese who were employed by Japanese resigned their jobs one after another. I dreaded going through Chinatown. The Chinese shopkeepers, gossiping and sunning themselves in front of their stores, invariably stopped their chatter to give me pointed, icicled glares."[38]

The Chinese in America responded to Japanese aggression with great speed. Soon after the Mukden Incident in September 1931, the Chinese-language newspaper *Chung Sai Yat Po* advocated that China declare war on Japan. In addition, the Chinese Consolidated Benevolent Association (CCBA) wired both the Nationalist and Communist factions in China, calling on them to join forces to defeat the Japanese.[39] Organizations with names like Anti-Japanese Association, National Salvation Association, and National Salvation Fund Savings Society were formed in Chinatowns across the country.[40] Throughout the early and mid-1930s, as the Japanese army continued to attack parts of China, Chinese in America raised money to send to China, and frequently urged other Americans to support their cause. And, demonstrating a new sense of political enfranchisement, they petitioned the American government and the League of Nations to intervene in the conflict in China.

In July 1937 the Japanese launched a major offensive. From their base in Manchuria, Japanese troops advanced southward.

In response, Chinese Americans increased their efforts to aid the mother country. As the *Chinese Digest* reported: "Since being a patriotic Chinese means also that one must hate the Japanese, the Chinese in America are rabidly anti-Japanese and not afraid to voice their pent-up emotions . . . For the first time in the community's history, every group, faction, clique, society, association, and lodge joined hands and fraternized with each other. It provided a spectacle never before witnessed. This evidence of unity for one common purpose whipped up the community's patriotic fever to new heights." The same article noted that within a month after the start of the Japanese offensive, Chinese American organizations and individual merchants began cabling contributions to the Nationalist government in Nanjing. To coordinate relief activities, the CCBA called a meeting of more than a hundred representatives from the various community organizations; from this was founded the Chinese War Relief Association (CWRA), of which B. S. Fong, president of the CCBA, was elected chairman. Within a week, $30,000 was raised in San Francisco alone. The largest individual contribution ($15,000) came from Joe Shoong, head of the National Dollar stores. His employees, numbering several hundred, reportedly pledged a month's salary as their contribution. In San Diego, Fresno, Tucson, Phoenix, and New York, other Chinese American communities also formed conjoint organizations to raise money.[41] By this time many non-Chinese Americans were alarmed by Japanese aggression in China and showed support for China's predicament. Many also began to realize that the United States would eventually be drawn into another international conflict.

In November 1937 the CWRA launched a second fundraising campaign with a parade through San Francisco Chinatown. Three hundred campaign volunteers and an equal number of students marched with banners and placards reading "Voluntary

Giving to Save the Nation," "Military Resistance to the End," and "Racial Freedom and Liberty Forever."[42] This last slogan implies that Chinese Americans linked China's grievance and victimization with their own situation. A similar development had taken place in New York with the Chinese Hand Laundry Alliance (CHLA). The historian Renqiu Yu points out that the CHLA's wartime motto, "To save China, to save ourselves," "linked its patriotic support for China to its struggle against exploitation and discrimination in the United States."[43] Chinese Americans, like other racial minorities, came to view the Allied championing of democracy in the Second World War as intimately tied to the struggle for civil rights on the home front.

The Chinese in New York took the lead in public demonstrations in support of China. On May 9, 1938, some twelve thousand Chinese Americans, seven hundred of them from Newark and Jersey City and hundreds more from as far away as Baltimore, Boston, Philadelphia, Wilmington, and Washington, D.C., marched three and a half miles from Mott Street in Chinatown through lower Manhattan. Sponsored by the CCBA, this parade, perhaps the largest showing of Chinese Americans ever, was held on the twenty-third anniversary of Japan's Twenty-One Demands on China. In 1915 Japan had made a series of demands in an imperialistic grab for control over China's internal affairs. The demands were divided into five groups: recognition of Japan's position in Shandong; a special position for Japan in Manchuria and Inner Mongolia; joint operation of China's iron and steel industries; nonalienation of coastal areas to any third power; and control by Japan of China's several important domestic administrations. Although the Chinese president, Yuan Shikai, accepted these terms, the Chinese people protested and there was an upsurge of Chinese nationalism. Thereafter, the Twenty-One Demands became a symbol of China's humiliation and the need for resistance against the great powers.[44]

In China it had long been commemorated as a "day of humiliation," but the parade in New York was organized as a "Solidarity Day," demonstrating that Chinese Americans from different backgrounds could come together publicly for a common cause. More than sixty Chinese American organizations participated, and in Manhattan alone, it was reported, fifteen hundred Chinese laundries, restaurants, and shops closed until five o'clock so that everyone could attend the event.[45] At the head of the parade, CCBA officials marched in front of a banner reading "China Defends!" An immense portrait of Chiang Kai-shek followed, flanked by marchers waving placards declaring "War in China—Made in Japan!" Above the parade flew six airplanes piloted by Chinese who had trained at Roosevelt Field in the hope they could soon return to China to aid in the fight against Japan. The marchers were divided into ten divisions of a thousand people each. There were floats, dragon dances, banners, bands (playing both Chinese and American music), and thousands of flags.

Of pioneering significance was one group of a hundred Chinese girls in fashionable Chinese dresses (the cheongsam) carrying a 45-by-75-foot Nationalist Chinese flag. The *New York Times* reported: "Though no appeal was made for funds, the spectators began showering coins—pennies to half dollars, and even dollar bills—onto the flag. About $300 was collected." This feature of the parade—large numbers of Chinese American women in Chinese dress carrying a large Chinese flag onto which money was thrown—appears to have been the prototype for other fundraising parades that would take place in Chinese American communities over the next few years. Sometimes the same flag used in New York, the largest Chinese National flag in the country, was flown to other cities for their parades. According to newspaper accounts, the flag became so heavy with money that each parade had to be stopped three times for the flag to emptied.

The presence of these women, young and old, marching in the parade and carrying the heavy flag (which weighed three hundred pounds without the money), symbolized "the merging of nationalism with feminism: the move of Chinese American women from the domestic into the public arena on behalf of the war effort."[46]

Later, Rice Bowl parades and parties were some of the most popular and effective venues for raising money and strengthening support for China's efforts against Japan. The *Chinese Digest* reported that the first Rice Bowl parties were held simultaneously in cities across the country on June 17, 1938. This event was organized by the United Council for Civilian Relief in China, of which Colonel Theodore Roosevelt, Jr., was national chairman, working with the CWRA. That day was set aside as "Humanity Day." In San Francisco the party started with a parade down Grant Avenue and continued with cultural entertainment that lasted into the late evening. More than two hundred thousand people lined the streets of Chinatown to enjoy fashion shows, indoor and outdoor dancing, Chinese and Western music, theatrical entertainment, a mock air raid, and a dragon dance. Everyone who entered Chinatown was encouraged to buy and wear a "Humanity button" that sold for fifty cents or else risk being tried by a "kangaroo court" of voluntary judges and fined up to a hundred dollars. Throughout Chinatown, locals in Chinese clothes and mock beggars, and children riding on floats, held out alms bowls and asked for donations to fill the "rice bowls of China": hence the name "Rice Bowl parties." On that one day, San Francisco Chinatown collected $55,000. This event was so successful that a second one was held for three days in 1940 (raising $87,000) and a third for four days in 1941 (raising $93,000). Much of the money was collected by the women in Chinese dress carrying the flag. The committee charged with allocating these funds in China was headed by Major Arthur Basset, attorney for the British-American Tobacco Company in Shanghai.[47]

Just as external financial support was vital to the success of the Chinese Revolution in 1911, relief efforts on the part of overseas Chinese were significant to China's battle against Japan in the 1930s and 1940s. In 1940 the *Chinese News* reported:

> Early contributions made by overseas Chinese to China have been in the form of direct relief funds; the purchase of Liberty Bonds; the sending of winter clothing, ambulances, and medical supplies; and support for the "Warphan" [a word coined by Madame Chiang Kai-shek referring to Chinese children orphaned by the war] and "Friends of the Wounded" campaigns. During the last three years, overseas Chinese contributed $180,000,000 [US $54,000,000] for relief or a monthly average of $5,000,000 [US $1,500,000]. The sale of Liberty Bonds amounted to $51,150,346 [US $15,345,104] while National Defense Bonds aggregated $6,265,138 [US $1,879,541] and Gold Bonds $2,915,880 [US $874,764].[48]

Chinese Americans also boycotted Japanese goods and picketed the docks where ships bound for Japan were moored. Because silk was one of Japan's leading exports, a call went out to stop wearing silk stockings. In January 1938 the *Chinese Digest* printed photographs of Chinese American women wearing cotton hose with the caption "Be in style, wear lisle." Another photograph, published in early 1939, showed two Chinese American sisters, Catherine and Patricia Joe, posed with one aiming a gun at the other for wanting to wear silk stockings. Chinese characters meaning "to resist" or "to boycott" appeared in the background of the photo; the caption below read: "You will, will you?" Realizing that using silk only aided Japan—and later, after the United States entered the war, that silk and nylon were needed for parachutes, medical supplies, and other wartime necessities—the Chinese American community whole-heartedly joined this boycott. Indeed, the boycott was effective enough to reduce Japan's exports of silk by three-fifths from 1936 to 1938.[49]

Even more significant was the picketing of ships that were to carry scrap iron and other materials to Japan. In late 1938 and early 1939 Chinese Americans joined with other Americans in demonstrating at the docks in San Francisco, Long Beach, Portland, and Seattle in order to publicize the fact that much of Japan's war material was coming from the United States. In December 1938 the SS *Spyros,* a Greek freighter chartered by the Mitsui Company of Japan, docked at San Francisco to load 8,500 tons of scrap iron for transport to Japan. The United Chinese Societies called for volunteers to go to the docks to protest. On December 16, two hundred Chinese American volunteers went to Pier 45 and were joined by three hundred sympathetic volunteers of various ethnicities: Greeks, Jews, and others. Speeches were made and picket lines formed. When the longshoremen broke for lunch, the crowd began to chant: "Longshoremen, be with us! Longshoremen, be with us!" After the lunch break, only a few returned to work. The *Chinese Digest* reporter Lim P. Lee wrote:

> The majority of them honored the Chinese picket lines, and the few that worked were so ashamed that they dropped their hooks and joined their comrades. Victory! Victory! the call was shouted through Chinatown and the pickets began to arrive in trucks, in streetcars, in automobiles. The radio and the press flashed the news to the

> nation:—Chinese pickets tied up scrap iron to Japan and American longshoremen refused to load implements of destruction.
>
> By the time the news was flashed back to Chinatown, pigs were being roasted for the nourishment of the Chinese pickets and American sympathizers. Soda pops, coffee, hot tea, sandwiches, oranges, Chinese buns were streaming toward the waterfront to feed the pickets and the longshoremen. Chinese came in from Stockton and Valley towns; they marched in from Palo Alto and Peninsula cities; and thousands poured in from the Bay Area till the climax of the picketing numbered 5,000 strong and more![50]

With support growing, the picketers held their ground for four days. On December 19 the Waterfront Employers' Association gave the protesters an ultimatum: they were to remove the picket line and the longshoremen were to return to work; if they refused, not only trade with Japan but the entire shipping business of San Francisco and the West Coast would be tied up. Thereupon the various parties met separately and together to discuss their options. After the United Chinese Societies pleaded with the longshoremen to respect their picket lines, the full membership of the International Longshoremen and Warehousemen's Union (ILWU) "voted not to pass the picket lines even if there were only one Chinese on picket duty." They instructed their union leaders to negotiate with the Chinese for an amicable solution, but told them "not to let the Chinese down."

A new round of emergency meetings was called and the United Chinese Societies met with ILWU officials who told them that the CIO Council had passed a resolution "to instruct the secretary to call all labor, fraternal, civic, and religious organizations for a Coast-wide conference to study and promote the embargo on all materials to Japan." On December 20 the Societies claimed victory and withdrew their picket lines. They had succeeded in calling attention to the issue of supplying Japan's war machine, and they had gained the support and cooperation of other Americans. B. S. Fong spoke for the Chinese American community, expressing heartfelt thanks to the longshoremen for honoring their picket line. The demonstrators then marched in a mile-long parade past the longshoremen's headquarters and through downtown San Francisco back to Chinatown, where a mass meeting was held. They marched singing "Yiyong Jun Jinxing Qu" ("The March of the Volunteers"), China's song of resistance. Soon thereafter, organized labor and other organizations, including the CWRA, helped lobby for an embargo of arms sales to Japan.[51]

The Rice Bowl parties and parades, the boycotts, and the protest against the SS *Spyros* galvanized the men and women of Chinese America to support China and created a sense of unity among the various Chinese American communities. Furthermore, these activities decreased the isolation of Chinese Americans, bringing them into close contact with their compatriots of other ethnicities who rallied against Japanese military aggression. As Chinese Americans became more visible in the public eye during the period leading up to U.S. involvement in the war, the negative images of China and the Chinese began to erode. Once the United States officially entered the war against the Axis powers, Americans of various ethnic backgrounds would fight side by side on the battlefield, and Chinese Americans would begin a new era of interaction with the nation's mainstream society.

As the American public began to pay more attention to the war in Europe and Asia, more men (and later women as well) enlisted or were drafted for military service—and in this Chinese Americans were no different from the rest of the population.

Chinese American periodicals began running stories on Chinese Americans in the military in November 1940. On October 16, the day the Selective Training and Service Act of 1940 came into effect, requiring men to register for the draft, Chan Chong Yuen of New York registered, and his number was the first drawn. He said that he was most interested in machine-gun training.[52] In San Francisco Chinatown there were four prominent Chinese on the local draft advisory board, No. 76. They were Leland Kimlau, a former commander of the Cathay Post of the American Legion and supervisor of the Chinese Alien Registration Office; Tom Chung Him, commander of the Cathay Post, American Legion; Kenneth Fung, attorney and officer of the Chinese American Citizens Alliance; and Thomas Jung, past president of the Chinese American Citizens Alliance. It was estimated that 2,500 Chinese Americans, or about 90 percent of those drafted, were registered in district 76. In late November 1940 the draft board announced that the first four draftees from the community had been called for military training: Chuey Woo, George R. Hall, Moo Thing Lee, and Too Kai Yuen.[53]

Until the United States entered the war, most of the coverage of Chinese Americans in the military remained on a lighthearted level. For example, in August 1941 the *Chinese News* ran a cover story on three childhood friends who had been in the same Boy Scout troop in San Francisco (Troop 3, composed wholly of Chinese boys) and, "together in manhood as they were in boyhood," were now stationed at Carlisle Barracks in Pennsylvania. The three had attended Lowell High School and the University of California at the same time. They were commissioned as first lieutenants in the reserves in 1940 and were called to active duty in July 1941. The cover photograph of the three smiling young men in uniform gives little hint of the events to come.[54]

Less than five months later the Japanese attacked Pearl Har-

bor and America was drawn into the war. The Chinese welcomed American support and assistance, and Chinese Americans were encouraged to defend both America and China. The *Chinese News* reported that Generalissimo Chiang Kai-shek had declared that "the Overseas Chinese should defend their second homeland where they have scattered and lived these many years. He [Chiang Kai-shek] urged them not to spare their efforts to defeat the common enemy. They should participate in all kinds of wartime activities, enlist when they are called for military service and fight to protect the country in which they live as religiously and as valiantly as their brothers and sisters are fighting to protect their fatherland."[55]

Many Chinese Americans, particularly the second generation and those of the first generation who had been in the United States for most of their lives, needed little encouragement to join in the war effort. Despite the long history of social isolation and discrimination, the events of the previous few years had given them a growing sense of belonging to American society. The war would offer some of them a chance finally to become Americans, both legally and emotionally. It gave them opportunities to demonstrate both their patriotism for the United States and their heartfelt Chinese nationalism, and it brought radical change to the Chinese American community both on the American mainland and in Hawai'i.

2

Chinatown Goes to War

With the U.S. entry into the Second World War, American Chinatowns, like the rest of the nation's communities, underwent an important transformation. With so many American men entering the armed forces, women and members of formerly excluded racial minorities were needed in the workforce, and they entered in unprecedented numbers. For Chinese Americans, this opening of economic and social opportunities was a turning point. For the first time, significant numbers of Chinese Americans were able to leave the restaurants, laundries, and gift shops to which they had been confined, and to join the armed forces and other defense-related enterprises that were desperate for manpower. One American-born man, with a degree in architecture from the University of Minnesota, found work in the war industry—the first technical job he had held since his graduation fifteen years before. Before the war he had managed his father's restaurant. When he found this new job, his American-born, business-trained wife took over his responsibilities at the restaurant.[1]

These opportunities came at a time of labor shortages, just as they had in an earlier period, when Chinese immigrants were instrumental in the building of the American West. By the 1940s, this generation, educated in American schools, was ready to assume new economic and social roles as they became available. Chinese Americans, many for the first time, joined workers of other ethnicities in the shipyards and aircraft factories, and in white-collar professions. Venturing outward, beyond Chinatown, they were exposed to a broader spectrum of American people, and those other Americans encountered Chinese Americans in a wider range of social roles and situations.

Women Answer the Call

While "Rosie the Riveter" is most often portrayed as a Caucasian woman, it is important to remember that she was also African American, Latina, and Asian American. Although Chinese American men engaged in a wide variety of occupations during the war, including military service, the emergence of Chinese American women in war-related jobs and activities deserves special attention, given the long history of a limited presence of Chinese women in the United States. Chinese American women entered the workforce and the public sphere in their efforts to contribute to the war mobilization and to improve their socioeconomic circumstances. Some sought employment when their husbands entered the armed services, others took jobs simply to earn a living, while others quit college to take positions in the shipyards and factories, believing that doing so would release men for military service. The presence of these women in the workforce caught the attention of both Chinese American and mainstream newspapers. As early as the spring of 1942, Theodora Wong reported on "Chinese Career Girls"; the subheading on her article was "They Help Run the Vital 'Behind-the-Lines' Business of the United States at War." Wong mentioned twenty-one Chinese American women from the San Francisco Bay Area who had taken jobs, mostly in the shipyards and other defense-related industries. She declared: "Since the defense program started last year, these graduates of high schools, colleges and business colleges from Seattle to San Diego have been stepping into all phases of government work. This war year their number is increasing as calls come for more personnel on the production front . . . They're the little, but important cogs in America's war machinery . . . They're part of the millions who stand behind the man behind the gun."[2]

Around the same time, the monthly magazine *Independent Woman* ran a piece on the "Chinese Daughters of Uncle Sam." The author, Louise Purwin, wrote glowingly of these Chinese American women, though she saw their entry into the workforce as an act of defiance of the Chinese tradition of confining women to the home rather than acknowledging that their opportunities for employment had previously been circumscribed by racial discrimination. Purwin framed her coverage of these working women in a manner that praised them but also tied them to traditional Chinese culture. The opening paragraph sets this tone:

> American girls of Chinese ancestry are devoting their hands and their minds to an all-out victory effort. In aircraft plants, training camps, and hospital wards, at filter boards and bond booths, in shipyards, canteens, and Red Cross classes, these girls are doing their utmost to blend their new-world education and their old-world talents to hasten the end of the war. Hundreds of Chinese girls, for centuries patient with their embroidery needles and skillful with their paint brushes, are "naturals" for delicate me-

chanical work in war plants, thus releasing warriors to fight for Allied victory.[3]

Purwin relates a number of stories of individual Chinese American women who were working in aeronautic hydraulics, aircraft instrument manufacturing, or nursing, joining the WACs (Women's Army Corps), or selling war bonds, but she portrays them as primarily Chinese, rather than American: "Daughters of women, who, in the Chinese homeland, lived out their whole lives in the cloistered seclusion of the enclosed courtyard of the traditional Chinese home, are today not only seeking their careers in their adopted country but are banded together as volunteers to help win the war." Purwin ignored the fact that for the second generation, America was not their "adopted country" but the country of their birth, the country of which they were citizens, and the country to which they pledged their loyalty.[4]

Nearly two years later, another article in *Independent Woman* focused on Chinese immigrant women who had succeeded in their respective fields. And yet, after two years of war, two years of participation in the war effort, the author of "Career Girl, Chinese Style" still found Chinese American women in the professions a novelty:

> *Chinese career women*—in America—that is something new and exciting. Few of us are even aware that there are a score of brilliant Chinese women in the United States holding down positions that require executive and professional ability. The war has brought these Chinese sisters of ours into sharp focus . . . Some are American born, geared to the tempo of American living, and exercising their talents as doctors, lawyers, actresses, scientists and X-ray technicians. Some are working on war jobs, aflame with high pa-

> triotism and the will to do, helping out with typing, clerical work, and other jobs—all important cogs in winning the war.

The piece described Chinese women in high-profile professions such as fashion design, medicine, scientific research, and aviation. It covered well-known American-born women such as Dr. Margaret Chung, the sociologist Rose Hum Lee, and the actress Anna May Wong. Yet its general tone placed these women outside the norm, even while stating that "today, there are second, third, and even fourth generation American-Chinese women on the West Coast. Many have fine civil service jobs which they have won by merit and stiff competition. Since April 7, the Department of State has even gone so far as to issue a public invitation to American businessmen to absorb Chinese men and women into various defense industries, to offset the hardships occasioned by men entering the service." Again the coverage of Chinese American women was positive, but a tendency to exoticize them detracted from their being seen as American.[5]

Sending the Ships to War

The war industries provided an economic boom for the Bay Area, and one of the main industries was shipbuilding. During the war there were six major shipyards in the area: the Kaiser yards in Richmond, Mare Island Navy Yard in Vallejo, Naval Drydocks in San Francisco, Marinship in Sausalito, Moore Dry Dock Company in Oakland, and Bethlehem Steel in Alameda and South San Francisco.[6] These shipyards proved to be a boon to Chinese Americans. The labor shortage, combined with federal regulations against discrimination, made the shipyards quite willing to hire women and minorities. In the spring of 1942 the yards began running recruiting advertisements in Chinatown newspapers offering government-sponsored free classes in marine sheet metal, pipefitting, electricity, shipfitting, and drafting. The shipyards in Richmond announced that they were hiring Chinese Americans regardless of citizenship status or English-language skills; their owner, Henry Kaiser, called upon Chinese Americans in the area to join the war effort. The Moore Dry Dock Company hired Chinese-speaking instructors for its Oakland welding school and offered bus service between the shipyard and Chinatown.[7]

These efforts were apparently effective: according to the *Chinese Press,* in 1942 approximately 1,600 Chinese Americans out of a population of 18,000 in the Bay Area worked in the defense industries, especially shipbuilding. Such jobs had an appeal for a number of reasons. They paid well, they could serve as draft deferments for men, and defense employees could apply for government-subsidized housing, often near the yards, which would allow Chinese Americans to move, at least temporarily, beyond the confines of Chinatown. And the jobs allowed Chinese Americans to act on their patriotism. May Lew Gee later recalled: "Everyone was going over to Richmond. It was part of the war effort. It was the patriotic thing to do, to work in some kind of war industry."[8] Dorothy Eng of Oakland Chinatown remembers the changes the shipbuilding industry brought to her community:

> Matronly women who had never worked outside of their homes before, got jobs as sweepers aboard ships. All they did was sweep. Sweep the decks. I remember seeing them get off the bus, going home to Chinatown carrying their broom and having their hair tied. So women were leaving

> homes just like everywhere else. That was the big change. And then there were young women working in the shipyards. So there was a lot more mobility for people. There was no longer that sleepy little hamlet. [Before the war] Chinatown was a real sleepy hamlet. Everybody kept within their homes, they kept nice and quiet, the kids went to school and came home.[9]

Jade Snow Wong's life was changed by a job at the shipyards. Soon after graduating from Mills College, Wong sought advice from the college's placement office. She was told: "If you are smart, you will look for a job only among your Chinese firms. You cannot expect to get anywhere in American business houses. After all, I'm sure you are conscious that racial prejudice on the Pacific Coast will be a great handicap to you." This advice made Wong more determined than before to find a job outside Chinatown, and she followed the example of her sister Jade Precious Stone, who was working as a draftswoman at Marinship. "By this time," Wong later wrote, "the trek to the shipyards was well under way. The patriotic fever to build as many ships as possible, together with the boom wages, combined to attract people from all types of occupations. Lawyers, artists, housewives, and street derelicts were seeking either skilled or unskilled work in the shipyards."[10] Wong landed a position as a clerk-typist and was assigned to a job in which she summarized and typed reports based on suggestions made by the workers to management. As a result of her efforts, the shipyard began supplying the workers with vitamins to ward off colds. When her boss was promoted, she became his private secretary. She attracted attention by winning a city-wide essay contest with an essay addressing the growing problem of absenteeism in the defense industries. Her prize was a war bond and the opportunity to christen a new Liberty ship, the *William A. Jones.*[11]

Employment in the shipyards allowed Chinese Americans to express both their American patriotism and their concern for the fate of China, as well as to demonstrate that they were capable workers, able to join the war effort with people from other communities while maintaining their ethnic identity. Jade Snow Wong (who went by her "American" name, Constance Wong, while working at Marinship) wrote an article for the shipyard's publication, the *Marin-er,* in which she declared: "With this war, Chinese workers have entered war industries in enormous numbers, applying to their jobs the same loyalty, patience, care, while preserving that individual dignity which they are proud to claim as a Chinese characteristic. Marinship foremen and supervisors will tell you that some of their best workers are Chinese. They are giving their all to the job because they know from their Chinese countrymen what Japanese warfare is all about."[12]

Indeed, Chinese American workers were appreciated by Marinship. Kenneth Bechtel, the company president, wrote in a letter to Chiang Kai-shek: "More than 300 such patriots, both men and women, are working everyday at Marinship, building cargo ships and tankers. We have learned that these Chinese-Americans are among the finest workmen. They are skillful, reliable—and inspired with a double allegiance. They know that every blow they strike in building these ships is a blow of freedom for the land of their fathers as well as for the land of their homes."[13]

However, the shipyards were not without racial tensions. At Moore Dry Dock in Oakland, "whites and Native Americans topped the racial hierarchy in the shipyards, Okies, Jews and Chinese were in the middle, and Portuguese and blacks were stuck at the bottom." Chinese Americans often worked in segregated crews at this same shipyard because of the racist attitudes of many of their fellow employees, and few Chinese Americans were ever promoted to supervisory positions. Instead, they were often assigned to do electrical work because it was a "lighter, detail-oriented trade considered more suitable for these immigrants." Also, according to a letter reprinted in the *Chinese Press,* some Chinese applicants were turned away from government shipyards because they were not citizens. The author of the letter, D. Y. Lee, was quite adamant in his belief that it was unfair that this shipyard was only taking citizens: "If I am willing to help the Government and do my part for the war effort, at least they can give me a job in their yard . . . If the Government hesitates, then why is the U.S. Government taking Chinese aliens in the U.S. Army?" Chinese immigrants were willing to do their share to support the war, but they wanted to be treated fairly and equally.[14]

In spite of such issues, many Chinese Americans found the shipyards a comfortable working atmosphere. May Lew Gee later said she had not experienced any discrimination: "There were a lot of Blacks from the South working there. There was a terrific mixture and everyone was there to do a certain job, to build ships so they could go and fight the war." Jade Snow Wong reported that her job in the office of Marinship exposed her to "the American work world":

> Until now American men were to Jade Snow a strange and unknown species of the human race . . . During these months, Jade Snow developed confidence in dealing and working with the men . . . She found dignity and respect accorded her in the shipyard. Sometimes at conferences she would be the only woman present in a room full of men. At first these experiences found her uneasy, but she contin-

> ued her work quietly, and she soon learned to maintain her equilibrium in almost any situation.

Like Wong, many Chinese Americans gained a new confidence from their experiences during the war, working and serving the United States alongside people with whom they had previously had little contact.[15]

Two women whose lives were changed by the war were An Yoke Gee and her daughter Maggie. An Yoke Gee was born on the Monterey Peninsula in 1895, thus was an American citizen. Her father, Jung San Choy, was well known in the small Chinese American community in Pescadero. He was a fisherman and also sold abalone shells; at one point the family operated three shell stands on the peninsula. He did not wear his hair in a queue as required by Chinese law, and he sent his older children to the Methodist Episcopal mission school in Point Alones and later in Pacific Grove—both acts indicating that the Jung family sought to live an American existence in both appearance and education.[16]

Although An Yoke Gee had spent her entire life in the United States, she became a victim of the anti-Asian legislation passed in the first half of the twentieth century. The Cable Act of 1922 declared that any woman who married an alien ineligible for citizenship would lose her citizenship, and indeed, when An Yoke Gee married a Chinese immigrant she was stripped of her citizenship. After her husband passed away, An Yoke Gee, at the age of forty-six, went to work in the Kaiser shipyard as a burner, cutting steel plate with a blowtorch. According to Maggie Gee: "It was a positive experience for her. She made non-Chinese friends for the first time, and it broadened her outlook in life. She was satisfied with being part of a Chinese community where she lived, but this allowed her to become part of the whole."[17]

Earning Their Wings

Maggie Gee soon followed her mother into the defense industry. A student at the University of California at Berkeley when the war began, she quit classes in order to work as an electrical draftswoman at the Mare Island Naval Shipyard in north San Francisco Bay. After six to eight weeks of training, her primary duty was to chart the electrical wiring for the repair of damaged submarines. Before long, however, Gee decided that she wanted to do something more demanding to assist in the war effort. She looked into the WAVES (Women Accepted for Volunteer Emergency Service) and the WACs, but learned that she was too young. She and two friends, one white, the other a Filipina, then decided to enroll in flight school. They went to Minden, Nevada, and learned to fly. At that time the Women Airforce Service Pilots (WASP) were recruiting, and Gee was accepted. She was proud of this accomplishment, as 25,000 women applied to join but only 1,830 were accepted for training and 1,074 earned their wings.[18] One of only two Chinese American women in the WASP, Gee trained at Sweetwater, Texas, and eventually flew a variety of aircraft.

The other Chinese American woman was Hazel Ah Ying Lee (she is usually referred to as "Ah Ying" in the literature on the WASP) from Portland, Oregon. Lee's father fled China soon after fighting broke out between the Nationalists and Communists on the Chinese mainland. He settled in Oregon, married, and raised an American family. Lee and her older brother both became interested in flying, and with the support of the Chinese American community in Portland, they completed flight instruction and went to China to offer their services to the air force of Chiang Kai-shek. Her brother was accepted and flew combat missions, but Ah Ying, being a woman, was not taken into the

Chinese armed forces. Instead, she taught school in her father's home village. She soon returned to the United States and eventually flew with the WASP, though she apparently became engaged to a Chinese pilot during this time. Lee lost her life in late 1944 when she collided with another plane while attempting to land at East Base in Great Falls, Montana. Her records indicated that her next of kin was Major Yin Cheung Louie, a pilot in the Chinese air force.[19]

The WASP transported airplanes from one base to another within the United States and flew mock missions in order to train men who were to be sent overseas for combat. They were disbanded in December 1944 as a result of pressure from male pilots who resented the women's presence and believed their jobs should go to men returning from the war. The WASP were never formally militarized, so the female pilots were not eligible for the GI Bill of Rights after the war, nor for other veterans' benefits until 1977. After the war, Maggie Gee finished her college degree and became the first woman hired as a physicist by Lawrence Livermore National Laboratory.[20]

Changing Social Roles

Aside from raising money for China, supporting the troops, and working in defense industries, Chinese American women engaged in a variety of social services in support of the Chinese American community. In 1944 Dorothy Eng of Oakland, California, helped found the Chinese Young Women's Society. One of its activities was to provide a welcoming social space for Chinese American servicemen passing through the area, not unlike the typical USO clubs. There was the fear that Chinese Americans would not be welcome in the USO clubs, so they determined to look after their own. As Eng tells it: "We were still being discriminated against even though the law [exclusion acts] had already been rescinded. It hadn't filtered down to ordinary people . . . You are not going to walk into the USO and be snubbed or be ignored. Why chance it? So unless we provided a center in each community for Chinese boys, they had no place to go, no common place to meet." Having established a venue for aiding the servicemen, the members of the Chinese Young Women's Society perceived an opportunity to improve their own understanding of mainstream American society. Eng continues:

> The next thing to do was to develop ourselves because we were just as wet behind the ears as the men in the service, because they were coming out of the laundries and out of grocery stores, out of the farms, out of small towns. Their social skills were just as non-existent as ours. [We wondered] how do you conduct a tea? What do you put on the table? How do you dress? [So we made contact with] Pacific Gas and Electric [which used to] have a homemakers division. And they would send out a homemaker to talk to various clubs and groups and tell them "Now these are finger foods and [this is] how you prepare them." They also talked about style and dress and hygiene. The whole works. It was a whole real makeover preparing us for the outside world.[21]

The opportunities that came to Chinese American women during the war were significant. By answering the nation's call to duty, they were able to venture beyond Chinatown and establish themselves as reliable and skilled workers in the broader American workplace. By working alongside Americans of other races and ethnicities, these women helped shape an increasingly

positive public image of Chinese Americans, and they developed a new pride and confidence both as Chinese American women and as American citizens. Their wartime presence in the workforce, like that of other American women, set a precedent for the postwar years, when the number of women seeking jobs outside the home would increase dramatically.

Citizen Soldiers

For Chinese American men, as well as some women, the armed forces proved to be a very important avenue by which citizens and noncitizens alike achieved a new status in American society. Traditionally, military service was not valued in Chinese culture. Soldiers were looked down upon as a necessary evil in what was considered a predominantly civil society. An adage from the Song dynasty (960–1278) advised: "Do not use good iron to make nails; do not use good men to make soldiers." By the time this American-born generation of Chinese Americans came of age, however, this attitude had faded, and when their country went to war, many were eager to join the fight. Approximately twelve to fifteen thousand Chinese Americans—nearly 20 percent of the adult Chinese male population of the United States—wore U.S. military uniforms during the war. They served in all branches of the military and in all types of units: combat infantry, engineering, intelligence, transport, medical units, fighter and bomber squadrons, and support units. Like others who served in the war, they endured separation from their families, the loneliness of being far from home, the brutality and horror of combat, and the tensions and strains of military life—and they enjoyed the relief of coming home. Theirs is a story not often told, but, like the other Americans who were their comrades in arms, they were (to borrow a phrase from Stephen Ambrose) "citizen soldiers."[22]

When the United States entered the war after the attack on Pearl Harbor, many Chinese Americans were eager to prove their loyalty to the United States and many were also hopeful that America's involvement would help China in its struggle against the Japanese. The sociologist Rose Hum Lee reported that "New York's Chinatown cheered itself hoarse when the first draft numbers drawn were for Chinese-Americans." Henry Joe Kim, born in Marysville, California, tried to enlist in the army air corps at the age of seventeen. Turned down, he was drafted the following year and eventually joined the marines and served in the postwar occupational force in Shanghai and Qingdao. Some men left college to enlist, others enlisted before they were drafted, hoping they would have a choice in their assignments, and others worked in defense industries before enlisting or becoming eligible for the draft. Ralph Jung of Philadelphia, after receiving several draft deferments because he worked at Bendix Aviation Corps in New Jersey, requested to be released for the draft. "Practically all my friends and relatives (two brothers) were in the service and I felt it was my duty to join them."[23]

The Chinese American recruits came from a wide variety of regions and situations. Some had grown up on farms or in small rural towns where there were few others of Chinese heritage; others were from Chinatowns, large and small. Some were butchers, grocers, and restaurant workers; others were engineers, draftsmen, and newspaper editors. This diversity reveals that despite the barriers to occupational opportunities in some areas, some Chinese Americans had managed to find jobs that were not circumscribed by Chinatown or ethnicity. A draftee from San Francisco, Edward "Kaye" Chinn, was described in the *Chinese Press* as a "typical example of the American of Chinese descent. [He was] a junior college graduate, majoring in aeronautic mechanics, and was working as a mechanic's helper when his [draft] summons came.[24]

While some Chinese Americans were looking to join the military to fight for their country, under the U.S. navy's discriminatory policies, they were only eligible to enlist as mess stewards or cabin boys. Two days before the bombing of Pearl Harbor, the *Chinese Press* ran an article on behalf of the navy recruiting "Chinese boys" for mess duty. They would be paid twenty-one dollars a month, and they had to be at least seventeen years old with sound teeth and eyesight. Their primary duties would be to serve food in the officers' dining rooms.[25] This recruitment program continued into the spring of 1942. The *Chinese Press* headline on March 20 read "U.S. Navy Wants 500 Chinese." The article stated that the navy believed that "the procurement of Chinese men is of vital importance in connection with our expanding naval establishment," because "the Chinese have proven to be among [the] best men who ever joined the Navy." At that time, sixty Chinese Americans were serving in such positions. The article also stressed that a career in the navy was possible for these recruits, who might someday achieve the status of officer's cook first class or officer's steward first class.[26]

In May 1942 the navy eased its restrictions on what positions Chinese Americans could hold. No longer confined to the mess hall and officer's dining rooms, they could now enlist as apprentice seamen. The editors of the *Chinese Press* applauded: "The Chinese are eager to prove that they want to be men of war with Uncle Sam's 'men-o'-war.' The Navy is to be congratulated on wanting fighting men of Chinese descent within its ranks." Although the armed forces would remain largely segregated until 1948, this change in policy was a small but significant step in the process of breaking down racial barriers in the American military.[27]

The Flying Tigers

In December 1940 President Roosevelt approved the formation of a covert American air force, the American Volunteer Group (AVG), to aid in the defense of China. During the winter and spring of 1941–1942, the AVG (better known as the Flying Tigers, *"Fei Hu,"* a name said to have been given to them by the Chinese because of their ferocity in battle), under the command of General Claire Chennault, defended Burma and helped the Chinese fend off the Japanese until America officially entered the war and began sending more men and materiel to the China-Burma-India theater (CBI). Eventually the AVG was replaced by the China Air Task Force, which would become the 14th Air Force in March 1943, with Chennault as commander.[28]

After America was fully committed to the war in Asia, Chennault's continued support of a joint U.S.-China air effort led to the creation of the Chinese-American Composite Wing (CACW) in 1943. The CACW was operated through the Lend-Lease program whereby planes and supplies would be sent to the Chinese Air Force (CAF) and their pilots would be trained by American aviators either in India or at Luke Field and Thunderbird Field near Phoenix, Arizona. Once they were trained, the Chinese pilots would fly together with American pilots in combat. Chinese Americans participated in the CACW: some had earlier joined the Chinese Air Force, and some were in the U.S. military. Thus the roster of the CACW was a unique blend of white American, Chinese American, and Chinese Nationalist service personnel.

A number of Chinese pilots were trained in Arizona before the creation of the CACW. In May 1942 *Life* magazine ran a cover story on the Chinese pilots at Thunderbird and Luke Fields. The article was cast as a human interest story, with the Chinese portrayed in a positive light: "[They are] more attentive

in the classroom than any other nationality . . . But life has not been all study for the Chinese cadets. They are as fun-loving and mischievous as any American youths. They have rapidly improved upon the Western custom of hazing and become so expert in volleyball and basketball that they have had a hard time getting American teams to play with them." Among the illustrations accompanying the story was one of young local Chinese American women visiting the cadets, allowing the readers of *Life* a view of Chinese and Chinese Americans as simply young people enjoying each other's company.[29]

Lieutenant Bill King, a Chinese American, joined the Chinese Air Force in 1938, after studying aeronautics at a junior college in California. He flew with the CAF for a number of years and then became one of the "Chinese" pilots in the CACW. When asked if the Chinese and American pilots got along, he replied: "As far as I can remember, I can truthfully say that we got along swell. Being an American Chinese and speaking the Chinese language, I was called to interpret a lot."[30] Other sources, however, reveal that while many Americans may have returned from the CACW with positive memories, there was more tension within the fighter group than King addresses. The language barrier was a frequent problem in both the classroom and the air: most Americans did not speak Chinese and the Chinese Nationalists did not speak English. "A Chinese tail gunner in a B-25 misunderstood an order over the intercom and bailed out of the plane, only to sheepishly walk into Malir after a night in the desert." It was also discovered that Chinese technicians were adequate at assembling engines and other parts, but were not trained well enough to be very effective troubleshooters, as they had rarely been called upon to take such initiative. One factor that may have hindered communication and affected morale was that CAF and American personnel had separate living and dining areas. Chinese officers and enlisted men had separate quarters and mess halls, as did American officers and enlisted men. This situation varied among squadrons and bases, but in general the CACW was Sino-American during duty hours only, which only exacerbated the gulf between Chinese and American personnel.[31]

The official history of the CACW brings the racial and national tensions closer to the surface. Kenneth E. Kay wrote the unit history of the Third Fighter Group of the CACW covering the period from July to December 1943. Aside from reporting day-to-day activities and duties, Kay devoted considerable space to his observations of relations between the Chinese and Americans and the cultural gulf between them. The most notable sentiment in his report is his growing appreciation of the Chinese Nationalists. It is apparent that he had held some misconceptions about the Chinese (and perhaps other racial groups as well) before coming to China. Early in the report he states: "One quickly dispelled bit of provincialism was that Chinese were all the same. The ancient, insular adage that 'all coons look alike to me,' that every Oriental is an almond eyed, bland, imperturbable and inscrutable replica of four hundred million other Orientals collapsed in patent falsity the first week we spent with our Chinese counterparts." He also comments on the disadvantage of not being able to communicate meaningfully with the Chinese:

> Unfortunately basic differences in racial temperament, lingual difficulties and the fact that while we worked together we lived and spent our leisure separately, preventing our camaraderie from maturing to the degree we could have all enjoyed. It is difficult to truly know a man with whom you cannot converse . . . It is unfortunate for the diplomatic premises of this Group that Americans with a deep knowl-

> edge of China and the Chinese could not have been found for an organization of this nature, but perhaps Americans so qualified are not otherwise qualified for Air Force duties.

Kay's comments imply that he did not know many, if any, Chinese or Chinese Americans before the war, but that he had come to a new appreciation of them:

> Individually every Chinese man and officer was a human being in his own mold, a complex personality with his own idiosyncrasies, strengths, weaknesses and talents. They laughed uproariously, they sulked, they spat curses in anger, they were lazy or industrious, leaders or followers, they were capable of petty deceit, minor larceny, heroism and fear. They were just like Americans, or Englishmen or Frenchmen or, for all we know, Eskimos. An American veteran of the CACW may someday go home with his mind poisoned against the Chinese, but he will never again think of them as duplicates of one another. Confronted with the myth of pigtailed "John Chinaman" of no tickee-no washee tradition, he will remember lithe Lt. Yu Wei who could step confidently into a pitched ball and knock it beyond the outfield . . . He will remember little Sergeant Hsieh, the 32nd squadron armorer who worked with more furious intensity than any American or Chinese in that hard driven section and took as a personal insult the sight of anyone sitting on his butt in the daytime . . .[32]

New Horizons

While men like Kenneth Kay were learning how to work with Chinese pilots, Chinese American soldiers and airmen were also encountering new circumstances brought on by their military service, both in the States and in Asia. Henry Joe Kim did not find coping with military discipline difficult because of the time he had spent in the Chung Mei Home for Chinese Boys, an institution in the San Francisco area for Chinese American orphans or boys whose parents could not take care of them. But he did have a hard time adjusting to the racial segregation in the southern states where he was stationed for basic training. He also mentioned that the Chinese he met in China immediately knew he was not "native," a reaction that gave him a new awareness of his Americanness.[33] Other servicemen, when stationed far from their homes, found ways to connect with local Chinese or managed to locate relatives. And some found their spouses in the military. For example, Alfred Toy, who grew up in Milwaukee, Wisconsin, and was a student at Marquette University when the war broke out, met and married Grace (Eng) Toy when they were both stationed at Camp Edwards, Massachusetts. An army nurse, Grace was later sent to England, where she befriended the local Chinese and other families. Alfred, meanwhile, requested a transfer to the CBI so he could try to locate his mother and sister who had been stranded in China during the war. He was indeed able to reunite with them.[34]

William Mar, of Seattle, Washington, had little difficulty adapting to China. Mar, a career army officer, spent time in India, in China, and on Guadalcanal. Captain Mar arrived in China via Burma and was happy that he could finally speak Cantonese with someone and eat Cantonese food. Richard M. T. Young, who was originally from Honolulu but whose prewar job as a metallurgical engineer had taken him to both China and New York, felt very much at "home when I was anywhere in China." Stationed in Chongqing, Young "had a close feeling for the Chinese peasants and soldiers," with whom he could converse in

"Cantonese, Mandarin, or [the] Shanghai [dialect]." Despite their close linguistic ties to China, both men considered themselves "Americans defending the United States," but they also were glad to have the opportunity to help China against the Japanese. Young remained in the army reserves for thirty years. His experience in the military reinforced his attachment to Chinese culture and those who shared his affinity for China. He said in 1995: "My closest friends are those, military and civilian, who were in the CBI with me. We share a love for the Chinese people, Chinese culture and Chinese history."[35]

Mar and Young were not the only Chinese Americans who served in the war and then decided to stay in the military. Henry Wong of Philadelphia left the University of Pennsylvania to enlist in July 1941. He admits that he did not enlist because of an overwhelming feeling of patriotism or because he sensed the coming of war: he simply wanted to join the service for the new and adventurous experience. He was eventually stationed in China in the Third Air Cargo Resupply unit, part of the 14th Air Force, charged with airdropping supplies to American and Chinese troops. Wong, who was awarded the Distinguished Flying Cross and the Air Medal for his service, later quipped that during the war he had been a "kicker"—responsible for kicking supplies out of airplanes. His father, Wong Wah Ding, was proud of his son's service, declaring "I cannot become a citizen myself because of the law, but I am happy that my only son is giving his services to the country I love best." Henry Wong served as a career officer in the air force for twenty-two years. He enjoyed the work, and his wife and family appreciated the opportunity to live in various countries and parts of the United States. For Henry and Mary Wong, life in the air force was a far cry from their earlier years in Philadelphia Chinatown. After retiring from active duty, Henry worked for the air force as a civil servant for another twenty-four years. When he retired from the civil service, the government presented him with the Outstanding Civilian Service medal.[36]

Wing Fook Jung grew up in Savannah, Georgia, where his family owned a laundry and later a small grocery store, and attended the Georgia Military Academy. His parents were reluctant to send him there, he later recalled, because of the typical "Chinese attitude toward having their boys in the military; it didn't have a good standing in Chinese eyes." But a salesman who did business with his father convinced the family that it was a good school. After the Georgia Military Academy, he was accepted by the U.S. Military Academy at West Point, and in 1940 he became the first Chinese American to graduate from the Academy. During the war he was stationed in China as a combat liaison officer, maintaining relations between Chinese and American infantry troops. He stayed in the service for thirty years, seeing duty in the Korean War, and retired a full colonel in 1970. When asked about serving in China and whether as a Chinese American he felt it was his duty to help China defend itself from the Japanese, he simply replied: "I was an American soldier doing what I had to do, going where I was ordered to."[37] That sense of doing one's duty as an American soldier was the foremost motive for many Chinese American soldiers.

William Chang grew up in Lovelock, Nevada, where his parents ran a restaurant and boarding house near the mines. He worked as a gas welder and cutter at the Mare Island Shipyard before he enlisted. Chang, who served in the Marianas as a staff sergeant in the army air force, looked back on his military service as a time when Americans were exposed to people from many different backgrounds, a situation that led to greater social acceptance for Chinese Americans. Samuel Fong, who left his father's farm in Santa Barbara, California, to attend college, credited his military service as a pilot in the Fifteenth Air Force with giving him a self-confidence that carried him through the post-war era. He gained this confidence while flying B-24s in southern Italy, which he described as a "very backward country, considering how long it has existed." Sue-Chun Luke, born in China to farming parents, was a student and part-time waiter in San Francisco when the war broke out; he joined the navy reserves. His aspiration before the war was "to become an American." His ship was hit in the second Battle of the Philippines in 1944, and he floated in a life preserver for six hours before another ship picked him up. He commented on the irony of nearly dying in the South China Sea, only two hundred miles from his home village of Toisan.[38]

The motivations and reactions to the war of Chinese Americans serving in the European theater were similar to those of Chinese Americans who found themselves in Asia or the Pacific. Wesley Ko of Philadelphia wanted to be a pilot with the Flying Tigers but was working in a print shop when the United States entered the war. Although his employer offered him a draft deferment, he decided to enlist because his friends were all joining up. After officer candidate school at Fort Benning, Georgia, he was commissioned as a second lieutenant. Upon graduation from OCS, however, he was not immediately assigned to a unit as were the others in the class. He wondered if it was because of his Asian ancestry.[39] He was soon assigned to the 82nd Airborne and then to the 325th Glider Infantry Regiment. For more than thirty months, Ko fought in six different bloody campaigns. After training in Africa, he saw action in Sicily and Naples; he flew his glider over Normandy on the day after D-Day; he fought in the Battle of the Bulge, the Allied assault on the Siegfried Line, and the battle for Cologne, Germany. Finally, he helped liberate the Wöbbelin concentration camp at Ludwigslust. Given that fewer than half of the American troops sent overseas were ever in a combat zone, Ko saw more than his share of action. He considered himself fortunate to have survived at all.[40]

The Ah Tye family of San Francisco made an impressive contribution to the war effort. One son stayed home to mind the family business, but his six brothers joined the military. Three flew in the army air force, two enlisted in the navy, and one was drafted into the army. While they all served ably, Edward Ah Tye, a top-turret gunner in a B-17 in the European theater, garnered the most attention. He flew a total of thirty-five missions, earning the Air Medal with three oak clusters and the Distinguished Flying Cross.[41] Harry Jang, who grew up in Locke, California, also received the Air Medal (with four oak clusters) and the Distinguished Flying Cross for his service as a navigator in B-17s in Europe. His future wife, Ruth Chan, also from Locke, joined the Women's Air Corps in 1944 and was assigned to clerical duty. Like most Chinese Americans who served in mixed outfits, the Jangs were the only Chinese in their units; they both reported that they were treated very well in the service, sometimes better than when growing up in Locke, where Chinese Americans had had to attend segregated schools.[42]

Coming from a variety of regions and economic backgrounds, these men and women who served in integrated units during the war, like the women who entered the workforce on the home front, learned to adjust to their new surroundings and duties and established themselves as valuable members of the armed forces. They too worked alongside Americans from a diverse range of ethnic and racial backgrounds and thus helped shape a new image of Chinese Americans. And their experiences would serve them well after the war, as they returned home with a newfound confidence and a strengthened sense of belonging in America.

Although many Chinese Americans in the military experienced some degree of discrimination, mostly off-color remarks, the majority of the veterans assigned to mixed units claim that they did not encounter overt discrimination in the armed services or from the local populations where they served, whether in the United States or abroad. When stationed in the South, some had to adjust to Jim Crow segregation, but they were often unsure where they fit in that system, and the locals were often equally unsure. Many of those who saw combat recalled that facing the enemy under fire equalized everyone in the unit regardless of rank, race, or ethnicity. Both Grace (Eng) Toy and Ralph Jung were the only Chinese Americans in their outfits stationed in Europe. Not only were they well received by the local populations in general, they also befriended local Chinese in England and in Paris.

In their responses to the war, the Chinese American community both defended China and claimed America: they sent money and supplies to aid the Chinese, they served in the U.S. military, and they carried out a variety of activities to support the war effort at home.[43] Florence Gee, a fifteen-year-old from Berkeley, California, captured this spirit in her prizewinning essay for the *Oakland Post-Enquirer*'s "I Am An American" contest, for which the prize was a fifty-dollar war bond. Gee wrote:

> I am an American-born Chinese. Like all American girls, I have a heroine. Mine is Madame Chiang Kai-shek who, with her husband, is behind the spirit of New China. The War has hit home. I have an uncle in the army and one in the shipyard. My sisters are members of the civilian defense. My mother is taking first aid. I belong to a club

> where I learn better citizenship . . . I help my church collect money for the United China war relief. That which helps China helps America.[44]

A month later twelve-year-old Eleanor Yee won another "I Am an American" essay contest, this one sponsored by the Chinese American Citizens Alliance. She wrote:

> God has given me my birthplace in an unconquerable United States of America. This is my country, the grandest on earth. We are all Americans, whatever our race, color or creed . . . Every loyal American should contribute gladly and freely in whatever way he can to help win the war. I, an American, give a solemn prayer that my country shall forever stay a free and glorious nation, the hope of all humanity.[45]

While the participants in the essay contest sponsored by the Ging Hawk Club in 1936 may have shown a degree of ambivalence in their feelings about one or both of their countries, in wartime young people like Florence Gee and Eleanor Yee were imbued with a concern and respect for China as well as a clear dedication to the United States.

Whether working in the shipyards, raising money to support Chinese troops, observing rationing regulations, or serving in the military, Chinese Americans embraced the war effort. Their contributions and the new circumstances created by the war would usher in a new era in which they received a newfound acceptance and stature in American society.

3

The "Good Asian" in the "Good War"

In 1876 the attorney and politician Frank Pixley, representing the municipality of San Francisco, testified at the congressional hearings concerning Chinese immigration: "The Chinese are inferior to any race God ever made . . . I think there are none so low . . . I believe that the Chinese have no souls to save, and if they do, they are not worth saving." Ninety years later *U.S. News and World Report* remarked: "At a time when it is being proposed that hundreds of billions be spent to uplift Negroes and other minorities, the nation's 300,000 Chinese-Americans are moving ahead on their own—with no help from anyone else . . . Visit 'Chinatown USA' and you will find an important racial minority pulling itself up from hardship and discrimination to become a model of self-respect and achievement in today's America." The first quotation captures the sentiment prevalent during the anti-Chinese movement of the mid-nineteenth and early twentieth centuries, and the second passage, written in the midst of the civil rights movement and its "disruption" of American society, is often cited as one of the earliest expressions of the "model minority" image of Chinese Americans. Obviously, much had changed in the nine decades between these two visions.[1]

The most dramatic changes in the social roles of Chinese Americans in those decades came about during the Second World War. After the United States and China became allies in the war against Japan, American images of Chinese and Chinese Americans changed enormously. The sinister mask of Fu Manchu was replaced by the tragic photograph of the lone baby crying in the bombed-out railroad station in Shanghai, and the stereotype of weak and ineffectual Chinese was replaced by patriotic posters of heroic Chinese men and women fighting to defend their country against Japanese invaders. This shift was evident on the covers of *Time* magazine. In 1938 Chiang Kai-shek and his American-educated wife, Mayling Soong (Madame Chiang Kai-shek), hailed for their heroic stance against the Japanese, were named *Time*'s "Man and Wife of the Year"—a status that was in sharp contrast to earlier impressions and opinions of Chinese people.[2] As Chinese Americans actively joined the war effort, they became more visible and less mysterious to their fellow Americans, better able to claim their place in the mainstream. Three interrelated trends and events in the mid-1940s helped to cast Chinese Americans as the "good Asians": the distinguishing and distancing of Chinese from Japanese, Madame Chiang Kaishek's tour of the United States, and the congressional repeal of the Chinese Exclusion Acts.

"How to Tell Your Friends from the Japs"

Although those of Japanese descent had long been discriminated against in the United States, the attack on Pearl Harbor solidified American antipathy toward Japan, and by extension, toward Japanese Americans. At the same time, the American public was becoming more aware of China's long struggle against Japanese imperialism and invasion. The Chinese American community had helped heighten awareness by displays of Chinese solidarity such as the boycotting of Japanese goods, the movement to halt the shipping of scrap iron to Japan, and the Rice Bowl parades. Once the United States and China became allies in 1941, many Americans took a greater interest in the events taking place in China and consequently, in distinguishing the Chinese ally from the Japanese enemy.

This process of separating Chinese from Japanese and Chinese Americans from Japanese Americans became critical in the ways the two groups of Asian Americans were perceived and treated by the U.S. public during the war. On December 22, 1941, *Time* magazine ran a three-quarter-page article in the "Home Affairs" section entitled "How to Tell Your Friends from the Japs"—immediately granting the Chinese the status of "friends." Photographs of two Chinese and two Japanese men ran across the top and bottom of the article, with the text in between. The text was full of cultural and physical stereotypes, as well as a warning that the guidelines offered were not always reliable: "There is no infallible way of telling them apart, because the same racial strains are mixed in both. Even an anthropologist with calipers and plenty of time to measure heads, noses, shoulders, hips, is sometimes stumped." Nevertheless, the article listed nine general differences, ranging from height (Chinese being taller than Japanese), weight (Japanese are seldom fat whereas in China being fat is a sign of prosperity), body hair (Chinese seldom grow an impressive mustache), and eyes (Japanese eyes are set closer together) to social demeanor (Japanese are hesitant, nervous in conversation, laugh loudly at the wrong time). None of these so-called differences, of course, could hold up from one individual to another, but the idea that such differences existed between Chinese and Japanese helped set the tone by which Chinese became "friends" and the Japanese "Japs."[3]

A similar article appeared in *Life* magazine on the same day. "How to Tell Japs from the Chinese" also purported to specify subtle physical differences between Chinese and Japanese, and explained them by reference to pseudo-scientific theories of race and racial origins. The article declared that the ability to distinguish between the two was important for both "U.S. citizens" and "U.S. Chinese," although U.S.-born Chinese were, in fact, U.S. citizens:

> In the first discharge of emotions touched off by the Japanese assaults on their nation, U.S. citizens have been demonstrating a distressing ignorance on the delicate question of how to tell a Chinese from a Jap. Innocent victims in cities all over the country are many of the 75,000 U.S. Chinese, whose homeland is our staunch ally. So serious were the consequences threatened, that the Chinese consulates last week prepared to tag their nationals with identification buttons. To dispel some of this confusion, LIFE here adduces a rule-of-thumb from the anthropometric conformations that distinguish friendly Chinese from enemy alien Japs.[4]

The text revealed that anthropologists admitted that "the difference between Chinese and Japs is measurable in millimeters," but claimed that they were still able to "set apart the special types of each national group." Unlike the *Time* article, which featured four small pictures of Chinese and Japanese for comparison, this piece provided a large portrait of a pleasant-looking Chinese government official, while the Japanese example was a menacing picture of General Tojo. The portraits were inscribed with handwritten comparisons, with lines drawn to facial features for the Chinese such as "scant beard," "parchment yellow complexion," "never has rosy cheeks," and "more frequent epicanthic fold" and to features for the Japanese such as "heavy beard," "earthy yellow complexion," "sometimes rosy cheeks," and "less frequent epicanthic fold." Another set of pictures compared the height and leg length of "tall Chinese brothers" with those of "short Japanese admirals." Although these articles could point to few signs that would really help anyone distinguish between Chinese and Japanese Americans, the message was clear that the Chinese were friendly while the Japanese were ruthless militarists.

While these articles were intended for the broad American public, they had an impact on Chinese Americans as well. Some saw them as a validation, a reason to hope that in the future Chinese Americans would receive better treatment. Philip Choy, a community activist and historian, recalled reading the *Time* and *Life* pieces as a young man and trying to stand taller so as not to look Japanese. "We felt uplifted at the time," he said. "The burden of being Chinese was lifted from our shoulders with the war. However, we didn't realize at the time that it was at the expense of Japanese Americans."[5]

If it was important for the public to be able to tell Chinese from Japanese Americans on the home front, it was vital that service personnel in Asia be able to tell Chinese from Japanese soldiers on the battlefield. To help meet this need, the army issued *A Pocket Guide to China* to Americans stationed there. The booklet offered a section in comic-strip format called "How to Spot a Jap," written and drawn by Milton Caniff, best known at the time for his comic strip "Terry and the Pirates." The title frame of the "How to Spot a Jap" strip showed a military officer asking Terry and his friend Ryan to show "the men a few points of difference between the Japs and our Oriental allies." Once again, the differences were constructed around supposed physical traits of the two nationalities. Throughout the strip, the Chinese are referred to as "C" and the Japanese as "J." Their skin color is said to be slightly different (Chinese "dull bronze," Japanese "lemon yellow"); Chinese have evenly set teeth, Japanese have buck teeth; when walking, Chinese stride whereas Japanese shuffle (the *Time* article maintained that Japanese walked "stiffly erect" while the *Chinese* shuffled); Chinese and other Asians have "fairly normal feet" but Japanese have a wide space between their first and second toes because they wore wooden sandals before being "issued army shoes"; and finally, Japanese have less ease with the English language, hissing on any "s" sound and being unable to pronounce the letter "L." Terry even advises the reader: "Try 'lalapalooza' on them! That's a panic!" Summing up, the strip emphasized that "spotting a Jap" depended on three things—appearance, feet, and pronunciation—and that in general the Japanese were "short, squat, [with a] fairly heavy beard . . . lemon-yellow skin and slanted eyes."[6]

Chinese, in contrast, were depicted in very positive terms. The U.S. army went to great lengths to portray the Chinese as similar to Americans in order to encourage soldiers' support for the joint American-Chinese war effort and to promote proper behavior while in China. The *Pocket Guide* opened by reminding the reader that China had already been at war with Japan for five years and that "you and your outfit have been ordered to China to help this gallant ally." The Chinese may have been impoverished but their character enabled them to endure great suffering: "Chinese peasants and workmen are almost never demoralized. They keep their chins up, take what comes, help each other out, and live with amazing contentment amid the terrific struggle for the bare necessities of life . . . The tough, lean coolies who pull [rickshaws] are to be treated always with respect for what they are in Chinese life and the waging of this war. They are the freight carriers, the builders of the Burma Road, the guerrilla

fighters, their stomachs never filled, their bodies nothing but bone and muscle." The Chinese were similar to Americans in that they had a good sense of humor and were devoted to their families and their land, and had natural democratic tendencies, and in that they too had "great men who were born in cabins . . . Generalissimo Chiang Kai-shek himself is a son of poor parents, and Sun Yat-sen, their George Washington, was a poor boy."[7]

What is most striking in the *Pocket Guide* is the call for American soldiers to refrain from any displays of racial superiority toward the Chinese, not because racism might be unjustified or immoral, but because it might hurt the war effort:

> If you think of the Chinese as a yellow-skinned people of a totally different race from us, you probably will never get to know them. What's more, you'll be playing right into the hands of Hitler and the Japs. Japan will harp on the color question first, last, and all the time. She will tell the Chinese what she has been telling them ever since Pearl Harbor—that Americans look down on nonwhite peoples and that the Chinese can never hope to be treated on terms of equality by America. "Why fight for the white man?" Japan dins into Chinese ears.[8]

A number of other passages throughout the booklet admonish American racist attitudes toward the Chinese while at the same time promoting them against the Japanese. For example: "China is the oldest nation in the world and its civilization is in many ways the greatest. As a natural result, the Chinese will not bear any assumption of superiority on the part of a white man because he is white." Toward the end there is a drawing of an irritated-looking Chinese man glaring at a fat cigar-smoking American man with a large "White" button on his chest; the caption reads: "Remember, it's Hitler who harps on the superiority of his own color, his own people, his own country."[9]

This piece of wartime propaganda elides a number of issues in American history. At the time of its publication, the Exclusion Acts which barred most Chinese immigration to the United States were still in effect, the armed forces were largely racially segregated, and Chinese immigrants were still denied naturalized U.S. citizenship. The *Pocket Guide* acknowledged that many Chinese resented the way people of their nationality were treated in America, but it emphasized that China had been at war with Japan far longer than had the United States, so that there was little danger that China would ally itself with Japan. While such exhortations may have lessened rude American behavior in China, one can only speculate as to how easily Americans were able to change their attitudes toward Chinese during the war. Decades of racism had presented all Asians as stereotyped look-alikes who bore the traits of their perceived inferiority. Such conditions had to be broken down over time, through contact and direct experiences.

Not Japanese, Please

A good deal of the campaign to distinguish Chinese from Japanese took place within the Chinese American community. Chinese Americans, in fact, participated in the construction of the imagery that would separate them from Japanese and Japanese Americans. Long involved in the struggle against Japan, many Chinese Americans responded to the attack on Pearl Harbor by taking immediate steps to express their support for the American war effort and to distance themselves from Japanese Americans, who were now viewed with increased suspicion. The day after Pearl Harbor the *New York Times* ran a photograph of four

Chinese American men in front of the Japanese consulate in New York; they were smiling with their thumbs up, indicating their confidence that China would now receive help from the United States in its struggle against Japan. Within days of the attack, the Chinese consulate in San Francisco, assisted by various Chinese American organizations, issued identification cards to Chinese immigrants and Chinese Americans. Buttons, often white with a red "V" for victory, were sold for ten cents each: some declared "I am Chinese" or simply "China," while others depicted American and Chinese flags crossed in unity. *Life* magazine ran a photograph of Joe Chiang, a Chinese American journalist, wearing a handmade sign reading "Chinese Reporter, NOT Japanese Please." The editors of the *Chinese Press* urged readers to carry identification indicating that they were not Japanese: "For your own protection, the authorities MUST distinguish you from the Japanese, a people at war and an enemy of China and the United States." Not surprisingly, Chinese Americans were not alone in seeking the benefits of wearing these buttons. In Los Angeles, according to the *Chinese Press,* "Cautious Chinatown merchants sold [the buttons] only to those who could converse with them in Cantonese or other Chinese dialects. Several young Japanese were refused buttons, and on trying other stores, found that word had passed from shop to shop before them. They quickly left Chinatown."[10]

Although the buttons were popular, some Chinese Americans recognized their implicit denigration of Japanese American loyalty. The labor organizer Karl Yoneda later reported that although many "Asians began wearing 'I am Chinese' or 'Korean American' buttons . . . Chinese Workers Mutual Aid Association (CWMAA) members refused to wear them on the basis that 'there were many pro-China, anti-Axis activists among persons of Japanese ancestry, and our solidarity has to be shown them.'"[11]

This expression of pan-Asian solidarity, however, was not the norm. Chinese Americans, in their opposition to Japanese aggression in Asia, their patriotic attachment to the United States, and their desire to be seen as loyal Americans, became, knowingly or not, complicit in the persecution of Japanese Americans.

Despite their precautions, Chinese Americans were frequently mistaken for Japanese Americans. One article in the *Chinese Press* began: "Identification cards, buttons, and car stickers are displayed and wore [*sic*] by the thousands, but still the practice of Chinese being mistaken for Japanese goes merrily on. Minor incidents, such as Chinese being refused service in department stores and restaurants, etc. are still making the rounds. Here is this week's 'So sorry—thought you were a Jap' news stories." There were incidences of violence reported in relation to some cases of mistaken identity, and the perpetrators were not always white Americans: Filipino Americans in Los Angeles were reported to have assaulted Chinese Americans, thinking they were Japanese. The newspapers urged Chinese Americans to be forbearing if mistaken for Japanese Americans. The editors of the *Chinese News* wrote:

> The average American cannot tell the difference between Chinese and Japanese. With this thought in mind, we wish to caution every Chinese to bear with patience if the salesgirl does not wait on you; show that you're Chinese in some way, but do not do so arrogantly. In all cases, remember that most people cannot tell the difference between flags, so even the display of a flag is best augmented with the word "Chinese" in connection with it. The duty of every Chinese in America is to participate in the defense of this country.[12]

Heeding the call to participate in the defense of the United States, Walter Lee, Sacramento valley correspondent for the *Chinese Press,* wrote a letter to President Roosevelt offering a "$100 defense savings bond to . . . the first man to shoot down a Jap plane anywhere over the United States soil or within three miles of both the Atlantic and the Pacific coasts of the United States . . . I am a Chinese-American citizen, age 24, and have been classified in the draft as 1B. Until the time comes for me to be with Uncle Sam, I will be buying more defense bonds and helping the Red Cross, and keep them flying."[13] Lee's sentiments were not unique. The Chinese American press was replete with similar declarations of patriotism and eagerness to defeat the Japanese.

Chinese Americans in the military also distanced themselves from their Japanese American colleagues. Private W. W. Yee, stationed at Camp Robinson in Arkansas, told his company commander: "Sir, I can't work at the office. There's a couple of Japanese corporals working up there, Sir. I won't work with any Japanese, Sir." Yee was transferred to other duties the next day.[14] As this anecdote illustrates, some Chinese Americans were as guilty as anyone else of failing to distinguish Japanese Americans from the Japanese enemy. By refusing to work with his comrades in arms, Private Yee was as complicit in the treatment meted out to Japanese Americans as were those who clamored for their incarceration.

Internment of Japanese Americans

Chinese American periodicals referred to the Japanese and Japanese Americans in terms similar to those used in the mainstream press, calling them "Japs" and depicting stereotypical caricatures. Noticeably, there was little mention of the internment of Japanese Americans except when it might benefit Chinese

Americans. (When asked years later about the lack of coverage of internment in his papers, Thomas Chinn replied simply, "My papers were for and about Chinese Americans," implying that he had seen little need to address Japanese American concerns.) The removal of Japanese Americans from their homes and their confinement in concentration camps in the spring of 1942 caused a severe shortage of farm laborers on the West Coast, especially in California. The United States Employment Service issued a call for 1,000 Chinese Americans to replace the relocated farm workers. The *Chinese Press* urged its readers to respond to this call: "Food is just as important as machine-guns to help win the war . . . This is an opportunity for all Chinese with farm experience to develop a business as well as perform a patriotic duty. All types of produce and berry farms, vacated by the Japanese, are available." Thus some Chinese Americans saw the internment as an opportunity for economic gain for themselves in the name of patriotism.[15]

Long angered by the presence of Japanese American stores in Chinatown, Chinese Americans also took advantage of the internment by moving into the properties previously occupied by Japanese Americans. As a *Chinese Press* columnist put it, "Young Chinese are taking over many of the vacated Jap stores on the 500 and 600 blocks of Grant Ave." The column provided details: "Thomas Dair is opening his own curio shop . . . Wilbur Wong has leased one of the larger places and is planning to establish his business there . . . Leroy Ja is another who swept out a mess of Jap stuff to make room for his own stock of Chinese merchandise. Bill Tong has also taken over a Jap evacuee's place and is busy converting it into the Limehouse Cocktail Lounge."[16]

Such tactics were applauded in the press by non-Chinese Americans as well. As early as February 13, 1942, the *Chinese Press* ran a letter to the editor about "a move to eliminate the Japanese-owned stores from Chinatown." The writer stated: "I sincerely hope that you will not let this matter rest until you have succeeded in accomplishing our objective. Every Japanese store on Grant Avenue is there under false pretenses, making the implied representation that it is a Chinese store and selling goods to tourists on that false and fraudulent basis." This letter was signed by David E. Snodgrass, dean of the Hastings College of the Law.[17]

The *Chinese Press* thus participated in spreading the belief that Japanese Americans might be guilty of fifth-column activities to aid Japan. An article by H. K. Wong reported that a "Japanese-owned hotel" on the corner of California and Grant Avenue had been leased by Albert and Nellie Lee and would reopen as a residence hotel for girls and businesswomen. When workers arrived to begin remodeling, they had "found an auditorium which had been changed into a pseudo-Jap garden . . . Jap pictures and scenes decorated the wall with a number of knee-high sukiyaki tables scattered about. In one large hall, they found chairs and tables all set up for (could be fifth columnist) conferees . . . The whole works were torn down in record time."[18] The fifth column message had been made more explicitly in an earlier article. It reported on a lecture in which Dr. Gordon S. Watkins, professor of economics and dean of the College of Letters and Science at the University of California, Los Angeles, claimed that "Pearl Harbor's fall was mainly caused by fifth column work by American-born Japs." Watkins placed the blame on those Japanese Americans who had gone to Japan, claiming that some had become "officers for the mikado" and that "a number of them were fliers." The Americans had been caught off guard, he went on, because the attack took place on a weekend; the Japanese, not having a "Christian sense of ethics," had taken advantage of the Americans' vulnerability. Watkins concluded that

Japanese parents prevented their American-born offspring from assimilating into American life through the use of Japanese schools and Buddhist priests who "see to it that the boys and girls do not lose the virtues of their ancestors."[19]

The editors of the *Chinese Press,* like many other Americans, lumped Japanese Americans together with the Japanese who attacked Pearl Harbor. By doing so, they implicitly deemed anyone of Japanese ancestry an enemy alien and thus supported the internment of Japanese Americans. Although they were acutely aware of the generational conflicts within the Chinese American community, in their drive to distance themselves from the Japanese, they refused to acknowledge that similar tensions existed among Japanese Americans. They were unwilling or unable to admit that their Japanese American counterparts were, like them, overwhelmingly loyal to the United States and its war effort.

The internment of Japanese Americans gave Chinese Americans an unexpected opportunity to make substantial gains in the motion picture industry. The war created a demand for films about the conflict in Asia, and stories set in the Pacific theater or in China were popular. A piece in the *Chinese Press* describing the call for Chinese American actors began: "If your cheekbones are high and prominent, if your eyes will slant with the aid of a little adhesive tape, Hollywood's harried casting directors may be looking for you. And if you're really an Oriental, you haven't a Chinaman's chance of ducking a movie job unless you can run faster than the sprinting scouts of half a dozen studios where China is in just about every other title on the production lists." Before the war, there were about a thousand Chinese working occasionally in the movie industry, but the war drew them into the military, the defense industry, and other jobs that offered steady employment and more money. There was such a shortage of Asian actors at this point that the Screen Actors' Guild

waived its membership requirements for hiring. The article emphasized: "The Japs are gone to internment camps. So many Chinese are playing Jap roles that there are practically no Chinese left for Chinese roles. Koreans are scarce. Malayans are scarce [and] Filipinos are so busy they have to stop and think which side they are really on."[20]

An executive for Metro-Goldwyn-Mayer, speaking of casting the film version of Pearl S. Buck's novel *Dragon Seed,* remarked: "I'll venture to say that every Chinese man, woman, and child west of Denver can get work in that picture. The only ones we definitely don't want are those in the army or defense plants."[21] Some Chinese Americans, however, took this opportunity to make a statement about their loyalties. Some were unwilling to portray the enemy, though Filipinos were said to relish the roles because "they all get killed at the end," indicating their hatred of the Japanese aggressors. In contrast, Mei Lee Foo, a San Francisco-born Chinese opera and concert singer, agreed to play a Japanese geisha because "the geisha girl is symbolic to many people of the moral decadence of Japan." In these cases, Chinese Americans were able to express their antipathy toward the Japanese while making economic gains for themselves.[22]

Beginning in 1942 the War Department commissioned a series of films entitled "Why We Fight," directed by Frank Capra. The sixth installment, *The Battle of China,* praises China as the world's oldest country, a civilization of "art, learning, and peace," one that has never "waged a war of conquest." Furthermore, the film proclaims, the war had brought the oldest and the youngest nations together to fight "side by side in a struggle that is as old as China itself; the struggle of freedom against slavery, civilization and barbarism, and good against evil." The seventh and final film of the series, *War Comes to America* (1945), stresses the notion that "we the people, all the people" are involved in the war and that the war is being fought in defense of all Americans, who include "English, Scotch, Dutch, Italians, French, Swiss, Danes, Norwegians, Poles, Welsh, Negroes, Spaniards, Mexicans, Greeks, Portuguese, Germans, Hungarians, Russians, Irish, Slavs, and Chinese." In the new circumstances created by the war, Chinese Americans were pleased to be able to parade their ethnic heritage while at the same time demonstrating their loyalty to America. Many consciously claimed their place in American society during these years, often at the expense of Japanese Americans. And Americans of Japanese descent, powerless behind the barbed wire of concentration camps, could do little to counter this trend. On May 16, 1943, the Treasury Department's war savings staff hosted an "I Am An American" Day at the Civic Auditorium in San Francisco. Representing Chinatown, May Jeannette Wong and others joined groups of Austrian, Armenian, Czechoslovakian, Danish, Filipino, Finnish, French, German, Greek, Dutch, Hungarian, Italian, Norwegian, Polish, Portuguese, Rumanian, Spanish, Swedish, and Yugoslavian Americans to celebrate the climax of American Citizenship Week. Each of the twenty-two participating groups sponsored a booth, some of which sold art objects and native trinkets while others sold coffee and refreshments. The proceeds were to be converted into war securities. In the evening, there was a show featuring each nationality performing folk dancing, singing, and a variety of other features intended to illustrate the cultural contribution of each group to the development and upbuilding of America. New citizens were honored with a ceremony in the afternoon. The *Chinese Press* lauded the event: "They are the people who came to America to enjoy the freedoms guaranteed under our American form of government—the freedom of speech and of press, the freedom of worship, and the freedoms of petition and assembly. They show by their participation that they appreciate what America has given them and want to give all they can to preserve the American way of life." While German and Italian immigrants were among those honored as loyal Americans, Japanese immigrants were not. And while Chinese Americans were invited to participate, there is no mention of the fact that immigrants from China were still barred from U.S. citizenship.[23]

Japanese Americans were also left out of a book entitled *This Is America,* with text by First Lady Eleanor Roosevelt and photographs by Frances Cooke Macgregor. The first ethnic group covered in this work is the "American Chinese." While praising their patriotism, the text acknowledged: "Under our laws, some of our older Chinese people have never been able to become American citizens . . . [but] we have today many young Chinese, also born here, serving in our armed forces. They are serving equally the nation from which their parents or grandparents came, since China and the United States are now Allies." Like the "I Am An American" pageant in San Francisco, the book celebrates Italian and German Americans as part of the national mosaic. There is no mention of Italy as part of the Axis powers, and the German immigrant featured is described as a loyal American "though he may grieve for the second war which has now come between the country of his origin and the country of his birth."[24] Although Japanese Americans could have been portrayed in a similar fashion, they do not appear anywhere in the book. The propensity to link Japanese Americans with the enemy not only put them into concentration camps, it expunged them from the American family.

Meanwhile the public's perception of Chinese Americans was improving considerably. In an article published in the *San Francisco Chronicle* and reprinted in the *Chinese News,* a reporter praised Chinatown's readiness to aid the war effort. The end of the article revealed the changing attitudes toward the community: "Next time you're eating or drinking in the district, don't let the fancy neon lights, the Cantonese talk, or the Oriental architecture fool you. These people are American through and through. The fact that their parents may have come from the old country and that their children have a tougher Americanization job on their hands than most of us makes them all the better Americans."[25] In 1942 Earl Warren, running for governor of California, issued a statement in observation of China's "Independence Day" (October 10): "Like all native born Californians, I have cherished during my entire life a warm and cordial feeling for the Chinese people. Under your great leader, Generalissimo Chiang Kai Shek you have long been in the forefront of the battle for freedom. My sincere congratulations to you on this anniversary of Chinese independence, and with it my prayer that the Jap invaders will be driven from Chinese soil before the beginning of the New Year."[26] During the late nineteenth and early twentieth centuries California had been at the forefront of the anti-Chinese movement; Warren's statement manages to erase that history and replace it with "a warm and cordial feeling." The U.S. alliance with China against Japan had created a new interpretation of both American history and Sino-American relations in which the hostility between the two countries and the mistreatment of Chinese immigrants and Chinese Americans were conveniently forgotten.

Madame Chiang Kai-shek

If there was one person who did more than anyone else to change the American public's image of Chinese and Chinese Americans, it was Madame Chiang Kai-shek, the wife of wartime China's Nationalist leader. Mayling Soong was born in Shanghai in March 1897, the fourth of six children. Her father, Soong Yao-ju, was sent to Boston around 1880 to apprentice in his uncle's shop. He eventually converted to Christianity, taking the baptismal name of Charles Jones Soong, and attended Vanderbilt University, from which he was graduated in 1885 with a degree in theology. Returning to China, he became an influential industrialist and publisher and an ardent supporter of Dr. Sun Yat-sen, the founder of the Republic of China. Soong decided that his children, like him, should receive an American education. Of his three sons, Tseven (T. V. Soong) and Tsean (T. A. Soong) attended Harvard while Tseliang (T. L. Soong) went to Vanderbilt. The daughters Eling (Ai-ling) and Chingling attended Wesleyan College for Women in Macon, Georgia, and Mayling attended Wellesley College in Massachusetts. These American educations, combined with their father's wealth and connections, enabled the Soongs to become one of the most powerful families in mid-twentieth-century China.[27]

When Mayling returned to Shanghai after graduation in 1917, she had to reacquaint herself with Chinese life and society. She studied Chinese language and literature with a tutor and thus regained her fluency. Once she felt more engaged with Chinese society, she began to assume social responsibilities, accepting a position with the local YWCA. She took an interest in child labor issues and led a campaign to stop the exploitation of children in Shanghai factories, especially in the silk industry. These activities gained her a post on the Child Labor Commission of the Shanghai Municipal Council, the first Chinese as well as the first woman to be offered the position.[28] It would be her marriage to Chiang Kai-shek, however, that would catapult her into national and international fame.

Although they met around 1920 at the home of Sun Yat-sen,

it would be another seven years before they wed. Mayling's mother and her sister Chingling did not approve of Chiang Kai-shek. He had been married previously and was known to have had an association with the Chinese underworld, traits that the Christian Soong family found distasteful. With Sun Yat-sen's death in 1925, when Chiang became his successor in the Chinese Nationalist party, he became a more suitable match for Mayling, especially after he promised to study Christianity. They were married in 1927, to the delight of many Americans, especially Christian missionaries. Some missionaries believed that "Chiang's marriage to an American-educated woman represented a rapid advance in the long struggle to convert China."[29] When Chiang Kai-shek converted to Christianity in 1929, the couple's faith would be a central issue in the positive construction of their image for American consumption. After marrying Chiang, Mayling became quite visible in Chinese political and social affairs. She often accompanied Chiang on official business, occasionally served as his English interpreter, was the secretary general of the air ministry for two years, and advocated women's concerns through the New Life Movement, a government program aimed at building a new China through educational, physical, and moral rebirth among the Chinese people.

During the mid-1930s there was considerable disagreement within Chiang's ranks over how to respond to the Japanese incursion into Chinese territory. Chiang was determined to eliminate the Chinese Communists before turning his attention to the Japanese, but some of his subordinates believed that a united front with the Communists was the best way to achieve victory over the Japanese. In early December 1936, while visiting the Xi'an region in western China, one of Chiang's generals, Zhang Xueliang (known as the Young Marshall), organized a revolt. He was determined to make Chiang take an anti-Japanese stand

and had his men attack Chiang's headquarters. They captured Chiang and killed most of his bodyguards. Over the next few weeks, there were intense negotiations and planning involving Chiang's government, Zhang Xueliang's supporters, and the Communists. By Christmas Day, Zhang Xueliang and the Communist Zhou Enlai agreed to let Chiang return to Nanjing, with the understanding that he would consider their demands for a united front against the Japanese. That united front, however, never fully materialized.[30]

Although Madame Chiang was present in Xi'an and was allowed to visit her husband while he was being held captive, her participation in the actual negotiations was minimal. It is reported that she succeeded in discouraging the Nationalists from bombing Xi'an, but she did not play an important role in securing her husband's release, nor did she influence the terms under which he was released. The American press, however, as well as others who favored the Chiangs, played up her role as a skillful negotiator. Pro-Nationalist Chinese Americans glorified her part in the incident, declaring: "Largely through the force of her personality and diplomacy in the difficult situation, Chiang was released on Christmas day." The well-known American writer and public speaker Dale Carnegie elevated her role even higher: "China trembled on the verge of another civil war—and one woman stopped it. One woman alone—Madame Chiang Kai-shek . . . It was a turning point in history." Her Christian faith was especially highlighted during this crisis, as she was reported to have read the Bible to her husband until he slept.[31]

Besides her Christianity and her courage, Madame Chiang appealed to American audiences because of her humanitarian efforts, especially concerning children. While many Americans were probably unaware of her efforts to rectify child labor conditions in Shanghai, she was well known for her campaign to establish orphanages and schools for children left parentless because of war. Soon after her marriage and move to Nanjing, she started the School for the Children of the Revolution, the first orphanage established for children who had lost their fathers in battle. Soldiers were not highly respected in Chinese society, and when they were wounded or killed their families often faced difficult times. Madame Chiang sought to lighten their burden by seeing that these orphans in particular were cared for. When the Japanese attacked China in 1937, the fate of these children became one of her main concerns, a concern that she would champion throughout the war. Calling them "Warphans," Madame Chiang established the Chinese Women's National War Relief Society to care for them, and soon branch offices opened in many of the major cities.

The sociologist Rose Hum Lee was quick to point out the deeper significance of these orphanages in the development of modern Chinese society, information that served to bolster Madame Chiang's image among Chinese Americans as someone dedicated to modernizing China. Whereas orphans were usually taken in by members of the extended family or clan, wartime conditions often made that impossible. The clan system had emphasized family loyalty instead of national loyalty, and this worked against the Chinese in a time when they were trying to build a modern nation. The orphanages as national institutions could help the Chinese come to see themselves as members of a larger community than the clan. "Warphans from all over China live under one roof. Warphans will speak one dialect: Mandarin. They dress alike: a uniform of blue cotton jeans and white shirt, with a large straw hat slung on the back to ward off the sun or rain. They eat the same food, sing the same songs, recite the same lessons, and learn to love the same benefactress—Madame Chiang Kai-shek."[32] This social transformation was taken a step further when Madame Chiang called upon the country to look after the warphans, as she could not bear the responsibility alone for these "future citizens of China." She initiated a campaign asking others to help, with slogans like "Adopt a warphan for a month!" and "Adopt as many warphans as your income will allow!"

Madame Chiang's high profile in the news and Chiang Kai-shek's consolidation of power within the Nationalist party won the respect of the American media. Named *Time*'s "Man and Wife of the Year" in 1938, this handsome couple were regarded as China's best hope for modernization and against Japanese aggression. The editors of *Time* wrote: "If Chiang Kai-shek and Mei-ling can maintain their will as China's will—the same will which said that 'any sacrifice should not be regarded as too costly'—Chinese prospects are good." And Generalissimo Chiang's message to the United States, according to *Time,* was: "Tell America to have complete confidence in us. The tide of battle is turning and victory eventually will be ours!" In fact the tide of battle would not turn for China until America was drawn into the war in late 1941. In 1943 Madame Chiang Kai-shek would tour the United States in an attempt to secure more support for the war effort in China and to encourage overseas Chinese to continue to aid China while doing their share to support America. Her tour would be hailed as a great success, prompting one journalist to remark: "She took the country not by storm, but by charm."[33]

Charming the Americans

Madame Chiang returned to the United States in November 1942 to receive medical attention for a back injury she sustained when thrown from a car while visiting the Shanghai front. During this time the White House accepted cards and presents for Chiang. One letter, from Mrs. Cathleen Quinn of East Orange, New Jersey, included a money order for three dollars and a request that the president present it to Madame Chiang with a note reading: "It is from my three daughters and it is for the little guy on the railroad tracks somewhere in China." Once she began her tour of the United States in early 1943, the response to her presence from a great segment of the American public was overwhelming. She received hundreds of cards and letters a day, and once, while she was on her way from Chicago to San Francisco, a station master's wife woke at 3 A.M. in order to have a batch of homemade cookies ready for her when her train passed through the station at 8 A.M. The poet Carl Sandburg wrote: "What she wants, she wants for the Family of Man over the entire earth."[34]

Referring to her affectionately as the "Missimo" (to match her husband the Generalissimo's abbreviated title "Gissimo") and more formally as Madame or the First Lady of China, Americans embraced her with respect and kindness that were in stark contrast to the treatment of most Chinese immigrants and Chinese Americans throughout American history. Madame Chiang represented not the heathen Chinese slave girl of the past but the modern Christian woman of China's future. The historian Karen Leong notes: "American acceptance of Mme. Chiang as an educated, modern, beautiful and Christian Chinese woman relied as much on ideologies of gender as did earlier Americans' rejection of Chinese prostitutes." Chiang was a model of the modern woman: loyal to her husband, intelligent, attractive, well spoken, caring, and nurturing. She was especially acceptable to American audiences because "as a women who fitted squarely within domestic ideas about gender roles, Mme. Chiang could be viewed as the foreign equivalent of an American woman." As the *Pocket Guide to China* emphasized the similarities between Americans and Chinese, Mme. Chiang's speeches while on tour and the American response to her words were also couched in the rhetoric of similarity, inclusion, and equality.[35]

Chiang's well-publicized and well-orchestrated tour of the United States officially began in the nation's capital on February 17, 1943. A guest of the Roosevelts, she stayed in the White House and was photographed chatting with Eleanor Roosevelt on the White House lawn and meeting various politicians and military figures. On February 18 she became the first private citizen and only the second woman to address both houses of Congress (the first woman to do so had been Queen Wilhelmina of the Netherlands). Thinking that she was to address a joint session of Congress, Chiang had prepared only one speech, which she delivered to the House of Representatives; reportedly she then spoke off the cuff to the Senate. Her appearance on Capitol Hill had been well publicized, so both chambers were full with congressmen, dignitaries, and spectators fortunate enough to get tickets. *Time*'s account mentioned her poise, clothes, figure, and presence, characteristics that would be commented upon throughout her visit:

> The Senators watched in curious silence as Madame Chiang walked down the aisle of the Senate Chamber. They saw a still face with dark eyes. They saw a slim, straight figure in a black Chinese gown, with a tiny splash of jade, there a black sequin's unstated sparkle. Madame Chiang stepped to the rostrum, listened as Vice President Wallace introduced her, shot a smile at the Senators, and then, after apologizing for not having a set speech, knocked their silvery blocks off extemporaneously.[36]

Chiang's speech was eloquent, witty, flattering of the United States, and forceful in presenting China's case. At one point she stressed the commonalties between the two countries, first giving it a personal bent: "I came to your country as a little girl. I knew your people. I have lived with them. I spent the formative years of my life among your people. I speak your language, not only the language of your hearts, but also your tongue. So coming here today, I feel that I am also coming home." She then linked her experiences in the United States to that which bound the two countries together:

> I believe, however, that it is not only I who am coming home; I feel that if the Chinese people could speak to you in your own tongue, or if you could understand our tongue, they would tell you that basically and fundamentally we are fighting for the same cause, that we have identity of ideals, that the Four Freedoms which your President proclaimed to the world resound throughout our vast land as the gong of freedom, the gong of freedom of the United Nations, and the death-knell of the aggressors.

When her speech ended, the chamber erupted in generous applause. As *Time* put it, "The U.S. Senate is not in the habit of rising to its feet to applaud. For Madame Chiang it rose and thundered."[37]

From the Senate chambers, Madame Chiang was escorted to the House of Representatives by the Speaker of the House, Sam Rayburn, who introduced her by declaring: "It is a proud day for the United States of America to receive and to do honor to one of the outstanding women of all the earth."[38] Her prepared speech to the House, broadcast nationally on the radio, touched on a number of issues that she would reiterate in other venues:

> The second impression of my trip is that America is not only the cauldron of democracy but the incubator of dem-

> ocratic principles. At some places I visited, I met the crews of your air bases. There I found first generation Germans, Italians, Frenchmen, Poles, Czechoslovakians and other nationals. Some of them had accents so thick, that if such a thing were possible, one could not cut them with a butter knife. But there they were, all Americans, all devoted to the same ideals, all working for the same cause and united by the same high purpose. No suspicion or rivalry existed between them. This increased my belief and faith that devotion to common principles eliminates differences in race and that identity of ideals is the strongest possible solvent of racial dissimilarities.[39]

Not surprisingly, Japanese Americans were not included in her list of ethnics who were to be considered American, though by this time the formation of the all-Japanese American combat regiments had been announced.

Just as Japanese Americans were erased from the American community of citizens of which there was no "suspicion or rivalry between them," Madame Chiang and her supporters also set aside the history of Sino-American relations and Chinese American history in their aim to build goodwill between the countries. She claimed: "The hundred sixty years of traditional friendship between our two great peoples, China and America, which has never been marred by misunderstandings, is unsurpassed in the annals of the world." Madame Chiang was well aware of the conditions under which Chinese immigrants lived in America, the ongoing exclusion of most Chinese from the country, the ban against naturalized citizenship, and the discrimination faced by Chinese Americans, but these issues were not the ones she had come to America to address. Rather, she had come to appeal for American aid and to promote a more positive image of China and the Chinese, focusing on the "solid practicalities of war and peace." She relieved Americans of the responsibility to confront anti-Chinese legislation, Jim Crow segregation, or any other thorny issue of inequality brought to the public's eye during the war. It was much preferable that "with characteristic dignity, Mme. Chiang complained of nothing and asked for nothing—except a better world and safer future for us all."[40]

Chiang's two speeches before Congress set the tone for the rest of her tour in terms of how the American public would generally receive her. Her intellect, beauty, charm, and message of cooperation in the war effort would be touched on wherever she went. *Time*'s description of the impact of her speech in the House captured well the general response of many Americans:

> When she finished, tough guys were melted. "Goddam it," said one grizzled Congressman, "I never saw anything like it. Madame Chiang had me on the verge of bursting into tears." These and the other much-moved listeners probably did not stop to analyze what had pulled at their hearts. It was not the words. In any other mouth they might have sounded flat. It was the woman, the way she clutched her handkerchief and brought her tight hand down on the desk for emphasis, the flash in her eyes which reflected something deep in her experience. Madame Chiang and China know the meaning of endurance. Through this woman, a few Americans saw and understood China.[41]

Life, which featured a full-page photograph of Madame Chiang addressing the House, was equally effusive in its praise. It too touched on her appearance, her understanding of American democratic principles, and her general impact on those present:

> One can only hope that the founding fathers of the Republic were present last week in some ghostly fashion, when Madame Chiang Kai-shek stepped onto the rostrum of the House of Representatives and began her extraordinary speech. The Fathers would, perhaps, have been somewhat dazzled to see this beautiful woman, clad in black and ornamented in flawless jade, enter that rugged arena where Americans have wrangled over their domestic affairs for 154 years. But, for that matter, so was everybody else. When the slim and graceful "Missimo" appeared a gasp went around the galleries and people leaned forward to have a better look. Yet the Fathers, if present, quickly discovered that this was no glamour-queen come to charm the Congress away from its legislative duties. On the contrary. Here was a voice from Asia, speaking a cultured English (with a slight trace of the Georgia accent she acquired in her girlhood) and propounding the very principles that the Fathers had been at such pains to develop.

Thus the tone was set for the way Madame Chiang would be received by the general public for the rest of her visit. As one journalist summed it up in the next issue of *Life:* "If the Generalissimo could take the Japs as Madame took Congress, the war in the Pacific would be over in the bat of an eyelash."[42]

Madame Chiang and Chinese Americans

When her train pulled into New York City's Pennsylvania Station on the morning of March 1, Madame Chiang was met by Mayor Fiorello La Guardia, Dr. Tsun-chi Yü, the Chinese consul general in New York, and her brother T. L. Soong. Although she would give well-received speeches to general audiences while in

New York, she also, for the first time, addressed the Chinese American community directly, an audience that she would continue to meet and cultivate for the rest of her tour. At the train station she was given a large bouquet of roses and narcissi by Adet Lin, daughter of the famous Chinese scholar Lin Yutang, and Florence Chu, daughter of T. W. Chu, secretary of the Chinese Consolidated Benevolent Society. From the train station she was taken to city hall where she addressed a crowd of a reported fifty thousand people. After this speech she made a brief visit to Chinatown, where thousands lined the streets to see her. American and Chinese flags hung from buildings; vendors sold buttons of her likeness and small Chinese and American flags. The *New York Times* linked China and Chinatown to the rest of the country because of a shared experience: "It was Chinatown's day, not as a city curiosity, but as a link to another nation that has suffered from Japanese aggression. The distance between Pearl Harbor and Pell Street grew small."[43]

At Carnegie Hall Madame Chiang addressed three thousand Chinese and Chinese Americans. She spoke in Chinese (in Mandarin, which was not understood by all of the predominantly Cantonese-speaking audience) and with fierce emotion. In addition to her usual emphasis on the war in China, she spoke to the audience as fellow Chinese. She thanked Chinese Americans for their financial contributions to China, though she realized many had scant resources to give. She told them they should be proud of being Chinese because China had shown its mettle in its war against Japan. At the same time, she warned them not to become arrogant or disrespectful because they represented China to the world and they should not tarnish its image. She also urged those who had American citizenship to be good citizens in order to "be worthy of the Chinese people," and she declared that since China was now a partner of the United Nations, Chinese should not only think of their rights but also be aware of their responsibilities. She stressed that she was proud of the Chinese in America because they had "never gone on relief."[44]

The coverage of Madame Chiang when in the presence of Chinese Americans took on a slightly different tone. The clothing of white Americans around her was rarely mentioned, but the two Chinese American girls who gave her flowers at the train station were described as wearing "Chinese costumes," with the word "costumes" seeming to imply some exotic dress; in fact they were simply wearing Chinese-styled dresses, the kind of dresses Chinese American girls and women wore on special occasions, ranging from dinner parties and holidays to meetings with important people or significant events as when they carried the flag in the Rice Bowl parades. When she was with Chinese Americans, the press coverage emphasized their "foreignness" by referring to Chinatowns as "colonies" and the people there as her "countrymen" or "compatriots," often ignoring the fact that many were actually American-born and hence American citizens. Madame Chiang herself carried this attitude forward as she often referred to the Chinese and Chinese Americans in her audience as "my own people." Her praise for the Chinese in America was not for their endurance under restrictive legislation or social marginalization, but for their loyalty to China.

This was very much in accord with the general approach of the Chinese government toward overseas Chinese. The historian L. Ling-chi Wang argues that while U.S. society has expected "total assimilation" by Chinese Americans, for China "the primary concern has been the loyalty of the *huaqiao* or the Chinese in diaspora." Wang identifies two competing paradigms for understanding the history and life of overseas Chinese, *luoye guigen* and *luodi shenggen*. The first phrase implies that Chines abroad, like "fallen leaves will return to their roots" in China, whereas the second sees them as "seeds sown on foreign soil, taking root wherever they have emigrated."[45] While Wang sees these two paradigms as competing, it can be argued that Madame Chiang tried to use them simultaneously in her relationship to the Chinese in the United States. She praised their loyalty to China and their willingness to support China financially, but she also urged them to be good American citizens. To Chiang, it was possible, indeed it was incumbent upon overseas Chinese, to be of both minds: to remain loyal to China and maintain the sense of being Chinese, while being model citizens of the United States, if for no other reason than to reflect well on China.

In San Francisco as in New York, the Chinese American community played a prominent role in hosting Madame Chiang during her visit to the city. From the Embarcadero she was driven through Chinatown, where a temporary Chinese arch was constructed over Grant Avenue. The streets were lined with thousands of people waving Chinese and American flags, many singing "The March of the Volunteers," the song that had come to symbolize China's resistance against Japan. Chiang did not stop in Chinatown, but was taken to her hotel. She later went to city hall to watch a parade in her honor, which included military units and Chinese American student groups. She was apparently quite taken by the presence of the students, commenting, "I never dreamed there were so many Chinese children here."[46]

In San Francisco Madame Chiang held press conferences and delivered two speeches at the civic auditorium, one for a general audience and one for the Chinese American community. She generally made the same points she had in her earlier speeches, using Chinese anecdotes to illustrate her points about China's resolve and need for aid, and she again encouraged the Chinese in America to be good U.S. citizens: "I should like to say that I hope, wherever my compatriots go, into whatever land they are adopted, they become loyal citizens of that country."[47] The Marinship shipyard in Sausalito honored her presence in San Francisco by declaring March 26, 1943, "Chinese Day." On that date Madame Wei Tao-ming, wife of the Chinese ambassador to the United States, christened a new Liberty ship built at the shipyard, the SS *Sun Yat-sen*. In addition, Chinese American employees at Marinship presented a portion of their wages to the United China relief in honor of Chiang's visit to the Bay Area.[48] Treated like a head of state, Madame Chiang had certainly captured the attention of the public. She appears to have inspired a great many people, both Chinese Americans and others, by her personality, words, and presence.

The reception of her visit to San Francisco, as seen in the "Welcome Madame Chiang Kai-shek" edition of the *Chinese Press*, bears this out. Her portrait is featured on the front cover with a map of Asia in the background. There are a variety of laudatory articles covering her life or drawing connections between her and the involvement of Chinese Americans in the war effort; one focusing on her years at college "about a Wellesley girl, written by two Wellesley girls"; a recap of her visits to other cities and excerpts from her speeches; an article by Dr. Hu Shih on the role of women in Chinese history; and features on local Chinese American women in the Women's Auxiliary Army Corps (WAAC) or in the defense industries, including a report that the actor Anna May Wong had signed up to be an air raid warden in Santa Monica, saying: "As an American-born Chinese, I feel it is a privilege to be able to do my little bit in return for the many advantages bestowed upon me by a free democracy."

Much of the issue also contains advertisements and endorsements that speak to the respect accorded to Madame Chiang.

Local stores and businesses took out advertisements that welcomed Chiang and praised her for her commitment to democratic reforms. The ad for Frank's Sportswear on Grant Avenue was in the form of a letter addressed to "My dear Madame Chiang Kai-shek" declaring: "You are the inspiration in which the essence of a universal understanding may be conceived." The China Lady, a women's store on Grant Avenue, saw the future of Chinese women in Chiang's example: "In Madame Chiang Kai-shek we have the symbol of a new culture in which Chinese women have found themselves by confidence in their own strength to make democracy survive." Other stores and businesses joined together to sponsor larger ads, which often highlighted the contributions of Chinese Americans to the building of the United States as well as praising Chiang. A two-page ad from various Chinatown businesses read: "For 100 years we Chinese have lived in California, working to make our community an integral institution of this region . . . We welcome you, Madame Chiang, as an outstanding Chinese leader. We welcome you as a woman who is proving the glory of womanhood. And, proving among leaders of both sexes, of all nations, of all times, you rank with the truly great."

Some of the ads in this issue of the *Chinese Press* were taken out by businesses from other cities. Los Angeles Chinatown merchants described Chiang as a leader of modern thinking and living and asserted that Los Angeles Chinatown was the largest and most progressive Chinese community in the Southwest, one that believed in modern living and was trying to follow in her footsteps. The advertisements and endorsements from Stockton, Fresno, and Sacramento all make some mention of the history of the Chinese in California and welcome Chiang's visit as a special moment in that long history, while the merchants from Tucson, Arizona, refer to the Chinese cadets being trained there for the Chinese Air Force as an example of how the Chinese in Tucson have "always been regarded as an integral part of the economic and civic life of a community that includes among its pioneer citizens many Chinese families who have done their part in the building of a modern Southwestern city."

Not all the advertisements in the issue were from Chinese-owned businesses. Major department stores such as Gump's and I. Magnin also took out ads welcoming Chiang to the city, whereas Ransohoff's, a fashion shop, hailed Chiang for her "indomitable spirit which in serving valiantly through the yoke of aggression . . . has inspired the love and admiration of not only the brave people of China . . . but all the United Nations." Most telling was a full-page ad shared by a number of businesses, some of which identified themselves as "friends of the Chinese." This ad welcomed Chiang in very flattering terms:

> You are a symbol, Madame Chiang. A symbol of courage and bravery, tolerance and humanity. You represent the fortitude of four-hundred-million Chinese, fighting for their country. You represent the thousands of millions all over the world, fighting, hoping, praying for a new world, a better world, a world of freedom and peace and kindliness . . . We are proud that you will visit our Chinatown, which plays such an important part in San Francisco's community life . . . We welcome you and the things you represent."

One could certainly argue that these ads were worded in such flattering terms in order to curry favor with potential Chinese American customers, but even if that argument is correct, the fact that mainstream American businesses were courting a Chinese American clientele indicates that the image of Chinese Americans had improved in American society. It is more likely that these businesses had long-established relationships with the Chinese American community and were showing their support of Chiang and the people of Chinatown through these ads. The war, and perhaps the presence of Madame Chiang, had the effect of slowly eroding the barriers between Chinese San Franciscans and the city at large.

A Farewell Gala

After San Francisco, Madame Chiang traveled south to Los Angeles for the final stop on her American tour. The highlight of her stay was her appearance at the Hollywood Bowl on the afternoon of April 4, 1943. Produced by David O. Selznick, "China: A Symphonic Narrative" was an elaborate spectacle in front of thirty thousand people with music provided by the Los Angeles Symphony Orchestra, a narration read by the actor Walter Huston, and five hundred Chinese Americans acting out scenes of China's history and its role in the war. As the performance came to an end, Madame Chiang rose to give her speech, which recounted China's struggle against the Japanese and also touched on the close relationship between China and the United States. Hailed as a great success, this was viewed as a proper ending to her impassioned tour.

The staging of the history of China was carried out in a way that hinted at the similarities between the two countries. The Chinese flight to the west to escape Japanese aggression brought to mind the American westward movement, and as the actors struggled to build a new China in the West, the message was clear: "Old China was being replaced by a new China, one more educated, industrialized, democratic and Americanized."[49] Madame Chiang's persona and ability to easily address Americans added to the notion that China and America had similar goals and ideals. Surrounded on stage by a welcoming committee that included famous stars such as Joan Bennett, Ingrid Bergman, Rita Hayworth, and Lana Turner, Madame Chiang, dressed impeccably as usual, seemed to be an international star as well. Behind the scenes, however, Selznick sought to keep Chinese Americans on the margins of this production. He used them as actors, but they had limited access to tickets to see the show and he balked at the suggestion that Chinese American Boy and Girl Scouts be allowed to sell programs, writing: "This is a tribute from Americans to Madam Chiang and not from the Chinese to Madam Chiang." Like many others, Selznick continued to see Chinese Americans as Chinese rather than as Americans, and so decided to limit their participation in the production of his vision of Chinese history and Sino-American relations.

Not everyone was enthralled by Madame Chiang during her tour. Many were indeed wrapped up in what the China correspondent A. T. Steele would characterize as "a period of dreamy unreality, in which the American public seemed prepared to accept and believe anything and everything good and wonderful that was said about the Chinese, their Generalissimo, the Generalissimo's wife and the heroic Chinese people." But Patricia Neils describes another point of view: "Madame Chiang had so captivated the warmth and sympathy of Americans that they seemed undisturbed by critics who grumbled that she personally did not reflect any of the destitution for which she pleaded. She traveled with an exquisite wardrobe that included a variety of fur coats and brought along her own silk sheets which were changed every day. Her rudeness to hotel employees and her insistence on the very finest accommodations went virtually uncriticized by her millions of American admirers." One wonders what the working-class residents of Chinatown and elsewhere said to themselves about her dining on solid gold dishes during the war, while accepting checks for the "warphans." Theodore White, also a China correspondent during the war, would later describe her as "a beautiful, tart and brittle woman, more American than Chinese, and mistress of every level of the American language from the verses of the hymnal to the most sophisticated bitchery. Madame Chiang, always stunning in her silk gowns, could be as coy and kittenish as a college coed, or as commanding and petty as a dormitory house mother. She swished briskly into any room like a queen, and could bustle even sitting down." It is obvious that White had his own biases against Madame Chiang's persona, but her strong personality and class privilege did grate on many who found her less gracious than the media often made her out to be.[50]

Despite these criticisms, the general reception of Madame Chiang by both the general American public and the Chinese American community was very positive. By making China more familiar to Americans, she made it easier for them to embrace China's cause. She was American-educated, Christian, attractive, fluent in English, and an outstanding orator. For many Chinese Americans, she was all these things and more: she represented a modern and respected China; and she was a heroine they could believe in, one who made them proud of their cultural roots, and one who had America's press and celebrities eager to pay homage to her.

The End of the Exclusion Acts

Some scholars have criticized Madame Chiang for not confronting the racial discrimination faced by the Chinese in America or the continued enforcement of the Chinese Exclusion Acts.[51] While it is true that she said little in public about these concerns, her presence does appear to have contributed to the softening of American sentiments toward China and toward the Chinese in America. Madame Chiang apparently took a hand in U.S. politics in mid-May 1943, when she invited several key congressmen to dinner, days before the House committee on immigration and naturalization was to begin hearings on various repeal bills. She is said to have stressed how much repeal of the Exclusion Acts would boost Chinese morale and thus contribute to the war effort.[52] Throughout the congressional hearings and debates over the scope of repeal, establishing an annual quota for Chinese immigrants, and granting them the right of naturalization, Madame Chiang was repeatedly invoked by supporters of the repeal measures.

The push for repeal came primarily from the Citizens Committee to Repeal Chinese Exclusion, a group of well-connected white Americans who had ties to China in one way or another. According to Fred Riggs's account of the campaign, in the summer of 1941 Donald Dunham, returning from American consular service in Hong Kong, made contact with Richard J. Walsh, president of the John Day Company, a publishing house, and editor of *Asia* (later called *Asia and the Americas*), a liberal magazine that sought closer ties between the United States and various countries in Asia. Walsh, who was married to the novelist Pearl S. Buck, asked Dunham to write a memorandum on the repeal of the Chinese Exclusion Acts. Walsh gave Dunham's piece to Charles Nelson Spinks, a scholar of Far Eastern culture and history. Spinks added historical context to the memorandum, and it was published under Spinks's name in Walsh's magazine as "Repeal Chinese Exclusion!" The article argued that exclusionary legislation violated American principles of justice and equality. Spinks reviewed legal cases that had established the ineligibility of Asian immigrants for American citizenship (the only racial group ruled ineligible), and pointed out that whereas the 1924 Immigration Act denied entrance to anyone who was ineligible for citizenship, only the Chinese were excluded by a set of specific laws that named them directly. He maintained that most Americans would favor repeal if not for the fear that it would lead to a large influx of Asian immigrants which would threaten the American economy and society. If the Chinese were allowed in on the same basis as other immigrants, he argued, only about two thousand Chinese and a handful of other Asians would be able to enter the country annually, numbers that would not have a great impact. Most important: "As our allies, the Chinese deserve racial equality now. As fellow human beings, they have been entitled to it ever since the United States first came into contact with their country."[53]

The article received considerable attention, and support for repeal grew. By early 1943 the Citizens Committee to Repeal Chinese Exclusion was meeting in New York to map out its strategy. At the same time, Madame Chiang had begun her tour of the United States. Seizing on her presence in the country, Martin Kennedy, a Democratic congressman from New York, introduced House Resolution (HR) 1882, calling for repealing the Exclusion Act and making Chinese eligible for naturalization. (The resolution number, 1882, matched the year of the passage of the first exclusion bill, which had prohibited the immigration of Chinese laborers for ten years.) Other versions of the resolution and amendments followed in steady succession. Some congressmen wanted to repeal all the laws that excluded Asians from immigrating and naturalization; others advocated putting the Chinese on the quota system established by the 1924 Immigration Act; and some wanted to include a provision allowing Chinese men to bring their wives into the country as non-quota immigrants. In the end the version that garnered the most support was HR 3070, sponsored by a Democrat from Washington state, Warren Magnuson. It called for repealing the Chinese exclusion statutes, establishing an annual quota based on the system outlined in the 1924 Immigration Act, and allowing Chinese immigrants to apply for citizenship. This bill passed the House on October 21 and the Senate on November 26, and President Roosevelt signed it into law on December 17, 1943.

Debates over Repeal

The process through which the exclusion laws were repealed and the language in which the debate was framed revealed the positioning of Chinese and Chinese Americans as the "good Asians" during the war. As Congress debated repeal, much of the rhetoric employed on both sides was reminiscent of the debates over "the Chinese question" in the late nineteenth and early twentieth centuries. Those opposed to repeal came from four main constituencies: organized labor, veterans' groups, "patriotic" societies, and some West Coast interests. Among those who supported some form of repeal were commercial interests, religious groups, "China hands," and Chinese Americans and Chinese nationals. The debate focused on a number of overlapping and interrelated issues: countering anti-American propaganda employed by the Japanese, raising Chinese morale in order to aid their war effort, notions of racial equality, and the fear that repeal would allow so many Asian immigrants into the country that their presence would threaten the postwar economy and create racial tensions.

The issue of Japanese propaganda was at the forefront of much of the congressional discussion. Pearl Buck testified: "The Japanese have not failed to taunt them [the Chinese] with the friendliness of our words and the unfriendliness of our deeds.

The Chinese have heard this propaganda and while they have not heeded it much, it has nevertheless been true. As a war measure, it would simply be the wisest thing we could do to make it impossible for Japan to use this sort of propaganda any more, by making it untrue." Warren Magnuson echoed these concerns, citing a translation of a Japanese radio broadcast that said: "What are you fellows [the Chinese] fooling around with the United States for, in this war when they won't even let you stand on the same basis as a Turk or Armenian or an Italian." Magnuson went on to state that the passage of repeal would give the Chinese government "one of the greatest counterpropaganda weapons it could have." Senator Carl Curtis, a Nebraska Republican, took the need to counter Japanese propaganda in a different direction, citing his fear of the consequences of the Chinese joining the Japanese: "I am the father of two little children. I cannot see it any other way that the future is black if all of the yellow and brown men of Asia turn against us. I believe one of the most important things we have to do is to see to it that our war in the Pacific does not end up as a race war."[54]

Others, however, were not convinced by the argument that repeal would counter Japanese propaganda and bolster Chinese morale. Congressman John Bennett, a Republican of Michigan, declared that this idea was "pure poppycock and nothing else. You cannot eliminate enemy propaganda by legislation." In fact, Bennett declared, repeal would do little to help China: "Its value is purely psychological and aesthetic and . . . it is very difficult to appreciate aesthetic things in life on an empty stomach." Bertrand Gearhart, a California Republican, asserted that repeal would not defeat Japanese propaganda but bolster it. If Congress repealed exclusion for the Chinese only, the Japanese could then turn to the Filipinos and tell them that "the United States holds them in such contempt that we have by our laws declared theirs to be the only race so inferior and so degraded as to be unfit to enter the United States, even on the quota basis."[55]

The proposal to establish an annual quota for the Chinese was as equally sensitive for many. While some believed a quota would signify that the Chinese were seen as equals of other immigrants, others did not want to tamper with the nation's immigration laws during wartime, and still others feared that the proposed change would open the floodgates to a deluge of Asian immigrants and refugees. Supporters pointed out that "Hitler could come in under a quota, Mussolini could come in under a quota, but Madame Chiang Kai-shek, or the finest type of Chinese people, cannot because we say they are ineligible to come here." But opponents, such as the national committees of the American Federation of Labor, the American Legion, and the Veterans of Foreign Wars, feared that a rise in Asian immigration would threaten the job prospects of returning veterans after the war, and that if Chinese were allowed to immigrate, other Asians would then seek the same privilege: "There would be no tenable argument after this war to deny admission to the Japanese, Hindus, Malays, and all other people of the brown and yellow races."[56]

Race and Citizenship

Underlying the arguments for and against repeal were American attitudes toward race and citizenship and toward Chinese and Chinese Americans. One can observe the positive shift in the images of Chinese in these debates as well as the persistence of very negative views. Those who supported repeal often denounced the racial discrimination that was practiced through exclusion, though they usually framed their argument in relation to the war effort, Japanese propaganda, and America's international reputation, rather than in terms of the moral questions of racism and social equality. The rhetoric of those opposed to repeal may have stressed issues of economics and wartime conditions, but their racial antipathy toward the Chinese was evident, as was general opposition to racial equality and integration. Many opponents of repeal asked witnesses if they supported equality for all racial groups in all social situations, implying that approval of repeal was linked to their stand on segregation.

One of repeal's most ardent supporters, the Minnesota Republican Walter Judd, appealed to his colleagues in Congress to pass the repeal bill on the grounds of fair and equal treatment. He remarked: "The Chinese are good enough to die by the millions in a war against Axis tyranny—but a Chinese who is not born in the United States is not good enough, so the law implies, to become an American citizen by naturalization. A man of German descent may so be naturalized, and so may an Italian. But a Chinese alien is not so fortunate. He is beyond the pale." Judd went on to point out that many Americans knew that the Chinese were not inferior, as American laws had deemed them to be: "In the United States we have come to admire the Chinese for his industry, his intelligence, his patriotism, and his good faith, and we have come see, in the person of Mme. Chiang Kai-shek, the symbol of a truly great people." Judd's sentiments were echoed by the California Democrat Thomas Ford, who spoke of the similarities between Americans and Chinese: they shared a "love of liberty," and were "reliable people," "honest, . . . loyal, . . . and good citizens in every sense of the word." Ford concluded with a strong endorsement of repeal: "I am sure the Chinese will make a distinct and tremendously valuable contribution to freedom as conceived by democracy." Pearl S. Buck concurred on the quality of Chinese as citizens, using language that would reappear in the 1960s as Chinese Americans were hailed as the "model minority": "The Chinese we have here are among our best citizens—they do not go on relief; their crime record is very low; they are honest and industrious and friendly."[57]

While organized labor saw repeal as a threat to the postwar job opportunities of returning veterans and others were against changing immigration policies during a time of war, some opponents simply continued to make racialized attacks on the Chinese and to argue that they could not become Americans. William Green, president of the American Federation of Labor, was quoted as saying: "People from other countries are absorbed in a few years and you can't tell where they came from. A Chinaman is a Chinaman. Haven't you noticed that?" Sounding like the politicians from western states in the late nineteenth century, Compton White, an Idaho Democrat, declared:

> I do not think we can take the Chinese with their habits and mentalities in this year and time into our great American melting pot and in 10 years or a hundred years bring them up to our standards of civilization. It is impossible. We may be placed in the same position as the sentimentalists were in the South after the Civil War who wanted to do something grand for civilization. You have got a long, tough job to bring them up, and you still have race riots and other racial problems confronting you.

Not content with this white supremacist tirade, White asked his colleagues: "How many of you Members know anything of the devious ways of the 'wily Chinese?'" He cited their slave-like labor conditions, their penchant for gambling and opium smoking, and their filthy standards of living. Yet he finished by stating: "I have no animosity against the Chinese. We children loved the Chinese cooks and laundrymen who lavished Chinese 'good-

ies' on us on Chinese New Year's—and even remembered our own Christmas. Let us help the Chinese—but help them in their own country!"[58]

Among those testifying against repeal were members of "patriotic societies," who sometimes couched their opposition in economic terms. James L. Wilmeth, speaking for the National Council, Junior Order, of the United American Mechanics, a fraternal patriotic organization, expressed his fear that repeal would "be an entering wedge by which you [Congress] are going to flood this country with cheap labor and threaten our people with that ruinous competition." Representing the Crusading Mothers of Pennsylvania and the National Blue Star Mothers, Agnes Waters did not mince words in expressing her opposition to repeal. Waters clearly set Chinese and other minorities apart from those whom she considered American when she declared: "We are for Americans only. The mothers of America intend to keep this nation first, last, and forever for Americans." Repealing the exclusion acts would jeopardize American society because "practically all of the Chinese are Communists and when they come here, they come in here to ruin this country . . . These people are enemies coming in here as Trojan horses. And the Chinese race is a yellow race the white people have to fight . . . We should never forget that a friend today can be an enemy tomorrow. Why flood this country with yellow races?" It is clear from the hearings that there was considerable support for both sides of the issue. While Chinese and Chinese Americans had indeed risen in the eyes of many Americans, others still regarded them as racially inferior and a threat to the United States.[59]

Japanese Americans, however, remained the main enemy of the nation. While the debates over repeal were still taking place, the California Democrat Alfred Elliot rose to tell his colleagues in the House of Representatives that he had been informed that the War Relocation Authority had begun releasing some Japanese Americans from the internment camps and that they were being "shipped to the west coast." He said this would only bring bloodshed because the people of his district did not want the Japanese Americans to return. He then made his own feelings clear: "As I have said before in this House, the only good Jap is a dead Jap, and that is just what is going to happen to every one of them that is sent back there. So the Government better wake up and keep those Japs in camps where they belong . . . When the war is over, as far as I am concerned, we should ship every Jap in the United States back to Japan, if there is any Japan left to ship them to."[60] Individuals like Agnes Waters may have lumped the Chinese and Japanese together as members of the "yellow races," and labor unions may have feared the "entering wedge" of "cheap labor," but no one who spoke in the public hearings over repeal advocated killing Chinese Americans or shipping them "back" to China. During this period, Chinese and Chinese Americans were definitely seen as less of a threat to American culture and society than Japanese and Japanese Americans.

When President Roosevelt sent a letter to Congress urging the passage of the bill to repeal exclusion, he made no reference to issues of racial and social equality. Instead, he reassured Congress that the small number of Chinese admitted each year would have little impact on employment, that repeal would be a weapon against Japanese propaganda, that it would show the Chinese that the United States was acting in good faith, and that

although it "would give the Chinese a preferred status over certain other oriental people, their great contribution to the cause of decency and freedom entitles them to such preference."[61] Thus, like many members of Congress and the American public, the president pursued repeal, not on moral grounds, but rather as an expedient way to further American wartime goals.

The Impact of Repeal

One of the most striking aspects of the repeal movement is the absence of a strong Chinese immigrant or Chinese American presence in the public campaign. In fact, these groups were kept on the margins of the movement by the very people pushing for repeal. According to Fred Riggs, the Citizens Committee to Repeal Chinese Exclusion decided early on to limit its membership to "American citizens not of Asiatic origin so as to give the impression that the demand was completely indigenous, and not fostered by the Chinese or anyone with a personal 'axe to grind.'" This approach was a continuation of a patronizing and paternalistic attitude that many supposedly well-meaning Americans maintained toward Chinese Americans. The committee's decision to limit membership to "Americans" served to deprive Chinese Americans of their legal status as "Americans" and made one writer feel as if "we were just outside observers."[62]

Nevertheless, Chinese Americans were not silent on the issue. They wrote letters to political figures and they let it be known that the repeal of the exclusion laws was indeed something important to them. Taking a very accommodating yet direct line, Theodora Chan Wang, representing the Chinese Women's Association, Inc., of New York City, took the opportunity offered by Madame Chiang's visit to the United States and wrote to Eleanor Roosevelt expressing support for the establishment of an immigration quota for the Chinese. Wang stressed the issue of equality with other nations without mentioning them by name, hoping that "a quota may be established—however limited it might be—whereby members of the Chinese race would be accorded the privileges enjoyed by our companions in ideology and arms." She addressed the concern that repeal might lead to an influx of unwanted labor, and she emphasized that setting a quota would simply send a message to the Chinese that the United States was sincere in its proclamations of equality. Otherwise, she went on, the Chinese would continue to be "savagely assailed by the irrefutable claims of [the] Japanese that those who would accept us as their brothers-in-arms yet regard us as strangers within their gates . . . They see only the cold facts before them."[63]

In the spring of 1942 the *Chinese Press* began publishing articles on organizations that supported repeal. It reported that the California League of Women Voters had approved a resolution urging repeal because of the racial discrimination inherent in the exclusion laws. According to the newspaper, this was the first step taken by an "American" organization since 1937 to have the laws repealed. Later that summer the paper reported that Dr. Roy Smith, editor of the *Christian Advocate,* had told two thousand members of the Women's Society of the Christian Service that the Chinese should be given the right of naturalization. It quoted Smith as having said: "If the war should end tomorrow, we would admit Germans and Italians to citizenship on a quota basis. Why should we not admit the Chinese? We Americans should remove all restrictions of color and race and welcome all foreigners to citizenship on the basis of character."[64]

As the national campaign for repeal picked up steam, Chinese American periodicals ran more articles and advertisements in its support. When the San Francisco Chamber of Commerce voted to support repeal and the establishment of a quota for the Chinese, it was front-page news. The *Chinese Press* also encouraged its readers to send letters to their representatives in Congress urging them to support the movement for repeal. And when San Francisco's City Board of Supervisors voted in favor of repeal, the *Chinese Press* commented: "Sixty years ago [the city] was the chief center of violent 'The Chinese must go' discriminatory measures, this week [it] repaid its debt to justice." Just above the article in which that comment appeared was a large photograph of Mr. Chow Fong receiving Silver Star and Purple Heart medals awarded posthumously to his son Lieutenant Albert P. Fong, who had fallen in combat. In addition to articles of this kind, there were advertisements that proclaimed support for the Chinese American community. One taken out by the International Longshoremen's and Warehousemen's Union was especially poignant: "Here is where we Stand . . . From 1935 on we refused to pass the picket lines of the Chinese People as they protested the sending of scrap iron to Japanese militarist murderers. We stand now for repeal of the Chinese exclusion laws, and for full equality of the Chinese people with all of us. We are united with the Chinese People and with them we will fight for the right of all to use the maximum energy against the common enemy on an equal basis."[65]

Chinese American periodicals also urged their readers to vote. In one instance, the *Chinese Press* featured a picture of a Chinese soldier "fighting the battle for Freedom and Democracy" with text proclaiming: "One of the privileges of democracy is the right to vote, to vote for leaders of your choice. You Americans of Chinese ancestry have a precious heritage. Preserve this heritage by using it! Don't abuse it by shunning your rights and obligations as citizens. Vote—It's the American Way."[66] Although they did not lead the fight to repeal the Exclusion Act, Chinese Americans were determined to claim their place in American society.

When the details of the repeal were worked out, there were three main advances for Chinese immigrants and Chinese Americans: repeal ended sixty-one years of the exclusion of Chinese immigrants; it established an annual quota based on the system established in the Immigration Act of 1924; and it allowed Chinese immigrants to apply for naturalization. However, the new law was a limited victory for the Chinese. Chinese wives of American citizens were not allowed to enter as non-quota immigrants; the annual quota was set at a mere 105; and naturalization was open only to those who could prove they had entered the country legally, who also had to pass an English-proficiency test and demonstrate a knowledge of American history and the Constitution. These hurdles would prove insurmountable for many immigrants.[67]

The low annual quota was revealing of persistent racial antagonism. Although the quota was on a par with those of some other nations according to the Immigration Act of 1924 (2 percent of a country's population in the United States as of the 1890 Census), it was assigned to the Chinese as a "race," rather than on the basis of nativity. Seventy-five percent of the entrants were to come from China and the rest from elsewhere. Moreover, the language that determined the quota also shaped who was to be considered "Chinese." The definition of Chinese persons and persons of Chinese descent was both broad and specific: "persons who are of as much as one-half Chinese blood and are not as much as one-half blood of a race ineligible to citizenship."[68] Therefore, a person with one Chinese parent and one parent from another Asian country (or in the parlance of the time, "race") could not enter the United States. Despite this restriction, Chinese immigrants now had a better chance of entering the country because of repeal and the lifting of the ban on naturalization. Those from other Asian "races" would have to wait until the postwar years to be granted the right of naturalized citizenship.

In the long run, repeal would not have a great impact on the rate of Chinese immigration or naturalization, and yet the repeal of the Chinese Exclusion Acts in 1943 would eventually prove to be the "entering wedge" that its opponents feared it would be. As laws excluding Filipinos, South Asians, Koreans, and Japanese were repealed in the decade after the war, allowing more Asians to enter the United States and become American citizens, racial barriers to naturalization would fall, culminating in the Immigration Act of 1965, which did away with racial and geographic restrictions on immigration.[69]

One of the harshest critics of the repeal process and its outcome, L. Ling-chi Wang, has argued that Chinese Americans gained little from repeal, and that furthermore they "were permitted only to play a very limited and prescribed role assigned to them by the Citizens' Committee." That role, according to Wang, was to demonstrate that "Chinese in America were no longer the coolies, the heathens, and the immoral, inassimilable human beings of the past. Instead they were fully Americanized and assimilated, posing no threat to the moral and racial purity of the United States."[70]

Wang, however, misses an important point. Chinese Americans were not forced by other parties to demonstrate that they were not "coolies and heathens." They themselves went to great lengths to change their image in the eyes of other Americans. Not wanting to be seen as immoral pariahs, they actively sought to be accepted as part of the American social landscape. Their participation in the war effort provided them with that opportunity. In a letter to Charles Thomson of the department of state, Donald L. Chu wrote that he expected to be inducted soon. He continued: "Personally, I don't mind for I always want to do my part for America. However, I hate to think of this: I am given a chance to naturalization only at the risk of my life! I believe there's no better way of promoting better cultural relations between China and U.S.A. other than the immediate repealing of the Exclusion Act!"[71] This was not a man who was being assigned and accepting a racially subservient role, but someone who was trying to carve out a place in American society on his own terms, even if it meant accommodating to a legal stipulation that he resented.

✪ If the Chinese had no souls to save in 1876, by 1943 Chinese Americans were coming to occupy a new status. As they developed a better sense of themselves as Americans, embracing the "internal experience of citizenship," the wider public viewed them in a more positive light. Their status also rose as they distanced themselves from Japanese Americans after Japan became the nation's enemy—although in doing so they helped to perpetuate false accusations of fifth-column activity among Americans of Japanese descent. By becoming the "good Asian in the good war," Chinese Americans found a new position in American society.

4

Hawai'i's Local Warriors

The racial and ethnic composition of the Hawaiian Islands was much more complicated than that of the U.S. mainland. Although the society and economy of Hawai'i had long been dominated by white businesses and missionary efforts, Asians constituted the majority of the population. Local Chinese were not segregated in Chinatowns but lived all over the islands and held a wide variety of occupations. (I use the term "local Chinese" to denote Chinese or Chinese Americans living in Hawai'i, as opposed to those living in the continental United States or China and those of mixed heritage living in Hawai'i. The terms "Hawaiian Chinese" and "Chinese Hawaiian" signify those of mixed Hawaiian and Chinese ancestry.)

Whites generally occupied managerial positions and owned the better tracts of land, but despite this racial stratification there appears to have been much less overt racial hostility in Hawai'i before the war than existed on the mainland. There were no strict Jim Crow–like mechanisms of segregation that kept Chinese and other Asians from finding a range of socioeconomic opportunities. Prior to the war, most whites were considered to be of the genteel upper classes, somewhat untouchable and beyond reproach. "Locals," whether Chinese, Japanese, Filipino, Korean, or Hawaiian, were generally a caste below, rarely finding upper-level jobs and usually working in lower-level positions, as small shopkeepers, in skilled trades, or in plantation work or other sorts of manual labor.

The Second World War brought about substantial changes in racial attitudes and race relations. As working-class whites and blacks migrated to Hawai'i, either as military personnel or as defense workers, the racial mix of the islands was transformed. In the process, new tensions arose and new racial hierarchies emerged. By the time the war ended the Chinese of Hawai'i had encountered a broad range of white workers and realized that whites were not all destined to belong to the upper class. Those who had seen military service returned from the war with experiences of the wider world which provided comparisons and contrasts to what they left behind. They would come to embrace a broader vision of what it meant to be local Chinese or Chinese American vis-à-vis other racial and ethnic groups, and they would strive to improve their position in Hawai'i's multiracial society.

The Early Chinese of Hawai'i

Chinese began traveling to the Hawaiian Islands in the late eighteenth century after the islands became a major hub in the European-American-Asian trade circuit. The first Chinese to reach Hawai'i were probably in the employ of American or British ship captains. In 1789 the American trader Captain Simon Metcalf left Macao for the American Northwest on the *Eleanora* with a crew that included forty-five Chinese. The ship wintered in Hawai'i, and it is possible that some of the Chinese crew decided to remain there. In 1939 the Chinese community in Hawai'i celebrated 150 years of Chinese presence in the islands, using 1789 as the date of the first Chinese to arrive. One reason the Chinese found Hawai'i attractive was that sandalwood grew plentifully on the islands. This fragrant wood was a popular item with the Chinese, who used it for incense, carved fans, and other luxury goods. American and British traders were soon scouring the islands for sandalwood to sell to the Chinese in Canton. After the War of 1812, British mercantile interests in Hawai'i began to decline, and large American firms came to dominate the sandalwood trade. By the 1850s several million dollars' worth of the treasured wood had left the islands for the markets of Canton. The tremendous demand for sandalwood in China had depleted the Hawaiian supply, but the Chinese continued to call Hawai'i the "Sandalwood Mountains."[1]

As contact between China and the islands increased, Chinese began to emigrate in search of employment opportunities. Some tried to make a living in agriculture, but most of the early Chinese immigrants were small-scale entrepreneurs and artisans who found jobs in the main island ports. Although sugar production in the islands eventually would be controlled by American business concerns, it was pioneered by the Chinese. According to an account published in 1852, the first Chinese "sugar master," Wong Tze-chun, reached Hawai'i on a sandalwood trading ship in 1802, bringing with him a vertical mill and boilers. He set up his operation on the island of Lanai, raised a small crop of cane, and made sugar. His enterprise was not successful, however, and he returned to China the following year. This early disappointment did not deter others, and by the 1830s Chinese-owned sugar companies had established a foothold in Hawai'i, supplying both capital and skilled Chinese labor to the operations. One company, Samsing and Co., was based in Honolulu but manufactured sugar at one time or another at Waimea, Kohala, and Hilo on the island of Hawai'i and at Lahaina on Maui. During the 1840s and 1850s at least six Chinese-run operations were producing sugar on the island of Hawai'i.[2]

The most famous of the Chinese sugar growers was Chun Fong from the Zhongshan district of Guangdong province (from where most of the Chinese in Hawai'i trace their origins). Known locally as Afong, he had a number of business interests in Honolulu, where he married a Hawaiian woman of noble lineage, with whom he had twelve daughters and four sons. The practice of marrying Hawaiian women of high social status helped the Chinese secure a solid standing in the social hierarchy, often serving to place them above other Asian immigrants and settlers. Afong eventually became the largest shareholder in Peepeekeo Plantation near Hilo. In 1888, with 326 workers and close to twelve hundred acres of sugarcane, this plantation ranked twelfth among the seventy-nine plantations and mills in "numbers of hands." Afong is reported to have received sixty thousand dollars for his share in the firm when he sold it in 1890.[3]

Despite their success, Chinese sugar makers could not compete with the American sugar interests. As Clarence Glick points out, "Large scale agriculture for the world market requires a combination of resources: long-term control of land suitable for the desired crop; large amounts of capital; entrepreneurial and technical skills; an adequate, stable labor force; and access to markets where the crop is in demand at prices high enough to provide a return on investment."[4] The Chinese could not match the capital or the political power of American business.

Furthermore, as Americans gained more control over the islands, U.S. immigration policy curtailed the influx of Chinese. When the first Chinese Exclusion Act was passed in 1882, prohibiting Chinese laborers from entering the United States for ten years, some hoped it would apply to Hawai'i as well. Although Americans did not yet have official control of the islands, they exercised enough political power over the legislature of the Kingdom of Hawai'i to restrict Chinese labor immigration to Hawai'i in 1886. In 1892 the Exclusion Act was renewed for another ten years, in 1902 it was broadened to cover Hawai'i and the Philippines (which by then were officially U.S. territories), and in 1904 it was extended indefinitely. American sugar interests had exploited the mainland's racism for its own ends.

The increasing American control over the Chinese in Hawai'i was evidenced in 1900, when a few cases of bubonic plague were discovered in Honolulu Chinatown and the area was quarantined. Liang Qichao, the Chinese intellectual and political reformer, was in Hawai'i at the time and observed the destruction of the Chinese community at the hands of American authorities. He wrote:

> They began to burn the homes and the stores of the Chinese. At first it was decided that the buildings belonging to those who had the disease would be burned. But later, it was argued that everyone [in the Chinese quarter] was diseased. The disaster was then carried out left and right, to the neighbors on both sides. It was later decided again that since everyone was diseased, they burnt down the whole street. That same day, other measures were taken because of the plague. Public gatherings were forbidden, including the use of temples and theaters.[5]

Although the Chinese had established themselves in Hawai'i decades earlier, American economic, political, and cultural power had grown too strong and too repressive to overcome.

American involvement in sugar growing in the islands began around the same time the Chinese were establishing themselves in the industry. In 1835 William Hooper of Boston visited the island of Kauai to survey the land for possible large-scale sugarcane planting. Sent there by Ladd and Company of Honolulu, Hooper represented the commercial interests that would eventually transform the system of land ownership, the economy, and the social structure of the Hawaiian Islands. In time American sugar companies (and later, fruit companies) would dominate the economic and social hierarchy. American business interests had close ties to the missionaries (mainly New England Congregationalists) who had been in the islands since the early 1800s. The influence of Christianity and American business increased in tandem.

The turning point in the transformation of Hawai'i from a self-governed kingdom to a plantation colony of the United States was in 1848, when the land tenure system was changed from communal to private ownership. Between 1836 and 1839 the Hawaiians were forced to sign treaties with foreign countries that stipulated special land privileges for foreigners living in Hawai'i. In 1841 the king issued a proclamation making it possible for foreigners to lease the land on which they were living. Americans pressed the monarchy for more access to land and gradually obtained more land rights based on notions of private land ownership. Finally, in 1848, the legislature, by that time American-controlled, passed what is known as the "Great Mahele," which divided the land into two parts: "crown land," to be owned and controlled by the king, and "government land," to be administered by the legislature.[6]

This arrangement allowed more and more land gradually to come under foreign control. By 1886 two-thirds of the government land had been sold to foreigners (mainly Americans) and large sections of crown land had fallen into foreign hands through leases and sales to private corporations. With private ownership of land now institutionalized and communal traditions abused, the sugar industry became the dominant economic and political force in the islands. The monarchy was overthrown in 1893, and the islands officially became an American territory in 1900. With the passage of the Organic Act in that year American law was also instituted throughout the islands.

American enterprises initially depended on native Hawaiian labor, but the indigenous population steadily declined because of imported diseases and emigration.[7] Many of the remaining Hawaiians chose not to risk their lives and health in plantation labor. The solution was found in imported labor. From the 1850s into the 1920s, the Royal Hawaiian Agricultural Society and later the Hawaiian Sugar Planters' Association recruited hundreds of thousands of workers from China, Japan, Korea, the Philippines, Portugal, Puerto Rico, Germany, and even Norway to perform the arduous tasks of raising and cutting cane and processing it into sugar. But most of the imported labor came from Asia. Between 1852 and the end of the nineteenth century, some fifty thousand Chinese alone were brought to the islands as laborers.

This influx of Asians, initially under the control of American plantation owners, created a multiracial and multicultural society that was unlike that of any other American state or territory. On the plantations, whites, either American, German, Norwegian, or Portuguese, were generally at the top of the racial pyramid, with the Asian laborers below. Workers were housed according to race and ethnicity, and the groups were often paid on different wage scales even when performing the same tasks, fostering competition and discouraging any sense of worker solidarity. This split-labor strategy created not only a wide division between owners and workers but a hierarchy among the workers themselves, with Chinese and Japanese on top, Koreans in the middle, and Filipinos and Hawaiians on the bottom.[8]

Once the laborers were allowed to move off the plantations, however, a more natural economy developed, with the various racial and ethnic groups finding their own niches in trade and commerce, albeit with whites at the apex of the economic and political pyramid. While Hawai'i is often portrayed as a "rainbow" society of ethnic and racial harmony, there were certainly animosities between the various Asian groups, some carried over from Asia, others created by the plantation system. But, unlike the situation in the continental United States, there were no distinct ethnic ghettos. Although Chinese, Japanese, or Filipino neighborhoods could be found, it was not uncommon for Asians of different nationalities to live side by side. It was the *haole* elite (upper-class whites) who lived in self-segregated residential neighborhoods, usually enforced by local covenants.

The Chinese, the first laborers to be recruited in large numbers, were also the first to move off the plantations and achieve financial security. As early as 1889, "the Chinese practically monopolized the restaurant business, the butchering of pork, and cake peddling." They also became the first urban Asian group in the islands with only 2 percent working on farms and more than 80 percent living in Honolulu. By 1930 less than a third lived in Chinatown. By the eve of the Second World War, many had attained middle-class status, with substantial male representation in white-collar professions, especially in management, clerical, and sales positions. The second-generation Chinese on the islands eagerly embraced English, Christianity, and American business and political practices.[9] Their elevated status and the attitudes that accompanied and fostered this level of attainment would set the Chinese apart from other Asians on the island, as well as from many of the Chinese Americans they would encounter during the war who had grown up in the urban Chinatowns of San Francisco, New York, and other cities on the mainland. The Chinese of Hawai'i would articulate their wartime experiences in ways that reflected their strong sense of belonging and being American.

Up until the Second World War, most of the economic and political power in Hawai'i rested in the hands of trading companies with plantation and missionary ties, the so-called Big Five: American Factors, Castle and Cooke, Alexander and Baldwin, Theo. Davies and Co., and C. Brewer and Co. By 1910 they controlled 75 percent of the sugar crop; by 1933, 96 percent. In 1932 the Big Five also took over Hawaiian Pineapple, once owned by James D. Dole, a company that supplied three-quarters of the world's pineapple supply. Put another way, during the peak of their power, "almost half the total land area of Hawai'i was owned by fewer than eighty individuals, and most of the rest was owned by the government." Because of the near-absolute power held by this small group of business firms and their associates, all with close ties to the missionary elite, and their use of a predominantly Asian imported workforce, there was no discernible white working class in Hawai'i. A fraction of the total population, whites held a disproportionate amount of political and cultural capital. The *haole* elite had little contact with the local population outside of a "superior-subordinate" relationship. The local population, meanwhile, often had so little knowledge of society on the U.S. mainland that they did not conceive of white society as being multi-classed. Whites were seen only in positions of power and therefore many locals regarded *haoles* as superior and worthy of emulation. Mun Charn Wong of Honolulu recalled: "The Caucasians and Chinese never socialized to a great extent. If I knew a Caucasian, I was proud to know one." Eventually, however, the war brought about a radical change in racial attitudes for many local Asians.[10]

Like their counterparts in the continental United States, the

Chinese in Hawai'i maintained close contact with relatives in China and kept a watchful eye on political developments there. In addition, because of Hawai'i's proximity to China, Chinese political activists, especially toward the end of the Qing dynasty (1644–1911), visited the Chinese in Hawai'i in hopes of raising funds and winning converts to their cause. Sun Yat-sen, father of the 1911 revolution and the Republic of China, spent part of his early life in Hawai'i. Sun came from a poor rural family in the Zhongshan area of Guangdong, and some of his family members had emigrated in search of more secure livelihoods. Two had died in the California Gold Rush and others had settled in Hawai'i. At the age of twelve Sun came from China to live with his brother in Honolulu, where he enrolled in the Anglican school now known as the Iolani School. After graduation he stayed in the islands, attending St. Louis College (now St. Louis High School) and then Oahu College (now Punahou School). His stay was cut short when his brother discovered that Sun planned to be baptized as a Christian and sent him to Hong Kong before that could happen.[11]

After further schooling in Hong Kong, Sun became a medical doctor, but a few years later he dedicated his life to the overthrow of the Manchu dynasty. He returned to Hawai'i in 1894 to discuss his revolutionary plans with old friends and to organize a political party. In November of that year he and his comrades founded the *Xingzhong hui* (Revive China Society), the first of the revolutionary parties associated with him. Throughout his career, Sun would return to Hawai'i from time to time to gain support for his revolutionary cause, raise funds, and recruit members for the *Tongmeng hui,* the forerunner of the Guomindang or Nationalist party.[12]

Chinese in Hawai'i were intimately linked to social and political developments in China. Throughout the early twentieth century, local Chinese sent money to support projects in their districts of origin and raised relief funds for famine and flood victims in various parts of China. When hostilities with Japan reached crisis proportions, the Chinese of Hawai'i organized rallies and mass meetings and established "Save China" organizations on the islands of Hawai'i, Oahu, Kauai, Maui, and Molokai to secure funds to assist Chinese troops. From 1937 on, local Chinese were very involved in the war effort, both through relief activities for China and eventually through the increased militarization of Hawai'i itself. When the Japanese offensive of 1937 began, the Chinese Relief Association in Hawai'i raised $350,000 in two years, and other organizations such as the Aid to Chinese Wounded Soldiers and Refugees Committee, the Aid to South China Refugee Association, and the Overseas Chinese Zhongshan Association all lent their efforts to assist the Chinese during the war.[13]

However, Hawai'i's local Chinese were not as constant or as openhanded as those on the U.S. mainland in their financial support of China. The Chinese Relief Association's $350,000, for example, was well below the total raised in San Francisco. When there were well-publicized conflicts between Chinese and Japanese troops, the Chinese community in Hawai'i would respond with assistance. But when the news was more routine, the "Save China" organizations would wind "up their business and publish their final reports in the Chinese newspapers."[14]

One might explain the different responses of the Chinese in Hawai'i and those in the continental United States in generational terms. Whereas on the mainland an American-born second generation did not come of age until the late 1930s and early 1940s, in Hawai'i there was already a sizable third generation when the conflict between China and Japan began. The differences are quite noticeable in terms of numbers. In 1940 there were 22,880 American-born Chinese on the U.S. mainland and 23,930 Hawai'i-born Chinese in Hawai'i. In 1940, when there were 17,782 Chinese living in San Francisco, there were 22,445 living in Honolulu, 19,217 of whom had been born in the islands. The higher numbers of native-born Chinese in Hawai'i can be attributed to two factors: more Chinese women immigrated to Hawai'i than to the mainland, especially once plantation owners began encouraging the male workers to start families; and the absence of anti-miscegenation laws in the islands allowed the Chinese more potential marriage partners there than on the mainland.

Another factor was that after the United States annexed Hawai'i in 1900, Chinese (and others) who had been naturalized Hawaiian citizens became American citizens, and from that time on, those born in Hawai'i had U.S. citizenship from birth. Of Chinese who lived on the mainland, by contrast, the overwhelming majority were neither citizens nor eligible for citizenship. Thus it is probable that the Chinese in Hawai'i simply felt "more American" than those on the mainland and accordingly had less of an emotional bond with China. Dai Hing Loo, a third-generation local Chinese, noted: "We heard about China and the invasion by Japanese, but I guess my parents had minimal resentment because they were of the second generation." Ethnic Chinese in Hawai'i did devote much less energy than their mainland counterparts to supporting China's efforts against Japan. But when the Japanese attacked Pearl Harbor, it was only natural that they would be eager to take up arms for Uncle Sam. They were, after all, defending their homeland.[15]

Racial Politics in the Islands

Even before the United States entered the Second World War, there was an increase in military personnel and activity in

Hawai'i. This was mainly due to America's concern with Japanese aggression in China during the 1930s. Hawai'i was regarded as the first line of defense against the Japanese. However, the racially mixed population of the islands, though largely created by the American plantation system, worried some Americans. In a 1938 article in *Foreign Affairs*, one scholar stated:

> To the tourist Hawai'i means "Aloha," the land of friendship and flowers and moonlit surf at Waikiki—"the loveliest fleet of islands that lies anchored in any sea." But to the statesman, the diplomat and the General Staffs of the Army and Navy it means America's powerful mid-Pacific naval base, it means problems of naval warfare and of national defense—political as well as military. Among these problems one of the most serious arises from the racial composition of the islands' population.[16]

Although this author's main concern was the loyalty of the large local Japanese community, other racial concerns were evident as well. Racial harmony in wartime was regarded as vital to national interests. By the end of the 1930s the boom in defense industries had brought an increasing number of working-class Americans to the islands, and during the war the civilian population of Oahu (the island on which Honolulu and Pearl Harbor are located) increased by ninety thousand people, primarily single white men between the ages of twenty and forty.[17] In addition, more than three hundred thousand American military personnel either were stationed in or passed through Hawai'i during the war. These included some thirty thousand African American soldiers and war workers who were in Hawai'i at some time during the war. The influx of both working-class whites and African Americans transformed a society that had previously been divided between elite whites and working-class Asians and Hawaiians. Racial politics became a major component in the lives of soldiers and civilians alike.

Many local Chinese spent the war either serving in the military or working in the defense industry. Some never left Hawai'i but experienced the changes in racial and gender relations that developed because of the influx of defense workers and military personnel from the mainland. Some did leave the islands and served in racially integrated units or worked in the defense industry on the mainland, thus working and fighting alongside Caucasians in greater numbers than they had before. Others left the island and served in the all–Chinese American units of the Fourteenth Air Service Group in the China-Burma-India theater. These three groups had very different experiences.

The locals who stayed in the islands often bore the brunt of racial hostility from soldiers and civilians from the mainland. One war worker from the mainland wrote home: "Believe me if Paradise is anything like this I'll take my chances in Hell. Honolulu in itself is about the dirtiest town I've ever been in and I've been in quite a few . . . Japs, Chinks, Hawaiians all run about barefoot, dirty and unkempt. The morals out here are disgusting." Another war worker complained: "Here is where the Black, Brown and Yellow man is 'Lord of all he sees,' the 'Paradise of the Oriental.' Here he struts and the 'Powers that Be' bend over backwards to please him."[18]

Many of the local Chinese did not feel that the "Powers that Be" were going out of their way to please them. Soon after the attack on Pearl Harbor, civilians were organized into a variety of militia units to help defend the islands in case of a full-scale Japanese invasion. The men in these units were commonly referred to as "last ditch soldiers." One such unit was the Businessmen's Military Training Corps (BMTC). The membership of the

BMTC, however, was restricted to Caucasians and part-Hawaiians.[19] The local Chinese were offended by this policy and took the matter up with the Chinese executive committee of the morale section of the military governor's office. The well-known author Tin-Yuke Char, who was serving as the secretary of the morale section, reported: "Naturally the young Chinese wanted to do their part and so volunteered to join. However, they were turned down on the grounds that they look Japanese and can be mistaken for such. They are supposed to be Americans, so they felt confused and hurt when they were not accepted." As a result, a new militia was formed, the Hawai'i Home Defense Volunteers, which consisted of Chinese, Koreans, and Filipinos.[20] Even in a time of national crisis, the *haole* elite managed to control the racial composition of a civilian unit, sending a clear message as to where power and authority resided in the islands.

Clearly, however, the main tension was between the locals and the newcomers. Some service personnel felt so out of place in Hawai'i that they took their frustrations out on the local population in ways that demonstrated their alienation. In one case, some young recruits were harassing a local Chinese man on the bus and were told to quiet down by another soldier. One responded, "This is a foreign land, not the U.S. This is a yellow man's land. The States' our home, not here. How can anyone talk about statehood for Hawai'i?"[21]

American soldiers who arrived in Hawai'i after seeing combat against the Japanese often displayed the worst behavior toward the locals. A local Chinese woman in Hilo reported:

> The Marines hated the Japs and, therefore, many of them were hating everyone they met who appeared Oriental. Remarks against "these dirty Japs," "slant eye babies," etc. were aimed openly without restraint at people on streets,

> in the buses, or in the stores. Because of certain incidents involving Marines and the local population, most people, especially the Orientals, dared not put up any resistance. Those of Japanese ancestry were naturally resentful at the kind of treatment they were receiving. The Chinese, Koreans, and others were resentful not only at the treatment they were receiving in being mistaken for Japanese, but were indignant over the stupidity and narrow-mindedness of the Marines who knew no better than to condemn the local Japanese for happenings in Tarawa, over which they had no control or responsibility.[22]

This is not to say that locals simply accepted the racial abuse of white mainlanders. During an argument between a white couple and a local Japanese man, the white woman reportedly yelled, "Oh shut up you damn Jap!" The Japanese man replied: "Shut up yourself. If I'm a damn Jap, then you're nothing but poor white trash." Moreover, the mainlanders and resident whites held racial and class animosities toward each other, not just toward the Asians of Hawai'i. One white resident of Honolulu reported: "California furnished the bulk of these workers. Do you think California would have sent us these fellows if they were any good? California has been overburdened by the 'Okies' and 'Arkies' and she's been dying to get rid of them."[23] The war had brought an ugliness to race relations in Hawai'i that had last been known in the islands when the Americans had overthrown the monarchy.

The presence of the mainlanders brought out deep-seated racial tensions that were articulated through gender relations. Although there was a long history of intermarriage in Hawai'i, it generally took place between local Asians, Hawaiians, and, to a lesser extent, Portuguese and Puerto Ricans, but rarely between *haoles* and locals, except when whites married Hawaiians of noble lineage.[24] When the mainlanders arrived, however, interracial relationships rapidly became more common. These relationships were not always welcomed by the local population, and the racial, gender, and cultural stereotypes held by many mainlanders became evident through their interactions with local Asian women.

To the chagrin of some local men, many single Asian women enjoyed the attentions of mainland men. Two local female Japanese researchers noted: "Accustomed to playing a subordinate role in the family and society, the Oriental girl finds herself suddenly placed on a pedestal by the gallant American youth in search of feminine companionship. Consequently, she finds these men very attractive." Another scholar thought that Asian women enjoyed dating white servicemen and defense workers "simply for the thrill of and satisfaction of over-stepping social taboos," but that most objected to close associations because the "intentions of these men [were] generally held not to be too honorable." The new social atmosphere created by the war called for new rules to be negotiated.[25]

Local women were encouraged to date the newcomers as an act of patriotism, a way to lift the morale of men who were far from home and perhaps suffering the trauma of war. One local Japanese college student stated that she had "no objection because it is a patriotic gesture. Some girls have brothers in Wisconsin and realize the situation of the service men here." (Camp McCoy, Wisconsin, was where the all–Japanese American 100th Infantry Battalion trained.) A local Japanese man added: "I didn't approve of Oriental girls dating service men before the war, but ever since the outbreak of the war, I approve of it for they are doing something for their country in keeping up the morale." However, a number of local white women expressed their opposition to interracial relations. One stated, "Each nationality should date their own nationality," and another bluntly said, "I do not believe in the two races mixing."[26]

Local Asian women were not universally welcomed in social situations with those from the continent. In June 1944 a local Chinese woman complained in a letter to the USO office in Honolulu that the Asian women who volunteered to attend USO dances feared they were being snubbed by many of the servicemen because they resembled Japanese or might be of Japanese ancestry. They also felt that the white women running the dances were "race conscious": that the "older white women treated the younger white women much better, introduced them to officers, and generally spoke better to them, while the Asian women were ignored." The Asian women seemed to be seen as "dance partners" rather than as "hostesses." Related to this was the sentiment held by some whites that white women and Asian women should not be present at the same social events. One white man declared: "I do not think that white girls and Oriental girls would mix successfully at a dance. It might be a better idea to have USO dances with Oriental girls exclusively." A white woman concurred: "There certainly aren't enough *haole* girls to entertain all of them. However, I don't think the *haole* girls and Japanese girls should attend the same dances." Calls for racial segregation at this kind of event were a "radical departure from the pre-war tradition of racial equality in Hawai'i."[27]

Often the mainlanders who did socialize with Asian women revealed attitudes of racial superiority. A local Chinese woman recounted a conversation she had with a white naval officer at a party in June 1944. He asked if she was "having a nice time with all these white officers? You don't seem to be tongue-tied or ill at ease. I always thought you Orientals were socially immature, especially with white people." She replied: "Why should I feel ill at ease here? You're really not so much different than me." He continued: "But I ask you, honestly, in all sincerity—this party tonight, will it advance you socially or economically, will it, even one iota? Why, it might just bring you heartaches and unresolved conflicts. You might want to be like 'one of us,' but can't because of your racial uniform." The woman's response ended the conversation: "I don't even have the slightest longing to be like 'one of you,' as you termed it. Why should I? I'm perfectly happy the way I am, being a Chinese, an Oriental."[28]

Other servicemen made it clear that they had had little idea of what Hawai'i would be like. When asked what he had expected to find in Hawai'i, one army sergeant replied: "I expected it to be more or less a village and hula girls running around and no automobiles. It is practically like Washington in some aspects—all modern—I expected it to be primitive."[29] And another told his dance partner: "I didn't know you people wore shoes here; I thought you all went barefooted." To which she smartly replied: "Oh, tonight's special. We're at a dance. These are my dancing shoes."[30]

Another soldier reportedly asked a woman he was dancing with if she was Chinese. When she replied that she was Japanese, and that most of the women there that evening were Japanese, the soldier said he had thought that "you were all Hawaiians. Where are the Hawaiians then?" She informed him: "Well, pure Hawaiians are hard to find—most of them are 'part.' You see that girl standing by the post, she is part Hawaiian." The soldier then exclaimed: "What, are they all dark-skinned like that? I'll take a Japanese girl any day." Most white mainlanders, in fact, generally preferred to have sexual relationships with white women. As Beth Bailey and David Farber have documented, the majority of the prostitutes who serviced the transient wartime population in Hawai'i were white women from the mainland.

For most mainlanders, the way to circumvent Hawai'i's "race problem" was simply to stay with "their own."[31]

Like Dorothy Eng and others in the Chinese Young Women's Society in Oakland, California, the local Chinese in Hawai'i felt the need to provide a social space for Chinese American servicemen and war workers. In October 1944 Chinese members of the Honolulu YWCA met to establish the Hana Like Club (Hawaiian for "working together") with the purpose of promoting "a variety of social and recreational activities through which young people of Chinese ancestry from the mainland, China, and Hawai'i may gain friendship, fellowship, and mutual understanding."[32]

It was widely believed among the local population that the mainlanders had brought with them the mainland's racial prejudices, and that these prejudices were most evident in the treatment of African Americans. Gwenfread Allen maintained: "Prior to the war, local residents saw few Negroes. The first to arrive were mistaken by some for South Sea Islanders. The general tendency, especially among the Japanese, was to welcome them on equal footing, but soon other newcomers implanted their ideas of racial consciousness and the Negroes were not as well received as they might otherwise have been."[33] However, Judy Kubo, a local Japanese American scholar, drew different conclusions from her observations in the village of Kahuku, whose 2,251 residents were mostly Japanese and Filipino: "The Negro soldiers have not been accepted by the majority of people in Kahuku. From the day of their arrival, people peered through their windows in surprise. The Negroes were objects of curiosity, fear, and suspicion . . . Their fear was apparently based on previous reports, rumors, and transferred mainland prejudices. Color may have had something to do with the fear; however, this is unlikely since there are so many other dark-skinned people in Hawai'i." Kubo also noted that many blacks had "expected to find Hawai'i a place with equality for all races. Because of the many racial groups here, they had hoped to be accepted completely. Although, on the whole, the treatment here was better than that which the Negroes were accustomed to on the mainland, it was still far from their expectation of Hawai'i, the 'melting pot' of races."[34]

Apparently many African Americans did initially appreciate the racial climate of Hawai'i. One shipyard worker wrote home: "I thank God often for letting me experience the occasion to spend a part of my life in a part of the world where one can be respected and live as a free man should." Another wrote that Hawai'i "will make anybody change their minds about living down there [the Jim Crow South]." Some white men and women from the mainland also welcomed the racial diversity in Hawai'i. A young nurse commented: "They have come as near to solving the race problem as any place in the world. I'm a little mystified by it as yet but it doesn't bother anyone who has lived here awhile." And a teacher found the situation personally transforming: "I have gained here at least the impulse to fight racial bigotry and boogeyism. My soul has been stretched here and my notion of civilization and Americanism broadened."[35]

Others, however, viewed Hawai'i's racial mix more negatively. A wife of a war worker complained: "Down here they have let down the standards, there does not seem to be any race hatred, there is not even any race distinction . . . I don't want to expose our children too long to these conditions." Whites from the American South were particularly disturbed by the presence and perceived behavior of African American troops and workers. One declared, "Boy the niggers are sure in their glory over here . . . they almost expect white people to step off the streets and let them walk by . . . They are going to overstep their bounds a little too far one of these days and these boys from the South are going to have a little necktie party."[36]

Conflicts between whites and blacks were frequent. A local Japanese man described one such encounter:

> At a downtown barber shop, a young Japanese girl of 20 was shaving a Negro defense worker. A sailor passing by the barber shop stopped at the doorway and began to tease the Negro. The Negro, as well as the barber girl, ignored the taunts. Before passing on one sailor commented: "Look out, little girl. Don't let them niggers marry you." The barber shop girl later commented to me: "I pity these Negro boys. They are so good at heart—it's only their color that sets them apart from others. That incident you just saw was not unusual. It's bound to happen when I have a Negro here. Just last week, I had this whole place full of *haole* soldiers—then one Negro fellow came in. The sailors told the Negro to go around the corner or else.[37]

Furthermore, the military did very little to discourage the racism in its ranks. A black defense worker at Pearl Harbor related the following story:

> Some marines came over to the barracks and took four colored boys to their barracks and gave them a thorough going over. They were beaten up—broken noses, bruised lips, blood all over. A Filipino and I were at dinner the next night, standing in line. There were marine sentries close by. They took me for a native since I spoke in pidgeon. These marines spoke very freely and talked of the riot the night before. They had a call from the Commander for beating up these Negroes. The Commander told them not to use

the term "nigger" but to treat them as Negroes and beat them up as Negroes.[38]

This defense worker was able to escape such treatment because he was able to "pass" for a native since he spoke a little pidgin. One might assume that he "looked black," but he was able to separate himself from what mainland whites took to *be* "black." Thus race relations in wartime Hawai'i were influenced by mainland racial politics. As another local Japanese writer put it: "The very fact that discrimination toward the Negroes in Hawai'i has so quickly become standardized and is like that of the Mainland is an indication that it is a carry-over from the continental United States. Also, the institutions which came over to Hawai'i from the Mainland, such as the USO and the Naval Housing, were on the Mainland involved in discriminatory patterns which it was natural for them to take for granted in Hawai'i."[39]

Many local Chinese who joined the military and left the islands had to learn to negotiate this new context of white antagonism against blacks and other minorities. For many, it was new social territory after the relatively relaxed race relations of prewar Hawai'i. William Lum, for example, later recalled that he had first encountered blatant racism against blacks while attending officer candidate school (OCS) in Miami. When he boarded a public bus he saw a sign telling "Colored" to move to the back of the bus, and he wasn't sure what to do: "I said to myself, 'Well, am I colored or what?' . . . I don't remember what I did. But I think I didn't move to the rear. I thought to myself, 'To heck with it.'" He also maintained that the black candidates in OCS were treated poorly by the white candidates, and his disdain for this treatment was summed up in his statement: "And these were potential officers, too." Mun Charn Wong, who played on an air force football team, remembered: "That was when I learned about racial things. When I was on the football team there was one Black half-back. I befriended him, but I noticed the white boys never befriended him to that extent. The ones that came from Mississippi and Texas, they were different. Then the way the Caucasian officers talked about Blacks always surprised me. They didn't eat together with the white officers."[40]

Marietta Chong Eng had different sorts of experiences during her stint as a rehabilitation nurse in mainland naval hospitals. Born and raised in Honolulu, she went to the Philadelphia School of Occupational Therapy and the University of Pennsylvania before enlisting in the navy. Once on active duty, she was stationed at Mare Island, California. She later looked back on her time in the military with great pride and was even married in her dress whites. She recalled only one incident of overt racism, when "this young punk" in New York City was walking across the street and "pointed at my face and laughed and said 'Chink, Chink, Chinaman.'" Within the military itself, "sometimes people would see my yellow face and be startled, but I think being an officer in uniform erased that."[41] Comrades in arms, these men and women from Hawai'i found themselves having to cope with racial politics that were quite different from the multiracial environment of their youth. These experiences would have an impact on their social expectations when they returned to Hawai'i after the war.

Going to War

The Japanese attack on Pearl Harbor on December 7, 1941, brought the United States into a global conflict that had been developing for a decade. It also brought Hawai'i to center stage in the eyes of the American public. Prior to the attack, many

Americans were uncertain about Hawai'i's relationship to the United States, much less its location. Suddenly, however, most Americans were painfully aware of Hawai'i's role in the U.S. war effort. Pearl Harbor was only the first in a list of Pacific sites that would eventually include previously unimagined places such as Bataan, Guadalcanal, Guam, Okinawa, Tarawa, and Iwo Jima—a list that would end four years later with Hiroshima and Nagasaki. Likewise, America's entry into the war would eventually send thousands of Hawai'i's residents to places with which they were only vaguely familiar: Charlotte, North Carolina, Calcutta, Kunming, Ardennes, Normandy, Anzio, Dachau. The island men and women who ventured to these places to serve the United States came home changed individuals.

Over the course of the war, Hawai'i contributed more than forty thousand men and women to the armed forces, most of them enlisting or drafted into army. Early in the war, however, both enlistments and Selective Service inductions from the territory were discontinued because of the racial composition of the islands' population (the military was mainly concerned with the loyalty of local Japanese Americans), the demand for defense industry workers, and the need for local militias in case of an invasion. The first Selective Service registration in Hawai'i took place in October 1940 and young men were expected to register for the draft upon reaching their eighteenth birthdays, but regular draft calls were ended in February 1942, just two months after the attack on Pearl Harbor. The next inductions did not take place until June 1943, and men of Japanese ancestry were still excluded. The draft in Hawai'i did not include men of all races until April 1944. For this reason the percentage of military personnel from Hawai'i was lower than from some states, and more than two-thirds of them did not enter the service until the latter part of 1944.[42]

The draftees and enlistees were not the only sources of military personnel. Some of the young men of Hawai'i began their relationship with the armed services in high school or college ROTC programs. As part of the militarization of the territory, the Hawaiian National Guard, originally organized in 1917, was activated in October 1940 and assigned to Schofield Barracks on Oahu as the 298th and 299th Infantry Regiments. The 298th was generally made up of "Chinese, Koreans, Puerto Ricans, Samoans, Hawaiians, Filipinos, and island-born Caucasians of Portuguese extraction" from the island of Oahu, and the 299th was made up of men from the other islands. These two regiments were among the first troops called to duty following the attack at Pearl Harbor. They were sent to beach defenses to guard against invasion. Alfred Jay later recalled that because the Guard was under peacetime constraints, each soldier had only seven rounds of ammunition: "We were sent out to the countryside to prepare if they invaded the island. Fortunately, no invasion occurred. Otherwise we would have been sunk. What can you do with seven rounds of ammunition? Of course we got some ammunition later, but not those first few days."[43]

Originally there were local Japanese in these units as well, but they were removed in the summer of 1942 and organized into the 100th Infantry Battalion. Also removed from the unit were local Japanese students who were in the ROTC program at the University of Hawai'i, which formed the basis for the Territorial Guard. They later became the nucleus of the celebrated 442nd Regimental Combat Team. Removing local Japanese from these units dramatically reduced their numbers; the 299th was subsequently deactivated in the summer of 1942 and its remaining members were transferred to the 298th.[44]

The 298th did not remain exclusively "local." Owing to numerous transfers, by the end of 1943 it had only 15 percent of its original members. The complement of the unit comprised inductees from Hawai'i and from the continental United States.[45] These transfers and the use of mainland troops as replacements offer two cases of racial tension experienced by troops originating from Hawai'i. In 1943 three hundred men from the 298th were sent to the mainland as a cadre to form a new regiment. They were first sent to Lompoc, California, and then to Camp McCall in North Carolina. Alfred Jay explained that these "boys from Hawai'i" were not fully aware of the racial politics of the region, nor would they accept "their place" in the racial hierarchy of the South. On weekends the cadre from Hawai'i, "many of them dark-skinned," would try to "go to the nearest beer joint and have fun. They would flirt with the women and they had a lot of trouble." Leonard Wong similarly recalled: "There were a lot of Hawaiians in the group and they got mixed up with the Caucasians. Boy, they had a lot of fights." Eventually these fights reached riot proportions and resulted in serious injuries. Gwenfread Allen reports a street fight in Charlotte, North Carolina, between soldiers from Hawai'i and mainlanders that involved a thousand soldiers and five hundred civilians. After that the army disbanded the Hawai'i-based cadre and dispersed the men to other units in groups of eight. Jay ended up in the 331st Infantry training in Tennessee and was soon shipped to England; Leonard Wong went to Fort Benning, Georgia, and was later sent to the University of California at Berkeley to study Chinese. From there he was deployed to India and then stationed in China working as a liaison between the American and Chinese armies.[46]

Going in the other direction, eleven hundred mainland replacements were sent to the 298th in Hawai'i in late 1943. According to the unit history, some soldiers had trouble adjusting to the racial mix, especially the "predominant position held by the Chinese-Hawaiians and the presence of Caucasian replacements unfamiliar with Hawaiian ways."[47] Sections of the 298th were sent to the islands of Espíritu Santo and Guadalcanal in late 1943 and early 1944. The racial tension between the white soldiers and Asian soldiers from Hawai'i continued to the point that "effective May 8, 1944, the regiment was reorganized to permit segregation of the white elements into separate units." It was also observed that the regiment was not a "potentially first-class unit for combat in the Pacific Theater . . . This is as much the result of inaction as of any racial difficulties."[48] The regiment was reorganized so that the First Battalion "consisted almost exclusively of Filipino personnel. Officers and noncommissioned officers were the exceptions. The Filipinos called themselves the 'Bataan Battalion.' With the exception of a limited number in the Service Company and the Medical Detachment, all mainland-born Caucasians were assigned to the Cannon Company and the Second Battalion Company H." All other mixed-race groups (personnel from the Territory of Hawai'i) were assigned to the Third Battalion, Anti-Tank Company, Regimental Headquarters Company and Company H. Ironically, the next entry in these records states that a new phase of training was begun to "create and maintain in every officer and enlisted man a feeling of individual responsibility for participation in the war and to strengthen his efficiency as a soldier by increasing his understanding as to why we fight."[49] It thus appears that the army was cognizant of racial tension in its ranks and sought to alleviate it by appeasing white personnel but did not view racial equality and acceptance as social ideals it should promote.

Among the Chinese American soldiers from Hawai'i who spent the war in the Pacific theater were Warren Zane and Ah Leong Ho. Zane was stationed at Fort Shafter in Hawai'i for most of the war, until he was shipped to Kwajalein, Guam, Iwo Jima, and the Marshall Islands to assist in the "mopping up" operations after the major fighting was finished. He later spoke fondly of eating fresh fish caught from the deck of his troop carrier. Ah Leong Ho was sent to various islands to help build temporary field hospitals. He recalled that while stripping parts from a complex of Japanese pillboxes in Guam, he and his fellow soldiers were amused to discover that the pillboxes were connected by an underground communications system wired through sewer pipes made in Alabama. While Zane and Ho told some lighthearted tales, they both recalled that, being the only Asians in their units, they were told to stay in camp, especially at night. Ho was warned: "You look too much like a Jap, you're liable to get shot." He had to promise that he would stay in camp after sunset, especially after one marine threatened him: "You see this bullet? After dark it's going to be for you." While on Iwo Jima, Zane was also told to stay in camp after dark. His colonel informed him: "The whole island is loaded with American soldiers and Marines and they will shoot to kill anyone that looks Oriental."[50]

These examples of Chinese American soldiers being warned of personal danger because they looked like the enemy are not isolated incidents. Nor are they confined to the Second World War: the next two wars that involved large numbers of American troops took place in Korea and Vietnam. This equating of Americans with the enemy on the basis of race or appearance was given full expression in the establishment of concentration camps for Japanese Americans on the mainland and later in the treatment of Asian American soldiers in the Vietnam war.[51] These practices speak very powerfully to issues of race, nationality, and loyalty. If white American soldiers were so easily threatened by their fellow soldiers of Asian ancestry, it is evident that the fires of battle do not necessarily forge a "melting pot."

Combat soldiers from Hawai'i saw a good deal of action in

some of the worst fighting of the war. After his training in Tennessee, Alfred Jay was sent to England. His troop ship left the States in April 1944. He later recalled: "My ship must have been in the middle of the convoy because no matter which way you looked, front, back, both sides, you see ship after ship. All kinds of ships. Man, you couldn't help but feel proud because you knew you were in a damn terrific outfit." After landing in England, Jay knew he was soon to be part of a large operation. "D-Day was June 6, 1944. The other people went and I felt sorry for them. I was still in England. Other guys were hitting the beach." Within two days Jay too was wading ashore: "We landed on Omaha Beach. Even after two days or so, you still see heads bobbing in the ocean. I guess so many guys got killed they couldn't fish 'em all out at that time. I guess if you got killed you would probably stay about three days before you start floating up. Boy, I tell you, when you see that you get the willies and you worry. It's dawning on you now, it could be you."

Soon after reaching the shore, Jay led his platoon through a mine-laden area. About five feet in front of him a Corporal Anderson stepped on a mine; the concussion knocked Jay down: "I was on the ground looking up; I could see his two legs just from the knee down twirling in the air. Holy man, when that hits you, it's terrible destruction. You learn about combat." Later that day Jay was hit "by a sniper who was in a tree somewhere." Jay was picked up by his platoon and spent a month in the hospital. He then trained new troops in England before being shipped home.[52]

Daniel Lau was wounded as a member of the 78th Lightning Division during the Battle of the Bulge, and forged emotional bonds that transcended his ethnic identity. "We moved up to the front which was moving toward Germany then. We liberated a lot of French and Belgian people, who were very nice to us because after being under German rule for the past couple of years, they more than welcomed the Allied troops." Lau's unit attacked three days before the Battle of the Bulge officially began. "When we jumped into combat the weather was freezing; it was cold. Your canteen would freeze over. We had to attack through the valleys and our clothing was all wet so that after a week many of the soldiers had trench foot. Their toes turned black, or had gangrene, so a great number of casualties were to trench foot. Because you had to attack in this cold weather, the casualties were extremely high. The first week we lost over half our men." Lau met a fourteen-year-old boy in Belgium whose family took him in when his unit was passing through the liberated area. Lau slept in the boy's bed. In a subsequent reunion with the boy, now grown to manhood, Lau learned that he and his wife had named their daughter Danielle after him.[53]

Hawai'i sent a number of pilots and other air crew members to Europe as well. Stanley Lau, the only Chinese American fighter pilot in the Southern European theater, flew fifty missions with the 27th Fighter Squadron out of Foggia, Italy. He recalls arriving there and finding that the Germans had recently left, "obviously in a hurry, because they left a barn full of beer. We didn't know if the beer was contaminated or boobytrapped or anything. So we took a bottle from every case and we went out to the farmers there and traded the beer for eggs and things. We had them open the bottles and we drank with them. We figured if they didn't die the beer was all right." Lau also flew some of the most dangerous air combat assignments, including missions to attack vital German oil refineries in Ploesti, Romania:

> Ploesti was our favorite target. We hit that place about three times a week. We could never destroy Ploesti. We would go there every week and we'd drop a load and come

> on back. Some brass in headquarters figured if the bombers couldn't do it, maybe the fighters could. So they had us equipped. We had three P-38 groups, and they had our group equipped with one 2000-pounder slung under the wing and one 300-pound yellow belly sack and we were supposed to take off and just stay over the ground so they wouldn't detect us. Things got all goofed up. We got there before they even started the smoke bombs. They would always start the smoke bombs and smudge up the whole place. We went in there and the Germans were just waiting for us. They came on down. We couldn't do anything. I led the squadron and I think there were only four of us who returned out of sixteen. After the war we ran into about four or five of them, they were POWs. But it was fun. We were all single and didn't have a thing to worry about.[54]

Two other men from Hawai'i were the only Chinese Americans in their bomber groups. Arthur Shak earned his wings and a commission as a second lieutenant at the age of nineteen and eventually flew fifty missions in six months with the 15th Air Force as a navigator in a B-24 Liberator. His bomber group hit targets in France, Italy, Austria, Germany, Romania, Yugoslavia, Hungary, and Czechoslovakia, including a number of missions over Ploesti. Samuel Lum, in contrast, made only eighteen missions before he was shot down over Germany. He spent nearly a year as a POW before his prison camp in Moosburg was liberated. Lum recalled that after his capture he was marched through a town to the railway station and overheard someone say "Das ist Chinesisch" and another voice replying "Ja, Mongolian." Later a German officer asked him in English, "Are you an Eskimo?" Lum realized that any attempt to escape in Germany would be highly unlikely to succeed: "I came to one conclusion:

'Lum, you'd better not try any breaks anytime, any place . . . You don't know the lingo and especially you must stand out like a sore thumb! Better stick with the mob at all times when in doubt.'" For Shak, being Chinese American did not seem to make a difference in his experience of the war; for Lum, it became a difference of crucial significance.[55]

While most of the Hawai'i-born served in Europe, a number also did their tours of duty in the China-Burma-India Theater (CBI), both in racially integrated units and in the all–Chinese American units in the Fourteenth Air Service Group. William Lum, mentioned earlier, whose experience with white racist treatment of blacks in Miami raised questions about his own racial identity, was later sent to Harrisburg, Pennsylvania, where he received special training in photographic interpretation for bomb-site assessment. Next he was assigned to Adac, Alaska: "Of all the places for a boy from Hawai'i to go!" In early 1945 Lum requested a transfer to CBI, thinking it would be "more meaningful for me to be there than Alaska." Assigned to the 18th Photo Intelligence Detachment of the Fourteenth Air Force in CBI, he was stationed both in Kunming and in Chongqing (Chungking) but had very little contact with any Chinese American units or with the Chinese army. He believed that the local population did appreciate the presence of Chinese American troops, especially "the ladies! They were with the Red Cross; there were a lot of Chinese girls in the Red Cross. I got to know a few of them." Otherwise, he found China to be primitive. He was impressed by caravans of mules or horses surrounded by armed guards, "just like the old West!" After the war ended Lum returned to Honolulu.[56]

Clifford Young's military career was considerably more complex. His attraction to the military began at an early age, and he attended Western Military Academy in Alton, Illinois. Upon graduation at the age of eighteen, he was told that he would be allowed to become a commissioned officer when he reached twenty-one. He went on to study architecture at the University of Michigan, turning down a chance to attend West Point because "I enjoyed college life." Deciding to take a semester off in order to work at home, Young was in Honolulu when the war began. As an officer in the reserves, he was immediately called to active duty and assigned to the 298th Infantry. He was stationed in Hawai'i until late 1943 when the battalion was sent to Guadalcanal to participate in the "mopping up" campaign and to secure Hennessey Hill and the perimeter. From there he was sent to Bougainville, the largest of the Solomon Islands, where he worked on keeping runways operable for fighters giving cover to bombers going to the Philippines.

Young's next assignment began a fascinating phase of his career. He was ordered back to Hawai'i to attend the Chinese Language Training Center. Like many local Chinese of his age, he had attended Chinese school after full days in "English" (public) school, so he had a foundation in speaking, reading, and writing Chinese. There were about seventy students and ten officers at the Center, with teachers flown in from China. They spent eight to nine hours a day reading Chinese newspapers, translating, interpreting, and studying Chinese history and geography. After six months of this training, Young received orders to deliver sixty-four of the students to G2 (Intelligence) China Theater Headquarters in Chongqing.

They were supposed to leave for China in June 1945, but their departure was delayed. Eventually, the group of sixty-four was split up and sent to different bases on Oahu. When the war ended in early August, none of the cadre expected to have to go China, and none wanted to go. The orders, however, were never rescinded. Young was informed that he was still expected to escort the sixty-four language specialists to China. By now, some of them were in the Philippines and others were already in China. Meanwhile, China Theater Headquarters had moved from Chongqing to Shanghai—but Young's orders still specified that he take the men to Chongqing: "You know how the army is. If you have orders to deliver men to Chongqing, you have to, unless the orders are changed. I had no one to change the orders." Young made his way to Manila and then got a flight to Chongqing. The aircraft developed problems, however, and was forced to land in Tsunyi. After speaking with a number of pilots there, Young managed to get a flight to Shanghai. Upon his arrival at Headquarters, he was asked: "Where the hell have you been? We expected you six months ago!" After he explained, new orders were issued, and within three days all sixty-four of his men were in Shanghai. Once in Shanghai, they were reassigned to various postings, and Young, "having completed my mission, was unassigned. I had nothing to do."

While sharing officers' quarters in Shanghai, Young happened to meet a mainland Chinese American, Lieutenant Allen Jung. Jung had spent the last year as part of the "Dixie Mission," a contingent of American military observers in Yenan with the Chinese Communists. It was nicknamed the "Dixie Mission" because they were in "rebel territory."[57] Jung, eager to get home now that the war was over, was looking for someone to replace him. He described Yenan as "terrible—no women, no nothing, no liquor, only beer." Despite these "challenges," Young offered to take Jung's place. They went to G2 Headquarters and Young was granted permission to go to Yenan. When he arrived, he was informed that the American operation was now to be called the Yenan Observer Group and that he was to be the executive officer under Colonel Ivan D. Yeaton, who was then in charge of the operation.

Young spent a year in Yenan, from November 1945 to November 1946. He later looked back on his experiences there with great enthusiasm. He especially enjoyed meeting and getting to know a number of people who played pivotal roles in the shaping of modern China, including Mao Zedong, Zhou Enlai, Yang Shangkun (a longtime Communist revolutionary who later became president of China), and Ye Jianying (who was also influential in the Chinese Communist Party). Of all of the major figures at Yenan, Young was closest to General Zhu De, with whom he hunted pheasant on numerous occasions. He also became acquainted with the radical journalist Anna Louise Strong and Dr. Ma Hai Teh (George Hatem), a physician who worked with the Chinese Communists for half a century. After a year at Yenan, Young was reassigned to Peiping (Beijing) Executive Headquarters, where he served until American military personnel left China in April 1947. He was then assigned to Fort Riley, Kansas, where he was an instructor of automatic small arms until he "chose to be separated from the service" in late 1947.[58]

✪ Military service took the Chinese of Hawai'i to far-flung destinations and exposed them to a world quite unlike the islands. At the same time, the war brought unanticipated changes to the island society. Thousands of men and women from the continental United States arrived in Hawai'i, all with their own visions of race relations. As locals saw how the white newcomers treated Asians, African Americans, and one another, their view of *haoles* began to shift. From being seen as genteel and worthy of emulation, whites, especially servicemen and defense workers, became "Okies," "Arkies," and "poor white trash." Many of the mainland visitors felt alienated from what they considered a foreign land, and soldiers preparing for or returning from battle often had little tolerance for Hawai'i's multiracial society, especially for those who looked like the "enemy." The racial prejudices of the mainland took root in the islands, and the local culture was forever transformed.

Meanwhile, the local Chinese who left Hawai'i during the war were exposed to mainland society, often finding it racist and intolerant. They also saw whites performing jobs and tasks that they rarely performed in the islands, leading them to realize that *haoles* were not necessarily superior to Asians or other ethnic groups. And, because of the long history of the Chinese in the islands, the local Chinese who were assigned to the all–Chinese American units of the Fourteenth Air Service Group discovered that their lives in multiracial Hawai'i had given them a sense of ease in being Chinese American that was not shared by their mainland counterparts with whom they would serve.

5

The Fourteenth Air Service Group

The Chinese American presence in the American military was most pronounced in the Fourteenth Air Service Group (14th ASG). The 14th ASG consisted of nine units made up of Chinese American enlisted men with a combination of white and Chinese American commanding officers. These units would come to have the largest concentration of Chinese American personnel in the American armed forces (about 10 percent of all the Chinese Americans in the military).

The 14th ASG took shape in Venice, Florida, in 1944, but the move to create all–Chinese American units began earlier. In November 1942 Lieutenant Sing Y. Yee of the 859th Signal Service Company in Springfield, Illinois, received permission to recruit other Chinese Americans to serve in China in support of General Claire Chennault's efforts in the China-Burma-India Theater (CBI). This group would be officially activated as the 1157th Signal Company Service Group in July 1943. Most of the personnel received their training at Springfield, but certain groups were sent for specialized training in Allenhurst, New Jersey; Warner Robbins, Georgia; and Patterson Field (now Wright-Patterson), Ohio. The entire company was sent to Camp Patrick Henry, Virginia, in December 1943 and departed for India in January 1944 on the *Empress of Japan*. They were the first of the all–Chinese American units to be deployed for duty in China.[1]

Among these first recruits was Joseph Yuu from Boston. Yuu was born in Lynn, Massachusetts, in 1924, the son of a Chinese launderer who had served under General Pershing in the First World War and, under the 1918 law granting the right to citizenship to aliens who served in the military, had subsequently become a U.S. citizen.[2] Yuu's mother took him and his siblings to China in 1927 to receive a Chinese education. He later recalled that it was easier for the family to make ends meet on the small plot of land they still owned in China than it would have been had they all been together in Boston during the Great Depression. As Japanese aggression in China intensified, however, Yuu returned to Boston in 1935. He continued his education and worked with his father until he enlisted in 1942, becoming one of the first twenty-two members of the newly organized all–Chinese American unit in Springfield.[3]

Also activated in July 1943 in Springfield, the 407th Air Service Squadron was staffed by Chinese American personnel from its beginning as well. Like many other men in the 407th, Harry Lim of Oakland, California, was originally assigned to the 859th Signal Service Company with Lieutenant Sing Y. Yee before being placed in the 407th. After high school Lim had worked in the General Engineering Shipyard in Alameda, taken a business course in the hope of becoming an accountant, and then been drafted in 1943. When he reported for duty in Springfield, it was the first time he had traveled outside California.[4]

Soon after its activation the 407th was transferred to Patterson Field for technical training in aircraft maintenance, learning how to repair and service a number of types of airplanes, including P-38s, P-40s, B-25s, and C-47s. Members of the 407th also received some training as administrators, carpenters, sheet-metal workers, cooks, truck drivers, and supply clerks. In April 1944 the unit was sent to Newport News, Virginia, with orders to leave for Oran, North Africa, from where they later sailed to Bombay.[5] Both the 1157th Signal Company Service Group and the 407th Air Service Squadron spent time in various locations in India before being flown "over the Hump" (across the Burmese section of the Himalayas) to Kunming, China, where the men were eventually reassigned to the 14th ASG.

In addition to these units in the army air force, the 987th Signal Company was an all–Chinese American outfit of the regular army, activated in June 1943 at Camp Crowder, Missouri. The 987th's "Historical Report" provides the most explicit explanation for the formation of all–Chinese American units that I have found in official military records: "All personnel were Chinese speaking American soldiers of Chinese parentage. It was understood that the unit was organized expressly for duty in China, one of its functions being to further liaison relationships between American and Chinese troops in that theater." The unit soon became known on the base because of the large quantities of rice the men consumed. As it was the only Chinese unit on the base and the non-Chinese units were not particularly fond of rice, the 987th often traded bags of potatoes for bags of rice and thus had an unlimited supply. Their mess officers managed to serve Chinese meals "concocted wholly out of quartermaster issue rations." The news spread around the camp and soon men of all ethnicities began frequenting the 987th's mess hall.[6]

While on bivouacs in the countryside, Chinese American troops were often treated with great suspicion. One time a team was five miles east of Fayetteville, Arkansas, and decided to enter the town. They were immediately surrounded by police and questioned about where they had obtained the army equipment, required to show identification, and detained until a white officer from the nearby air corps training unit at the University of Arkansas came to verify their documentation. Incidents like this were not uncommon during the unit's off-base training sessions while still in the United States.[7] After a year of training the 987th departed for Camp Anza, California, and then embarked for Calcutta via Australia, eventually being airlifted over the Hump to take up their positions in Yunnan province, China.

The 555th Air Service Squadron, which would provide the bulk of the personnel of the 14th ASG during its earliest days, was activated in October 1943 at the Illinois State Fairgrounds in Springfield. It was manned by Chinese Americans from its inception, and became the main unit through which troops of Chinese ancestry were screened and accepted for service in the various all–Chinese American squadrons and companies. Those who were not accepted were assigned to standard integrated units. From October 1943 to January 1944, a total of 790 Chinese American enlisted men and seventeen officers reported for duty to the 555th. The unit's historian Henry Ching noted that enlisted personnel were "literally pouring in from all branches of the service, from army camps and air bases, reception centers, schools and organizations, with no particular qualifications except that they were troops of Chinese ancestry." After three months of training in Springfield, the 555th was transferred to Venice Army Air Field, Florida, in January 1944, to meet up with other companies that had also been reassigned to Venice to become units of the 14th ASG: the 1077th Quartermaster Company, the 1544th and 1545th Ordnance Supply and Maintenance Companies, and the 2121st and 2122nd Quartermaster Truck Companies. It was also at this time that the racial composition of the group was officially declared. All of these units were to be "manned with Chinese enlisted personnel [and] all white enlisted personnel [were to] be reassigned to other units." "No reduction in grade of any individual" was to result from these reassignments, and "Chinese officers [would] be assigned to these units if qualified and available." Not only would whites be transferred, but records indicate that the 2121st and 2122nd Quartermaster Truck Companies were originally staffed by African American troops and that they too were reassigned. These units of the 14th ASG would receive specialized training in Venice until they left for China in the fall of 1944.[8]

Although the records of the 987th Signal Company provide the clearest reason for organizing all–Chinese American units to be sent to China, the recruits and draftees had ideas of their own. One common belief was that Chiang Kai-shek or Madame Chiang Kai-shek had put pressure on President Roosevelt to create such units to show that Chinese Americans were returning to fight for the "Motherland," and to stimulate more donations from the Chinese in America to the Nationalist government. Mun Charn Wong of the 2122nd Quartermaster Truck Company thought it was a political move to satisfy Madame Chiang's desire to have a Chinese American unit similar to the all–Japanese American outfits fighting in Europe. Some, including Joseph Yuu, saw the units in more practical terms, believing that the knowledge of Chinese language and culture would indeed facilitate better relations with the local Chinese and the Chinese army. The reactions of some of those assigned to the 14th ASG or the 987th Signal Company, and the evaluation of their training and performance, may point to other, less positive reasons for their formation.[9]

From the units' initiation, the reactions of those assigned to them were mixed. Charles Leong, who had cofounded the *Chinese Press* in 1940 and would work as a public relations officer in the headquarters of the 14th ASG in Shanghai, wrote in 1944 in the *Buckley Armorer* (a weekly publication of the Army Air Forces Training Command) that back in 1940 one of the first men to receive his draft status had been a "New York Chinese laundryman." (Here Leong may have been referring to Chan Chong Yuen, whom he had named in an earlier article about national draft day—see Chapter 1.) "Since then," Leong continued, "some 7,000 Chinese-Americans 'are in the army now.' And the average Chinese GI Joe likes and swears by the army. The most obvious reason, of course, is the fact that every Chinese would like to participate in defeating our common enemy—the Jap." He noted that "to this end, the Army has made itself very accommodating to GI Joe Wong. It's no military secret that several all-Chinese units . . . will eventually join their brothers-in-arms in China." Leong concluded by touching on a sentiment many veterans would echo in the postwar era, that serving in the army was giving Chinese Americans "a regular break" and most important, a sense of "belongingness": "To GI Joe Wong, in the army a 'Chinaman's chance' means a fair chance, one based not on race or creed, but on the stuff of the man who wears the uniform of the U.S. Army."[10]

Indeed, some men were quite happy to be assigned to the 14th ASG. James Jay, who was born in China and joined his father in New York in 1935, enlisted in 1943 and volunteered to join the Chinese American soldiers being screened in Springfield. Assigned to the 407th Air Service Squadron, he served as an administrative officer. He believes that these units were being formed because of the shared language among the recruits and the Chinese. As for his reasons for volunteering: "I think I wanted to fight Japanese because of all that I read in the papers about the rape of Nanking and all these killings of civilians. I said I wanted to go to China and fight Japanese. I was born in China so naturally it's part of my heritage. I live in the United States. I don't want to see those two countries go to the Japanese. So they're sort of interlinked together." Others saw the opportunity to go to China in more practical terms, believing it might ease their experience in the war. Richard Gee of San Francisco, who served in the 407th Air Service Squadron, stated: "At least we knew that with our roots, we wouldn't starve. We wouldn't be left alone. Left alone in the sense that if I'm Cantonese, I can still cope with somebody who can speak Cantonese. I knew that I would be able to survive."[11]

Many veterans felt that they had had no choice about being assigned to segregated units and that they had simply done what they had to do. Harry Lim, who served as an aircraft electrical specialist, did not mind being in the 407th, and since he had always been curious about China, he saw his assignment as his chance to go. Mack Pong, who had worked for the postal service before the war and was made the mailman for the 407th, admitted that when he was drafted he had been happy to be assigned to the 407th because it was a noncombatant unit. He "had no feelings whatsoever about being in China" except that he liked being there, seeing his time there as an opportunity to travel. Others believed that some of the Chinese-born soldiers wanted to get into the 14th ASG, knowing they would be stationed in China and thus closer to their families. According to Edwin Len of Stratford, Connecticut, who was an aircraft mechanic in the 555th Air Service Squadron, "Some of the older guys even had their wives near them."[12]

Some of the men, however, did not want to be assigned to the 14th ASG or the 987th Signal Company. The fact that they were segregated according to race and nationality made them appear less legitimate and more likely to be a target of disparagement. Because he entered the war as a second lieutenant, Henry Wong of Philadelphia was given a choice as to whether or not to join an all–Chinese American unit. He declined because he had heard many racially prejudiced remarks about the units from other officers. He eventually served in an integrated unit of the Fourteenth Air Force.[13]

Draftees and other noncommissioned personnel did not have such a choice, and many were not pleased with being assigned to the ethnic-specific units. Edwin Len stated, "It wasn't a matter of fighting for the Motherland, but fighting harder not to go to this outfit." He had heard that men in the 14th ASG were not being fed well enough, and that most of them did not speak much English. Both rumors gave him cause for concern. But he was pulled from his original unit and ordered to report to Venice, where he was assigned to the 555th Air Service Squadron. Similarly, Harvey Wong, a native of San Francisco who served in the 1157th Signal Company Service Group, referred to the Chinese-born soldiers in the unit as "China Boys." Wong did not want to go into the unit because the men did not speak much English and he did not really speak Chinese. Len and Wong, both sons of launderers, grew up speaking a little Chinese within the family but only English with their peers. As Len explained: "I didn't know much [Chinese]. I knew some from my mother and father speaking Chinese. Once you went off to school it would be easily lost. At best, your mother would talk to you in Chinese and you'd answer her in English." The idea of being in an all–Chinese American unit posed special challenges to American-born and -raised GIs who might have felt more at ease in integrated units.[14]

Morale, Discipline, Citizenship

It soon became evident that the all–Chinese American units were not going to be easily made into efficient military outfits. Records of the 14th ASG, the 555th Air Service Squadron, and the 987th Signal Company, coupled with oral histories, reveal that numerous problems arose in these units because of the decision to organize around ethnicity and national origin rather than skills. The most immediate concern was language fluency. During the four-week basic training period of the 987th Signal Company, it was discovered that a third of the men, mostly immigrants from China, had only a rudimentary grasp of English. Attempts were made to train them through interpreters, but that could be only a temporary solution, as the men would eventually need specialized training in signal corps operations. Eventually, those who lacked sufficient proficiency in English were transferred to other units and better-qualified replacements were brought in. Lui Eng, a member of the 987th who had worked with his father in a New York laundry before the war, remembers that "men who couldn't perform well in the 987th were sometimes sent to the 555th or the 407th." When it became evident that the 987th could not be brought up to full strength within a reasonable time, the company was reduced and reorganized.[15]

The 555th Air Service Squadron had problems from the outset. The very mission of manning an all–Chinese American unit, as the 555th's historian noted,

> could not be readily solved by ordinary personnel requisitioning procedures already established by the army. Trained technicians in the United States army are not normally held in pools or segregated by nationality or race. This plainly indicated a lack of planning and coordination from Higher Headquarters. If the project was worth special consideration, certainly qualified personnel should be more carefully selected. Most of the personnel sent to Springfield were either cooks, laundrymen, or basics. By some good fortune, a small number were qualified as clerks and air-

> plane mechanics, but the overall picture was disheartening, especially when the majority of the personnel had only a poor command of English.[16]

James Jay recalls that men who were not fluent in English were often channeled into the trucking units and received English lessons with their basic training.[17]

When one looks at the demographics of the 14th ASG as a whole, the reasons for language problems and other issues concerning skills, qualifications, morale, and citizenship become more evident. According to the official report of the 14th ASG, roughly 85 percent of the enlisted personnel had been born in China. All but one percent had learned to speak some English. Most spoke various dialects of Cantonese, and about 99 percent could write some Chinese as well. However, some spoke Shanghainese, Fukienese, Hakka, or the dialect from the region of Ningpo. In order to prepare them for duty in China, Mandarin lessons were offered at Venice Air Field. And, to avoid confusion, the U.S. Articles of War were written in Chinese and posted for the men to read. Of the fifty-four officers, twenty-one were Chinese American, two Korean American, and the rest white. Most of the Chinese American officers had been born in China but educated in the United States and therefore spoke English. The personnel came from all around the country, with approximately forty states represented and California claiming by far the greatest number. While any unit in the American military may have included men from all over the country, it is doubtful that any other had so high a percentage born outside the country with a language other than English as their native tongue. And, given the limited employment possibilities that many of them had had prior to the war, it was unlikely that they arrived in camp with many transferable skills.[18]

Morale among Chinese American troops appears to have been

an ongoing issue. Many of the recruits were not happy to be assigned to segregated units. Things started off poorly for the 555th when the Illinois State Fairgrounds where they gathered were not adequate for so many soldiers and the barracks were overcrowded. Air corps training schools were not immediately available, and those enlisted men who had transferred from air corps units were in danger of forgetting their technical training. Many requested retransfer to an active air corps unit or airbase. The general conditions had a corrosive effect on morale.[19]

After the unit arrived in Venice, the mood improved as GIs began to receive specialized training, but many enlisted men and officers persisted in their attempts to transfer to integrated units. To many, the 14th ASG was "an organized effort at racial segregation and prejudice." Others felt that they would have better opportunities for promotion in integrated units. For the most part, requests for such transfers were denied. Not only did many Chinese American personnel see the units as organized racial segregation, they also encountered prejudice against the units from the white personnel. Many Chinese American GIs avoided USO dances because they felt discriminated against by both white women and white officers. There were reports that white soldiers at Patterson Field resented those Chinese American soldiers who were dating white women, and it is likely that some resented any form of interracial socializing. Thus the creation of these segregated units had the effect of alienating many of the men from their comrades and thereby reduced their morale and their sense of purpose.[20]

Closely related to morale were problems concerning codes of military discipline and behavior. Many men, when introduced to military regulations, restrictions, and rituals, balk at adapting to such discipline and rigor. The Chinese American and Chinese immigrant draftees and recruits were no different in this regard.

The unit report of the 14th ASG attributed laxity in military discipline to "lack of the right type of orientation, insufficient basic training, and inexperienced officer personnel." It continued: "They cannot be oriented in the type of work they are supposed to do in a service group, unless they are made to understand what it means to be an American, why they are in the war, and above all—why an all-Chinese Group has been formed . . . They need more basic training and a better understanding of soldiering. There is little attention to the meaning of stripes, except that stripes mean more money."[21]

Records indicate that discipline was difficult among all the Chinese units because the noncommissioned officers were not strict with their subordinates and unit officers were frequently transferred from one organization to another, depriving the men of any sense of continuity. There was also the problem that Chinese American and Chinese immigrant troops did not take well to regimentation, and had to be handled differently than white soldiers. One report declared: "Chinese will give their best efforts in response to understanding leadership, but will balk if they are approached in the wrong way. An officer who has their respect can accomplish whatever he sets out to do, but if he loses face in the presence of his troops, he is finished." Furthermore, when an officer gave an order to an American soldier, he expected to be obeyed without question. That was not always the case with the Chinese personnel of the 14th ASG, as they often responded to orders by questioning why. These issues of morale and discipline were not fully resolved during training at Patterson Field, Camp Crowder, or Venice Air Field, and would remain with the group in China as well.[22]

At the time of activation, about 40 percent of the enlisted men of the 14th ASG were not U.S. citizens. With a unit solely comprising Chinese Americans and Chinese immigrants, it was inevitable that a substantial number of noncitizens as well as "paper sons," who had entered the country with fraudulent documentation, would be found among the ranks. Thus citizenship classes were established at Venice Air Field, and soon new Chinese American citizens were being naturalized at the federal court in Tampa. When recruits were not able to provide proof that they had entered the country legally, arrangements had to be made to facilitate a legal entry. In one case, eighteen men stationed at Venice Air Field were flown to Detroit and then taken to Canada, from where they were allowed to enter the United States legally, thus making them eligible for naturalization.[23]

These efforts to naturalize Chinese immigrants in the armed service had a positive impact on those who desired citizenship but could not meet the rigorous requirements established by the repeal of the Chinese Exclusion Acts. For those who might have been reluctant to reveal that they were in the country as "paper sons," the army provided a haven from deportation and from in-depth investigations as to the extent of their "paper network" and those involved in it. However, those who did not come clean about their "paper" status encountered some problems, especially in terms of where to send their salary payments or who would be the beneficiaries of their national life insurance policies. Tung Pok Chin of New York, who served in the navy, had entered the United States as a paper son and claimed to be single, but in fact had a mother, a wife, and two sons to support in China. Because his papers did not indicate these dependents, he could only direct some of his salary to his mother, but was unable to provide for the rest of his family during the war because, on paper, they did not exist.[24]

Unlike Tung Pok Chin, a large number of immigrants revealed their illegal status and became American citizens. The granting of citizenship to Chinese-immigrant soldiers was part of a long tradition in American history of "exchanging expedited naturalization or even citizenship itself for honorable military service," a practice that had begun as early as the Revolutionary War. During the Second World War more than 164,000 members of the American armed forces—enlistees and draftees—were naturalized under a variety of programs.[25]

"We Were Too Americanized"

Local Chinese in Hawai'i had experienced different social and racial relations than Chinese living on the U.S. mainland. When Chinese soldiers from Hawai'i arrived at Venice Air Field to join the 14th ASG, they encountered difficulties not only with white Americans but with Chinese Americans born and raised on the mainland as well. It was among problems of morale, discipline, and military behavior that differences in experience and expectation would most readily appear.

While Clifford Young was in language school preparing for what would be a memorable tour of duty in China, one that would take him to the caves of Yenan to work with the Chinese Communists, his older brother Cecil was serving in the 555th Air Service Squadron. Cecil had preceded his brother at Western Military Academy and the University of Michigan, where he completed a degree in forestry in 1940. Called to active duty in 1941, Cecil Young trained in an infantry unit at Fort Custer, Michigan. He hoped to be a pilot, so, as required before the war, he relinquished his commission and applied to flight school. He was accepted, but soon "washed out." The air corps, however, kept him and sent him to Luke Field in Arizona to be liaison officer to the Chinese Nationalist pilots who were being trained there. After two more assignments in the mainland United

States, he received orders to report to Venice Army Air Field in Florida, where he became unit commander of the 555th.

Not until he arrived at Venice did Young discover that the 555th was an all–Chinese American outfit. He later remembered saying to himself: "My God, what did they want me for?" "Because of my technical background," he went on, "they assigned me to the 555th because it was a technical squadron. Harry Selin, the second lieutenant who was then in charge, said 'I am so happy you have come. Take this damn squadron out of my hands. I give up with these Chinese guys.'" Young believed that Selin, who had had only ninety days of training, had never really been in the service and therefore did not know how to handle the men. Soon after assuming command, however, Young realized that the problems were more fundamental. He candidly acknowledged that he was unprepared for what he regarded as a "decidedly unmilitary unit lacking discipline and even basic communication." The discipline problems included gambling, tardiness, and lack of knowledge of or concern for military regulations, and Young complained that the men in his unit did not understand the nature of orders. In speaking positively of one soldier, he resorted to a derogatory Hawaiian slang term for Chinese to refer to others: "He was trained in the army way so he understood what orders were. These guys with a little intelligence follow orders. Some of them fought it, but they knew they were there, so they had to follow orders. But some of them—I'll say '*Paké* Boys'—they don't understand, talking Chinese all the time. Those are the guys you have to watch. They simply don't want to take orders." Clearly those men who did not speak English and had few of the social skills common to Americans presented the greatest difficulty. Isolated and uncomprehending, they may well have found military rules and regulations bizarre. After serving with the 555th and with Headquarters Squadron in China, Young was reassigned to the 373rd Bomb Squadron, with which he went to Okinawa and later to Japan as part of the occupation forces.[26]

William Ching, born in Honolulu to Chinese immigrants who ran a fish pond, attended Yenjing University (now incorporated into Beijing University) from 1933 to 1937. When the Japanese began their southern offensive he returned home. Having witnessed the Japanese expansion firsthand, he joined the National Guard, and meanwhile found work in a stock brokerage company. When the National Guard was activated in 1940 he was stationed at Schofield Barracks on Oahu until he attended officer candidate school at Fort Monmouth, New Jersey, where he was the first Chinese American graduate. After returning to Hawai'i for a brief time, he received orders to join the 987th Signal Company. His assessment of the morale of the men fits with other reports:

> You would think you were in Chinatown when you arrived in this unit, they all spoke Chinese. It was a funny feeling, coming into a strange outfit that's just learning how to speak English at the same time trying to learn the American way of doing things. Frankly, the morale was not great. These were young boys, they were not yet American citizens, yet they were drafted. They were thrown into a highly specialized outfit. They were learning how to operate the radio, how to repair it, but they were not trained for that kind of thing. I would say 65 percent that came in were weeded out.

Ching pointed out that this was not the best way to staff a signal company, which depended on everyone being able to communicate with each other.[27]

Mun Charn Wong and Hon Chung Chee were both stationed at Hickam Air Field in Hawai'i when they received orders to report to Venice Air Field. Chee was made unit commander of the 2121st Quartermaster Truck Company and Wong was put in charge of the 2122nd. The two of them responded differently to being assigned to the all–Chinese American units. Although Chee was "shocked" when he got to Florida, "seeing all those Chinese kids," he stayed with them. Chee recalled that the troops were "very, very disorganized and had no discipline. In fact, they tried to converse with me in Chinese. Well, if it is in *Zhongshan hua* maybe I can understand, but talking *Szeyup* is quite difficult [he names two very different Chinese dialects]. I made it very clear that when I was spoken to, it would be in English only." In this way, Chee tried to maintain military discipline and the distance needed between enlisted men and their officers. Wong, in contrast, finding the troops very poorly trained and far from ready to be shipped out, requested a transfer. The men's lack of military discipline and respect for their superior officers led him to believe that it would be impossible for them to become an effective military force. Wong's transfer was granted, and he was eventually assigned to an integrated unit and sent to Europe.[28]

While the local Chinese from Hawai'i who served in integrated outfits later reported that they had generally felt comfortable in their units, those who served in the segregated units, especially those who were officers, often said they regretted having done so. As Cecil Young put it: "You have to be a certain kind of person to have enjoyed being in those all–Chinese American units." Ironically, one of the root causes of their dissatisfaction was Hawai'i's multiracial society. Although many of the Chinese living in Hawai'i did not associate regularly with whites, their everyday interactions were much more diverse than those of many Chinese Americans who lived in mainland Chinatowns. Because so many ethnic groups coexisted in Hawai'i, English or at least a form of pidgin English was the lingua franca of the islands; whereas in mainland Chinatowns, especially among recent immigrants, only Chinese was spoken, and usually a different dialect than that spoken in Hawai'i. Therefore, when the Chinese from Hawai'i arrived in camp with the American mainland Chinese, the men from Hawai'i felt "misplaced." As a few of the veterans from Hawai'i stated: "We were too Americanized."[29]

In addition, many of the Chinese from Hawai'i had been in ROTC or the National Guard before they were transferred to the all–Chinese American units, so they had already received training and become accustomed to military discipline. The structure of social relations in Hawai'i differed enough from that on the mainland that the Chinese from Hawai'i did not necessarily identify with the mainland Chinese. In fact, despite their geographical and cultural distance from the continental United States, the Hawai'i Chinese often thought of themselves as "more American" than the Chinese Americans from the mainland.

William Hoy and *Gung Ho*

After the San Francisco journalist William Hoy, who in 1940 had founded the *Chinese Press* with Charles Leong, joined the service, he continued to write a column for the paper while in training, usually human interest stories about his experiences in camp or about various Chinese Americans he encountered or heard about in the military. But Hoy discerned a need for a new publication aimed at his fellow Chinese American servicemen. Soon after he arrived at Patterson Field, Ohio, as part of the 407th Air

Service Squadron, Hoy approached his commanding officer about producing a newsletter for Chinese American personnel. Granted permission, he recruited a team of assistants. He called the newsletter *Gung Ho,* which in Chinese means "work together," in the hope that it would become the slogan of the 407th. The inaugural issue, dated December 25, 1943, carried a front-page message from the commanding officer of the 407th, Mark Mooty, expressing his wish that the "men use this paper as an outlet for their thoughts in promoting the welfare of this Squadron. The road ahead will be long and hard and it is imperative that this organization be solidified to such an extent that it will be impregnable." Hoy included his own "mission statement" for the publication, which recalled the public spirit that was characteristic of his newspapers in San Francisco Chinatown. Aside from providing squadron news, *Gung Ho* would "seek to bring about a spirit of fellowship, a real Confucian sense of social harmony, and a sense of community of purpose among the personnel."[30]

The content and style of *Gung Ho* reflected Hoy's Chinese American aesthetic sensibilities. The words *Gung Ho* were written in "bamboo letters" on the opening page, and the Chinese characters for the phrase appeared as well. It was a bilingual publication, with the articles sometimes differing in content. The bulk of the paper was in English, and the Chinese section sometimes included Mandarin lessons. There was a section entitled "Chop Suey," also spelled out in "bamboo letters," which reported news about particular soldiers, their girlfriends and wives, births, what kinds of presents they received from home, the parties they attended, off-base trips, and other activities. Squadron news included promotions and transfers, sports team results, and longer profiles of soldiers.

Brief accounts of what soldiers did when they left the base offer insights into how servicemen were treated and how they responded to their unique position as Chinese American soldiers in the Midwest. Private Louie Woon wrote about his time in Sidney, Ohio:

> What sweet memories are brought to mind when the town of Sidney is mentioned? Is it the memory of the bivouac area where we won medals for our good marksmenship? . . . Or does Sidney remind you of the many fair and sweet young things who made such an instantaneous hit with us; the streets through which we and they strolled hand in hand; the favorite drinking fountain where we dream and sip cokes at the same time; the amusement spots where we frequented? Or does Sidney perhaps recall to us the wholesome and delicious dinners we were invited to eat in the homes of many kind and generous citizens?[31]

Woon did not specify whether the girls he sipped Cokes with or the families who served him dinner were white or Chinese, but he embraced them as Americans and he clearly saw himself as an American, serving to protect the very America he described. In another issue there is a detailed description of an off-base squadron party at the Loretta Club in Dayton. The Chinese food was cooked in the base mess and driven to the club. The party was attended by 150 guests, many of them women from a variety of civilian and armed service organizations, as well as a contingent of men and women from the Royal Canadian Air Force. William Hoy pointed out that "to many of the guests the men of the 407th were the first Chinese Americans they had ever met and talked with. Thus the development of Sino-American friendship became an element of this party, though few were actually aware of it."[32] By casting their interactions in the frame of "Sino-American relations," Hoy perpetuated the separation between Americans of Chinese descent and other Americans. Private Woon, it seems, had grasped the notion of what it meant to be an American more fully than had Corporal Hoy.

Nonetheless, Hoy carried his commitment to promoting a Chinese American consciousness from San Francisco to his time in the military. He joined the unit's debating team and organized a weekly discussion forum on the "problems of Chinese Americans in the United States" until it was discontinued because too many men were being sent away on temporary duty. (Hoy himself was later transferred to the headquarters of the 14th ASG.) *Gung Ho* was originally printed in lots of five hundred copies but was later increased to a thousand copies as its popularity grew both at Patterson Field and on other bases where Chinese Americans were stationed, and as men started to send the paper home to family and friends.[33]

Overseas and over the Hump

After finishing their training in late 1943 and early 1944, the various components of the 14th ASG and the 987th Signal Company received their orders to proceed to China. The men of the 1157th Signal Company Service Group were the first to depart. They left Springfield in December 1943 for Camp Patrick Henry, Virginia, where they spent the holidays, then embarked for Cape Town, South Africa. After a brief stay in Cape Town they continued on to India, landing in Bombay. The unit next moved by rail to Calcutta and later to Chabua, from where they were eventually airlifted "over the Hump" to Kunming, in China's Yunnan province. The 407th Air Service Squadron followed a similar route, leaving Patterson Field for Newport News, Virginia, in April 1944. They boarded a ship bound for Oran, North Africa, proceeded to Bombay, then traveled by rail to Camp Kancharapara before being flown to Kunming in November 1944.

The rest of the 14th ASG took the Pacific route to China. Most of them left Venice Air Field in late September 1944 for Camp Anza, California. In October they sailed for Melbourne, Australia. They were not given full shore leave there, but were allowed to stay on the pier while they prepared for their journey to Bombay. From Bombay they followed the trail of the others to Camp Kancharapara and Chabua. The 987th Signal Company took a similar route, leaving Camp Crowder in June 1944 for Camp Anza, departing there for Australia and Calcutta, before being flown into China from Camp Kancharapara.[34]

Chabua, India, was near the starting point of the Ledo-Burma Road, which stretched all the way to Kunming, China. By the time the 14th ASG arrived in Chabua, the road was open to Allied forces as the Japanese had been generally driven from the area, and vital supplies could finally be taken to those stationed in southwestern China. The road project had begun in 1942; by the end of 1943 General Lewis A. Pick was in charge of the project. The original Burma Road, which ran from Mong Yu in northern Burma to Kunming, had to be restored, and a new five-hundred-mile road from Ledo in Assam, India, to the Burma Road had to be carved out of the jungle. Built primarily by African American engineers and local workers, the project was completed in late 1944 and early 1945. By the end of the war more than five thousand vehicles had made the eleven-hundred-mile trip, carrying thirty-four thousand tons of supplies to China.[35] Some sections of the road were extremely treacherous, especially the "21 Curves" in Annan, China, which consisted of twenty-one steep switchbacks and turns. Accidents were frequent, and at times it was necessary to push wrecked vehicles over the edge to keep the road open.

When Hon Chung Chee took the 2121st Quartermaster Truck

Company to China via the Ledo-Burma Road, it was the first Chinese American unit to make the arduous journey. Trucks often broke down and makeshift repairs were a regular occurrence. It took the unit eleven days to reach Kunming, and at times bulldozers were needed to clear the road ahead. Edwin Len of the 555th Air Service Squadron, who had only recently learned to drive during training at Venice Air Field, drove the Ledo-Burma Road, driving a jeep pulling a two-wheeled trailer. The unit transported equipment and a variety of vehicles including tow trucks, flatbeds, and three-quarter-ton trucks. Len recalls that at times the dust was nine to ten inches deep and all the drivers could see were the two tire ruts in front of them. Their journey took fifteen days, while others took nearly a month to complete the trek.[36]

Those airlifted over the Himalayas faced a different set of dangers. One source describes it this way:

> Five hundred miles of the worst flying country in the world. As one climbed up off the field at Chabua, he could see the dead end of India sealed off by the sixteen-thousand-foot Himalayas. The men had to top these peaks to get to China. To the north were the snow-laden Tibetan peaks, rising to twenty-five thousand feet . . . There is no summer in the Hump. Snow always crowns the peaks. Ice hangs heavy on the clouds. Black monsoon storms sweep up from India, screening the peaks, bringing terrific turbulence which flipped fully-loaded transports on their backs.[37]

The weather determined when flights could go over the Hump, and the weather could change with little warning. When the skies were clear, the mountains were an awesome and beautiful sight, but when bad weather set in, the danger increased. In one case, thirty-one planes circled the field at Chabua above "a fog fifteen feet deep clinging to the ground." The ground crews were able to talk down nineteen, but seven crashed and another five were lost when the crews had to bail out because their planes had run out of fuel. The cost in lives and equipment was substantial. Planes went down crossing the Hump because of enemy aircraft, the weather, overloading, and insufficient fuel. It has been estimated that 910 crewmen and 130 passengers perished in these flights, losing 694 planes, with 75 recovered. Nonetheless, an estimated 650,000 tons of cargo were flown into China via this route.[38]

Originally scheduled to fly at 4:30 P.M., Charles Leong was eager to see the "tall spires of the Hump painted by sunset colors." But delays pushed his departure back to 6:30. The flight took three hours, and most of the time the men were in total darkness, except when they were instructed to don their oxygen masks. Leong recalled: "It was the first time that any of us had ever put on the masks, and the relatively simple process of screwing the long black oxygen tube to a master tube built in the cabin fascinated us. It was just a simple slim tube, but it held the power of preventing us from gagging and gasping, and possibly fainting in the thin upper altitudes. After we had all carefully adjusted the masks to our faces, the lights were again turned off."[39]

Serving in China

Traveling by air or by land, the 14th ASG and the 987th Signal Company had finally arrived in China. Once the various units arrived in Kunming, some stayed at bases near the city while some were sent to other locations. The men of the 555th Air Service Squadron were headquartered at Tsingchen Air Base and also worked out of other bases in a three-hundred-mile area as needed. Their primary duty was to service the aircraft of the Fourteenth Air Force, as well as those of the Chinese American Composite Wing (CACW). The 407th Air Service Squadron's main headquarters were in the Kunming area and later at the Peishiyi Air Base near Chungking. Both service squadrons were known for repairing aircraft engines and other vehicles with makeshift parts and tools because of the shortage of materials. Signal companies were usually split up into smaller teams and stationed across a broad swath of territory. The 987th Signal Company was scattered throughout the French-Indo-China front, an area about seventy miles in width and fifty in depth. The men of 1157th Signal Company Service Group were sent to different areas and spent most of their time in small teams on detached service (away from headquarters and often temporarily assigned to support other units).[40]

This was also the case for the quartermaster trucking companies and the ordnance companies. Hon Chung Chee of the 2121st Trucking Company remarked that his unit was "scattered all over" and that while he would sometimes deliver airplane parts to the 407th or the 555th, he spent a great deal of time in the field and not with his unit as a whole. Likewise, Howard Chang of the 1545th Ordnance Supply and Maintenance Company was often on detached service duty and usually found himself the only Asian in the unit to which he was temporarily assigned. Thus many of the men who had been placed in segregated all–Chinese American units ended up working with white American troops on these temporary assignments.[41]

Having arrived in late 1944 or early 1945, most of the men had been in China for less than a year when the war came to an end. On August 22, 1945, when representatives of the Japanese army signed surrender papers at Chihkiang Air Field, many members of the 407th Air Service Squadron were present. The unit's historian recorded the event: "The squadron moved down to the transient area near the control tower preparatory to moving out of the Chihkiang base. While in this area, a Jap plane with the symbol of the rising sun landed on the field bearing emissaries to sign the surrender terms for the Japanese Army in the China theater. To the G.I.'s the rising sun on the plane appeared very much like the setting sun."[42]

A few weeks later Charles Leong was in Kunming on V-J Day (September 3, 1945, in China), and he captured the day's events with an eye to the future:

> This good-natured, smiling and immensely happy mob was a cross-section of a new China. Everyone was giving the thumbs-up sign and yelling "Ding Ho" to all American and Allied soldiers. Through these years of both a spiritual and military alliance between American and China the words "Ding Ho" has been the password for goodwill, even if neither American soldier nor Chinese knew not another word of each other's language . . . The pattern of this crowd, a fusion of forces of the old and the new, truly was a picture of a New China. This was the hour of triumph for the people. They were out to enjoy it.[43]

As wartime conditions wound down and the Chinese began returning to their homes, Allied personnel began their journeys home as well. Those who had earned the eighty points (which were awarded on the basis of amount of time served, combat experience, and age) that qualified them to go home went out on the first available troop ships, often leaving from Shanghai or Hong Kong. Some of the men of the 14th ASG remained to train Chinese troops and deliver equipment to the Chinese government. Many used the opportunity to visit relatives in China and possibly make arrangements to meet potential wives. Kern Owyang returned to his native village near Macao to see his mother, whom he had not heard from in two years. James Jay and three friends went to their home villages in the Canton area and stayed for about nine days. When news of their visit spread to neighboring villages, many villagers gave them letters for relatives in the United States with whom they had been unable to communicate during the Japanese occupation of the region. Jay took about fifty letters back to Shanghai and mailed them from there using the armed forces postal system. Most of the men from the 14th ASG were eventually sent to Shanghai, from where they departed for the United States in early December. They reached Tacoma, Washington, right before Christmas in 1945.[44]

Chinese American soldiers in China found themselves in the land of their ancestry but not necessarily in the land of their loyalty. Even the men who had been born in China or had spent time there before the war did not always see themselves as Chinese. There were certainly many who felt a special affinity for China. James Jay wanted to serve there as retribution for the brutality of the Japanese. Alfred Hong, who had spent the years 1933–1939 in China, also believed he had a "score to settle" with the Japanese. He explained: "The American Chinese who does not know China is fighting for one country, America, but the Chinese that know America and China are fighting for two."[45] Others made it very clear that while they were helping to defend China, they were doing so as American soldiers. Veterans of the 14th ASG declared that they had acted out of "a sense of duty, as Americans in the American service, as citizens. We are Americans first."[46]

Their identification as Americans contributed to their dissatisfaction at being placed in segregated units and at the treatment they were accorded by white soldiers. Henry Ching, the historical officer of the 555th Air Service Squadron, recorded these tensions in a unit history compiled after the war:

> Chinese American GIs, having lived in the States and considering themselves completely on an equal basis with any other personnel of the American forces, have on many instances stated that American GIs often make derogatory remarks about the Chinese American soldier, while the latter have as a result developed a resentment against some American Army personnel in China. At the mess hall, the American GIs have often stated that they will not tolerate Chinese Americans talking Chinese in their presence. The American GIs have a tendency to belittle the Chinese, their customs, living conditions, food, etc., and automatically classify all people of the race as below par; as a result, they resent having to consider a large group of Chinese American soldiers as equals.[47]

The history of the 14th ASG as a whole echoed these sentiments: "The men themselves are for the most part very proud of the fact that they are American citizens and wish to be treated as such. This feeling is torn down considerably by reason of the fact that the average GI looks down on them and classes them as natives or at least on a level with the native." The report added that American GIs would get drunk and start calling the Chinese American soldiers "slopies" and other derogatory names. The base commanders did little to discipline the offenders. Henry Ching explained: "While it is true that officers of the Group are responsible for the proper orientation of the Chinese American personnel, it is also true that this is of no value unless American

GIs are also properly oriented by their own leaders. This is not being done at the present time."[48]

Questions remain about why the all–Chinese American units were formed and how effective they were. The directive given for the 987th Signal Company to "further liaison relationships between American and Chinese troops in that theater" is the most obvious reason for the creation of segregated units. The army appeared to have a reasonable plan to utilize over a thousand ethnically Chinese American troops, many of whom were not fluent in English, by sending them to a country where their language abilities would be an asset. However, the decision to organize the units around ethnicity did not fully take into account the problems involved in using immigrant troops. During the First World War the U.S. armed forces had confronted these problems on a larger scale: in that war 18 percent of the U.S. army was foreign-born. At first the army had tried placing the immigrant soldiers in ethnically mixed companies aided by translators, but it quickly became apparent that this was an inefficient way to train large numbers of soldiers, so the immigrants were placed in ethnic-specific units.[49] The creation of the all–Chinese American units appears to have followed this earlier model.

Having a substantial number of non-English-speaking troops spread throughout the army had the potential to create dangerous situations on the battlefield. Because the military could not easily distinguish between Chinese Americans and Chinese immigrants, or determine which ones were fluent in English and which were not, the groups were placed together in these stigmatized units. It seems that these units were created out of convenience rather than as a public relations ploy or out of racist hostility. Segregated because of perceived deficiencies in language skills and training, but unlike the well-publicized all–

Japanese American combat units sent to Europe or the segregated African American units that reflected Jim Crow racism, the 14th Air Service Group and the 987th Signal Company occupied a middle ground in military race relations, a position similar to the one often assigned to Asian Americans in American racial hierarchies and thought.

As the records and oral histories indicate, the decision to organize the 14th ASG on the basis of ethnic background was not very successful. The policy failed to effectively staff the units, train personnel in their specialties, enhance morale, or promote good working relationships with other troops. Henry Ching's assessment of the all–Chinese American units was blunt:

> The majority of the personnel feel that it would have been better if each individual had been left on his own with any other American white unit, and no attempt made to single them out as different from any other GI in the armed forces. By being thrown together with other Chinese personnel and subjected to the control and command of Chinese non-coms, the inherent characteristics of the men immediately caused serious problems in discipline. From a morale standpoint, this has been a constant source of irritation and was never solved satisfactorily.[50]

The tendency of many immigrant Chinese draftees not to take orders seriously, to gamble in training camp, and to resist regimentation persisted throughout the existence of these units. Lui Eng of the 987th Signal Company recalled that some of the men were reluctant to take orders from officers of their own ethnicity, but were more likely to accept orders from "American officers." The final evaluation of the 555th Air Service Squadron stated: "In addition to the matter of morale and discipline, there is also the difficulty encountered from a strictly technical point—that of mechanical and technical training, experience, and initiative in performance of technical jobs." It was clear from the outset that language deficiencies would present problems in training, and both the published record and interviews concur. As Woody Moy of the 987th remarked: "Truthfully, the group was not qualified to move overseas into any combat. So we were sent to China in a non-combat area." Henry Ching concluded his history of the 555th: "It is the honest opinion of the historical officer that this is a serious mistake to activate an all Chinese Squadron, Company, or Group within the Army of the United States. It is hoped that, should a similar question arise again, the War Department would refrain from initiating a similar project as started at Springfield." When the war came to an end, so too did these units based on ethnicity and national origins.[51]

Given that most of the personnel of the 14th ASG were in China for less than a year and generally did not see combat, these soldiers did not return to the States as heroes, with stories of glory and adventure, but nevertheless they were proud of their service and accomplishments. Even more, as time passed, they were proud of what their war experience enabled them to do as Chinese Americans after the war. Brought together in the 1940s because of their age, their ethnicity, and war, they developed a camaraderie that lasted well into the postwar decades. As Harry Lim emphasized: "It is best to think of what we gained from the war rather than what we did."[52] These Chinese Americans who served in the U.S. armed forces looked back on the war years and the roles they played in the conflict as the door through which they walked into the broader American society.

6

Into the Mainstream

Like most Americans, Chinese Americans rejoiced when the war ended, celebrating the Allied victory over the Axis powers and China's liberation from Japan. Families welcomed their husbands, wives, fathers, mothers, sons, and daughters home. "It was just fantastic," Dorothy Eng recalled fifty years later. "Everybody was kissing everybody else."[1] Those fortunate enough to come home were anxious to begin new lives by finding jobs, going to school, and starting or reuniting with their families. The changes in the lives of Chinese Americans that had begun during the war became evident in the postwar years in the dramatic increase in the number of Chinese women in the country, the diversity of jobs opening to many Chinese Americans, the larger numbers of Chinese Americans attending college, and the strengthened tendency of Chinese Americans to identify themselves as *Americans.*

War Brides and Stable Families

Like the repeal of the Chinese Exclusion Acts in 1943, the War Brides Act of 1945 and its subsequent amendments changed the composition of Chinese America. It allowed thousands of Chinese women to enter the country, some as new brides and many others to rejoin their husbands after years of separation. These women would play a vital role in the creation of new Chinese American families and the stabilization of families long separated by exclusion policies. The War Brides Act, to be in effect for three years, allowed the admission "to the United States of alien spouses and alien children of citizen members of the United States armed forces," provided they fulfilled the other requirements for immigration. The original act was amended in 1946 by what is often known as the Alien Fiancées and Fiancés Act, which allowed those who were engaged to marry members of the American armed forces to enter the country for three months. If they did not marry within that period, they were to leave. Later that year another piece of legislation, the Chinese Alien Wives of American Citizens Act, allowed the entry of Chinese wives of American citizens outside the annual quota of 105. Finally, in 1947, Congress did away with all racial restrictions for alien wives of American citizens seeking admission to the United States.[2] There were generally three groupings of men and women who could take advantage of these provisions: those who married while still in China during the war or shortly thereafter, those who returned to China after the war to marry or become engaged, and those who were already married but could only now bring their wives to the United States. These legislative acts greatly altered the gender ratio of Chinese America.

There had been considerable interest among Chinese American soldiers during the war in meeting potential spouses while in China or in rekindling relationships that had been interrupted by emigration or the chaos of war. Private Hom Q. Sing of the 555th Air Service Squadron met his "boyhood sweetheart" while stationed in Kweiyang. In accordance with regulations, he sought approval of the marriage from Theater Command. He was told that permission would be granted once he received a certificate from the United States Consular Service stating that the "intended spouse is a person qualified to make application for an immigration visa under the United States Immigration Laws." Unfortunately, that certificate did not arrive, and the unit historian feared that their tour of duty would come to an end before permission was granted. He lamented: "If the military restrictions were more lenient on this subject, our organization would have many wedding celebrations by this time."[3]

When such a wedding did take place in China, either the new wife joined her husband in the United States after the war or the husband returned to China after the war to escort her to America. It was much more common for Chinese American service personnel to take advantage of the War Brides Act and its amendments by traveling to China in the postwar period to become engaged, to marry, or to reunite with a spouse. Many veterans returned to China in search of marriage partners. The marriages were arranged by their families, or the men would simply visit family villages hoping to meet a suitable mate. Both parties stood to gain from these arrangements. There were still far fewer Chinese women than men in America, and greater parity promised greater family and community stability. And marrying Americans gave young women the chance to leave a country that had been ravaged by civil and foreign war and to start a new life.[4]

In fact, the majority of the so-called war brides had already been married for five or more years. Rather than being new brides, they were "longtime wives of Chinese Americans in transnational families."[5] Yee Wing, for example, had been separated from her husband for fifteen years before she entered the United States under the War Brides Act. "Because he was in the service," she explained, "he was allowed to become a citizen and that opened the door for him to bring me and my daughter over."[6] During the three years in which the War Brides Act was in effect, 5,132 Chinese women entered the country, and the Chinese Alien Wives of American Citizens Act allowed another 2,317 women in between July 1947 and June 1950.[7] Chinese Americans finally had the opportunity to create and raise families at rates similar to their fellow Americans of other races and ethnicities.

The arrival of these women and the formation or reunification of families allowed Chinese Americans to participate in what is now known as the Baby Boom. In her study of Chinese American families in the Bay Area (which had the highest concentration of Chinese Americans in the country), Rose Hum Lee documented a 286.5 percent increase in the birth rate from 1946 to 1947 alone. The rate continued at near the 1947 level through 1950. Other important demographic shifts took place as well. By 1950 there was a drop in the sex ratio from three men to one woman to two to one, a lower median age, an increase of the workforce with over three times more women being employed, and a higher rate of married couples. What had been labeled a "bachelor society" a century before had by 1950 become a growing community of families.[8]

This development was "celebrated" in 1951 with the completion of the Ping Yuen East Housing Project in San Francisco. Although some have suggested that these apartments were built to keep Chinese Americans in Chinatown, others saw these units, outfitted with all the modern conveniences, as "a reward for the loyalty and fidelity demonstrated by American citizens of Chinese ancestry during World War II." Priority was given to veterans and U.S. citizens.[9] While most attention to the growth of Chinese American families in the postwar period is usually given to the "war brides" and their impact on the demographics of the community, it should also be noted that the Chinese American generation born in the 1920s was also marrying and having children during these years. Many of them were seeking lives beyond Chinatowns in mushrooming suburbs around the country.

Occupational and Social Mobility

Those who had been shut out of the larger job market before the war now returned to the United States with higher expectations and better skills. The long-range effects of the war on Chinese Americans in the workplace can be gleaned from information found in the federal censuses for 1940 and 1950. The total number of Chinese employed increased from 36,992 in 1940 to 48,409 in 1950. The significance of the changes becomes evident when specific areas of occupational mobility are examined. The most obvious and far-reaching changes occurred in employment in professional and semi-professional fields, and in the number of Chinese American women employed. Employment in the professional ranks more than tripled for men (from 812 in 1940 to 2,541 in 1950) and almost quadrupled for women (from 221 in 1940 to 914 in 1950). In other fields, men showed incremental increases, but the gains for women were substantial. For example, the number of men employed as managers, officials, and proprietors increased from 7,250 in 1940 to 8,920 in 1950, while the number of women in such positions jumped from 253 to 658. In clerical and sales positions, types of jobs traditionally more available to women, the number of men did increase (from 3,422 to 4,512), but the number of women more than quadrupled (from 750 to 3,210). In the service sector, too, the changes were indicative of an expanded labor market for Chinese Americans. For service workers (not including domestic workers), the number of men increased by approximately one-fourth (from 10,515 to 13,000) while the number of women almost doubled (from 562 to 940). And in the area of domestic help, only about half as many Chinese American men were employed in 1950 than in 1940, while again the number of women almost doubled.[10] (For more details about employment on the mainland and in Hawai'i see the tables in the Appendix.)

These figures do not explain the increasing numbers of Chinese Americans finding gainful employment: for example, the jumps in employment of women may be accounted for in part by the new legislation allowing Chinese women to immigrate. But the figures do indicate that Chinese Americans had made occupational advances during the decade. Men were able to leave domestic service in notable numbers and presumably find better jobs. And the number of Chinese American men and women in professional and semi-professional occupations increased dramatically. These trends point to the participation of Chinese Americans in the American economy beyond the confines of Chinatown. At midcentury, with more Chinese Americans employed as doctors, lawyers, engineers, and other white-collar professionals, and with substantially more women working in the public sphere, Chinese Americans were poised to enter the American middle class.

In Hawai'i, local Chinese had already made inroads into the middle class by the outbreak of the Second World War. Census records indicate that the overwhelming majority of Chinese had left the agricultural sector before the war and were living in Honolulu. In fact, by 1950 "farmers and farm managers" was no longer a separate category in the census, but had been folded into the statistics for "managers, officials, and proprietors." Most noticeably, Chinese men more than doubled their presence in the professions (from 320 in 1940 to 876 in 1950) and women made similar gains in clerical and sales positions (from 841 to 1,813). At the same time, there was a marked decline in the number of men working as laborers and in the service sector (including domestic service), though the number of women in service jobs remained stable.[11]

These developments in Hawai'i do not necessarily reflect the impact of the war, but are more likely to indicate where the Chinese stood in the islands' racial hierarchy and how they navigated within that hierarchy during and after the war. The arrival of war on its doorstep had helped shift Hawai'i's "economy from its prewar reliance on sugar and pineapple to a postwar emphasis on tourism and military expenditures."[12] As Chinese moved from the plantations to the urban centers before the war, they were in a position to take advantage of the wartime economic boom on Oahu by engaging in such economic activities as working at Pearl Harbor (local Japanese were not allowed to work there during the war) and running businesses that catered to the military personnel. As the sugar and pineapple industries began to decline and the economic and political power of the so-called Big Five (the five major corporate powers in Hawai'i) began to erode, the Chinese who had businesses in other sectors continued to prosper. An increase in air travel brought in tourists and goods from around the world, the importance of Hawai'i as a military outpost in the Pacific brought it fully into the American sphere of influence, and the Chinese of Hawai'i were among those who benefited from these transformative forces.

The social mobility that many Chinese Americans, both on the mainland and Hawai'i, enjoyed after the war was facilitated by the GI Bill of Rights or the Servicemen's Readjustment Act.

Passed in 1944, this program was designed to help returning veterans restart their lives, which had been interrupted by the war. It provided "a trio of benefits—unemployment pay while looking for a job, tuition and subsistence allowances for further education or training, and loans to purchase homes or farms or to start a business."[13] Like thousands of other veterans, Chinese American servicemen used these benefits to return to school and purchase homes. After Clifford Young was discharged from the army, he and his wife went to Ann Arbor, Michigan, where he received a degree in architecture from the university. From there he went to the Massachusetts Institute of Technology for a master's degree. In both cases he used the GI Bill. Young described the bill as "the greatest thing we had." He added: "I received $105.00 a month because I was married, and my wife worked at MIT as a part-time secretary." In addition to tuition, the GI Bill covered his books and materials, including cameras and other supplies. Young and his family eventually returned to Honolulu, where he became a well-known architect, designing, among other buildings, the East-West Center on the campus of the University of Hawai'i at Manoa.[14]

The GI Bill not only enabled Young to afford professional training but also gave him a new sense of relationship to the federal government and the broader civil community. Similar stories abound among the Chinese Americans who served in the war. Whether or not they took advantage of the GI Bill, the range of occupations that they entered after the war was as varied as the rest of American society. Although some of the advances gained by women and minorities during the war turned out to be temporary, the gains for Chinese Americans were nevertheless significant. Many entered professions previously closed to them and many found employment outside Chinatown.

Experiencing Citizenship

Their experiences during the war gave many Chinese Americans a newfound confidence and a stronger sense of having a legitimate place in American society. These changes in their sense of self and identity and in their attitudes toward their lives in America were at least as important as their upward economic and social mobility.

Looking back on the decade of the 1940s, the journalist Charles Leong wrote:

> World War II, from the personal standpoint of the Chinese-Americans, was the one great significant historical event of their times. I know that "Pearl Harbor" sent its shock waves all over the world. It touched millions. It affected, and changed many lives. It touched, and affected us just a significantly larger margin than it did white Americans. Especially for those of us in uniform . . . The pride of the time in feeling that the Chinese American—who frankly, wore the garb of inferiority—was a part of the great patriotic U.S. war machine out to do battle with the enemy.[15]

Leong had been stationed in the public relations office at the headquarters of the Fourteenth Air Force in Shanghai, the only Chinese American in the outfit. He considered the all–Chinese American 407th and 555th Air Service Squadrons "another wartime operational gimmick, segregated units, like the all-black outfits." But he saw the logic of "the idea of all-Chinese units, going back to fight in the homeland, wearing the uniforms of an ally of China." He recalled that he had been "overjoyed to be able to go to China," as before the war he had had a vague idea of going to "help build up the country." But he also recalled the tension of his generation's relation to China and the United States, a tension that had been articulated in the essay contest of the Ging Hawk Club (described in Chapter 1) and other essays and speeches of the 1930s. He continued:

> It was, I suppose, really an escape clause because at the time our acceptance as Americans of Chinese background and racial identity was not at all 100 percent complete, not even 80 percent, or even 60 percent. I'm serious about those figures. That is why in the 1930s and 1940s, the Chinese-American professionals in the personal services, such as lawyers, doctors, and dentists, seldom practiced outside of Chinatown. A few of my friends, like the artist Dong Kingman, and myself were secretly hoping that we would be among the first to penetrate the American scene, professionally speaking. In short, let my work and not my color speak for itself. So the American challenge, to some of us, was bigger than a challenge of helping the old mother country.[16]

Reflecting the thoughts of many of his generation, he wrote:

> The eternal question was posed: Are we American? Are we Chinese? That's why I think the historical impact of World War II was so important to our generation. Remember, ours was just about the first group—in somewhat sizeable numbers—to go to college. To venture a step deeper into the white world . . . So when thousands of us Chinese-Americans became members of the armed forces, the doors of somewhat equal opportunity were opened to us . . . All this gave us a measurable achievement, which forged a pride and poise as we realized that the thousands of us, in

> various branches of the U.S. armed forces, were equal parts of an operational team. It has to be experienced, rather than described, the feeling for so many of our Chinese-Americans, to be in a command position, as officers, in a squadron of majority white soldiers. In the 1940s we were the first sizeable group of Chinese-Americans to meet this challenge.[17]

Leong's reflection on his experiences as emblematic for his generation of veterans and Chinese Americans in general provides an invaluable glimpse into the identity formation of a generation in transition. Many returned from the war with new self-respect, a sense of inclusion in American society, and a confidence in their ability to break down the social barriers built on race prejudice and carve out a better life for themselves and their families. Like many other returning veterans, Leong understood the profound impact of the war: "The military experience of the 1940s in which thousands of Chinese-Americans tasted and savored for the first time a 'near equality' gave a definite, perhaps hidden, direction that their lives and destinies were to be shaped in America, as Americans."[18]

The attitude that Leong spoke of was common among Chinese Americans of that era, whether they had gone to war or not. There was a feeling that things had changed for them. As Harold Lui of New York put it:

> In the 1940s for the first time Chinese were accepted by Americans as being friends because at that time, Chinese and Americans were fighting against the Japanese and the Germans and the Nazis. Therefore, all of a sudden, we became part of an American dream. We had heroes with Chiang Kai-shek and Madame Chiang Kai-shek and so on. It was just a whole different era and in the community we

> began to feel very good about ourselves. My own brother went into the service. We were so proud that they were in uniform. It was nice. We felt part of the society at that time. Right after the war, that was the big change.

Serving in the U.S. armed forces had a profound effect on many. Woody Moy recalled of his days in the 987th Signal Company: "What wearing the uniform did was that it opened up things that gave you the confidence that you weren't going to get kicked around. So with the uniform on you felt that you had as much right as anybody else to go or be whatever you wanted . . . When I came back after the war I had no problem of going around and trying to get a job anywhere. I walked in as if I owned place. Even without the uniform."[19]

These feelings of confidence and pride were not confined to men. Flying in the WASP gave Maggie Gee a great sense of accomplishment, and when she returned to college (although WASP members were not given veterans' status after the war and therefore were not able to take advantage of the GI Bill), she felt older and more confident.[20] Stationed at Mare Island in San Francisco as a rehabilitation nurse in the navy, Marietta Chong Eng realized one day as she watched the flag being raised how proud she was to be in the service, to be contributing something to the country. She carried this feeling with her into the postwar era, insisting on being married in her dress white uniform.[21]

And on the home front, Dorothy Eng came to recognize the importance of her organization, the Chinese Young Women's Society, which provided opportunities for its members to learn more about mainstream America. In establishing a social space for Chinese American service personnel, these women had empowered themselves. Fifty years after the war, Eng gave "a lot of credit to this group because it built so much self-esteem, self-confidence, and assertiveness so that we could move on up out of Chinatown." The women also realized that their organization was the first community service group in Oakland Chinatown. "Before that, the family associations had narrow programs, but we did things for the whole community; we opened it right up. It was wonderful."[22]

Thus the war years allowed Chinese American women to become part of American society in ways that had been unknown to their mothers' generation. Whether serving in uniform, work clothes, or dresses, these women were a vital part of the social transformation the war brought to Chinese America. Whereas many men derived their sense of belonging to the nation from military service, women took a variety of routes to civic incorporation. An observation made by Linda Kerber about women of the American Revolution applies to Chinese American women of the Second World War era as well: "An allegiance defined by location and volition was an allegiance in which women could join. As this latter sort of citizen, women could be part of the political community, unambivalently joining in boycotts, fund raising, street demonstrations, and the signing of collective statements."[23]

American Stories

Perhaps no one exemplifies the positive impact of the war on Chinese Americans better than Thomas Lew of Alameda, California. Lew was born near Canton, China, in 1922 and entered the United States illegally as a "paper son" in the early 1930s, posing as the son of his uncle. He spent two months on Angel Island before being admitted into the country. Once in San Francisco Chinatown, he attended St. Mary's elementary school, and often worked a number of jobs: shelling shrimp, shining shoes, selling newspapers. During junior and senior high he worked as a houseboy in various homes in the San Rafael area. His high school years show a young man meeting the challenges of immigrant life in America with distinction. When seventeen, he was the president of the Boy's Organization at San Rafael High and was declared the best high school public speaker in Marin County, addressing the topic "New Frontiers for American Youth." His speech was essentially autobiographical as he spoke about his struggle against various obstacles "to secure an adequate education, strengthened by the faith of American youth in democracy."[24]

When the war began, Lew was eager to join the army. His hope at that time was to eventually enroll in the Whampoa Academy, a military school in China established by Soviet advisors to the Chinese with Chiang Kai-shek (before his break with the Communists) as its first commandant and Zhou Enlai as director of the political department. Lew recalled: "From the moment the U.S. entered World War Two I tried to enlist but to no avail. [I] found out later that an alien could not enlist, but could be drafted. For months I hounded the president of the San Rafael draft board until the law changed. In late 1942 an alien could be drafted who was eighteen or older so I was drafted on November 11, 1942." Once officially in the army, Lew admitted his "paper" status and was naturalized as a U.S. citizen. He thus joined more than 164,000 service personnel who were naturalized during the war. More immigrants became naturalized citizens between 1941 and 1945 than in any previous five-year period in the nation's history.[25]

As soon as he was able, Lew volunteered for the 987th Signal Company, which was being trained at Camp Crowder, Missouri. Unlike many of those in the all–Chinese American units, who resented being in segregated outfits, Lew was pleased to serve with fellow Chinese Americans. He liked the camaraderie he found there as well as the opportunity to return to China and help the motherland defend itself against the Japanese.

After the war Lew was discharged, but he signed up with the army reserves while working at the National Dollar Store and attending night school part time. During the Korean War he was recalled to active duty, and at the end of that conflict he was offered a career in the army. His military career spanned nearly thirty years, including tours in Europe, Japan, Taiwan, and Vietnam. Perhaps his most poignant assignment came in the late 1950s, when he was assigned to the Presidio in San Francisco and his duties included overseeing administrative communications on Angel Island, which was then under the jurisdiction of the army. Thomas Lew may be the only former inmate of Angel Island to return as an official in charge of the operations of that island. Coming full circle from Angel Island and back, Lew views the performance of Chinese Americans in the military during the Second World War as an important factor in creating a more accepting attitude for Chinese Americans in general and in paving the way for the social and economic advances they attained in the postwar era.[26]

The progress made during the war, however, was not immediate or necessarily permanent. Yin Yee went home to Detroit after serving in the 14th Air Service Group and found that it was still difficult to get a job outside Chinatown, so he returned to his father's laundry. After about four years, with the encouragement of his China-born wife, he used the GI Bill to attend college. His father was furious that a married man in his thirties would return to school, but his wife ran the laundry and they hired a woman to help. Yee would iron until one in the morning and then wake at six to iron a little more before going to classes. When he finally received a degree in engineering, the larger firms would not hire him because he was Chinese. He eventually got a job in a smaller firm and made enough money to move out of Chinatown, but had trouble finding a real estate agent willing to sell him a house. Yee also felt that he was passed over for promotion because of his ethnicity. Ultimately he left the firm and opened a restaurant, which turned out to be very successful. It was not the career he had had in mind, but he persisted until he found success.[27]

In the postwar era the borders of Chinatown were not yet fully permeable; finding housing elsewhere was often a challenge, as was finding employment beyond the ethnic enclave. Residential covenants, banks' lending practices, and segregation based on racial preferences would last well into the 1960s, and racially biased hiring practices remain today an issue in U.S. society. Even the positive image of Chinese Americans that emerged during the war would prove to be unstable, easily reversed depending on international events. As China turned to Communism and Japan became an important ally of the United States, Chinese and Chinese Americans came under renewed scrutiny. The sociologist Rose Hum Lee had foreseen this possibility when she wrote in 1944: "As violently as the Chinese were once attacked, they are now glorified and mounted on a pedestal. It is impossible to predict how lasting this change will be . . . Largely grounded on the sandy loam of sentimentality, one is left conjecturing what the tone of the literature toward the Chinese will be in 1954."[28] In fact in 1954 the United States had recently fought the Chinese Communists in Korea and relations with China were tense and hostile. Lee had certainly been right to suspect that the improved status the Chinese enjoyed in 1944 would not last forever, and that American images of Chinese Americans would be dependent on U.S. relations with China. In recent years, the Chinese seizure of an American spy plane and the incarceration of the scientist Wen Ho Lee for supposedly spying at Los Alamos National Laboratory are two examples of how U.S. images of China and Chinese Americans become entangled with political agendas.

Nevertheless, the Second World War did improve the social position of Chinese Americans. Rose Hum Lee may have overstated the case when she maintained that the war "emancipated the Chinese in the United States," but the war undoubtedly gave Chinese Americans a number of new opportunities to move into the mainstream.[29] As employment and residential restrictions gradually eased during and after the war, Chinese Americans enjoyed a new acceptance, though sometimes at the expense of Japanese Americans. Improved occupational opportunities gave Chinese Americans a foothold in the middle class. This social mobility reinforced their wartime image as the "good Asians," an image that would come to full flower in the late 1960s, when, as some whites reacted against the African American–led civil rights movement, Asian Americans were cast as the "model minority."

More important than the images held by others was the new confidence Chinese Americans gained from the war years. Whether they joined the armed forces or supported the war effort on the home front, many became much more comfortable with their lives as Americans. Embracing what might be called the internal experience of citizenship, they believed that they could play a vital role in postwar America. Even if they were still not regarded as equals by all other Americans, they had achieved the self-confidence and self-image of full citizens of the nation.

APPENDIX

NOTES

ACKNOWLEDGMENTS

INDEX

Appendix: Employment Tables

Table 1 Chinese Population and Employment, United States and San Francisco, 1940 and 1950

	1940		1950		Total Change		% Change	
	Male	Female	Male	Female	Male	Female	Male	Female
Population								
National	57,389	20,115	76,725	40,415	19,336	20,300	34	101
San Francisco	12,264	5,518	15,595	9,218	3,331	3,3700	27	67
Total employed								
National	34,081	2, 911	40,131	8,278	6,050	5,367	18	184
San Francisco	5,953	918	10,129	3,140	4,176	2,222	70	242
Professionals								
National	812	221	2,541	914	1,729	693	212	314
San Francisco	217	68	640	243	423	175	195	257
Managers/officials								
National	7,250	253	8,920	658	1,670	405	23	160
San Francisco	744	32	1,935	174	1,191	142	160	444
Clerical/sales								
National	3,422	750	4,512	3,210	1,090	2,460	32	328
San Francisco	1,024	179	1,827	1,421	803	1,242	78	694
Domestic Service								
National	1,954	287	746	514	−1,208	227	−62	79
San Francisco	780	84	404	88	−376	4	−48	5
Other Service								
National	10,515	562	13,000	940	2,485	378	24	67
San Francisco	1,800	155	2,851	291	1,051	136	58	88
Crafts								
National	448	9	1,348	42	900	33	201	367
San Francisco	175	4	622	15	447	11	255	275
Operatives								
National	7,502	750	6,564	1,711	−938	961	−13	128
San Francisco	999	384	1,430	851	431	467	43	122
Laborers								
National	1,520	42	1,394	95	−126	53	−8	126
San Francisco	186	6	316	23	130	17	70	283
Unreported								
National	200	37	532	176	332	139	166	376
San Francisco	28	6	104	34	76	28	271	467

Sources: Compiled from *Sixteenth Census of the United States,* vol. 2: *Population: Characteristics of the Nonwhite Population by Race,* 5, 47, 97; and *Seventeenth Census of the United States, Special Reports: Nonwhite Population by Race,* 3B–19, 42, 80.

Table 2 Chinese Population and Employment, Territory of Hawai'i and Honolulu, 1940 and 1950

	1940		1950		Total Change		% Change	
	Male	Female	Male	Female	Male	Female	Male	Female
Population								
Territory	16,131	12,643	17,044	15,332	913	2,689	.06	21
Honolulu	12,304	10,141	15,409	14,105	3,105	3,964	4	32
Total employed								
Territory	7,853	2,835	8,161	3,832	308	997	.04	4
Honolulu	6,028	2,239	7,441	3,504	1413	1,265	23	56
Professionals								
Territory	320	647	876	794	556	147	174	23
Honolulu	242	414	775	666	423	175	195	257
Proprietors/managers/officials								
Territory	1,153	193	1,632	303	479	110	42	57
Honolulu	874	135	1,427	263	553	128	63	95
Clerical/sales								
Territory	2,253	841	2,132	1,813	121	972	.0532	116
Honolulu	1,929	701	2,001	1,712	72	1,011	.04	144
Service/domestic service								
Territory	966	468	637	469	−329	1	−34	.002
Honolulu	730	376	592	432	−138	56	−19	15
Craftsmen								
Territory	802	46	1,502	51	700	5	87	11
Honolulu	675	42	1,422	50	747	8	111	19
Operatives								
Territory	945	462	921	327	−24	−135	−.03	−3
Honolulu	788	439	841	316	53	−123	.07	−3
Laborers								
Territory	722	128	431	45	−291	−83	−4	−65
Honolulu	531	106	360	37	−171	−69	70	−32

Sources: Compiled from *Sixteenth Census of the United States*, 2d Series: *Characteristics of the Population, Hawaii*, 5, 19–20; and *Seventeenth Decennial Census of the United States, Characteristics of the Population*, pts. 51–54: *Territories and Possessions*, 52–115–118.

Notes

Introduction

1. Little has been written on the experiences of Filipino, Korean, or South Asian Americans during the war. Two welcome additions are Anne Choi, "Border Crossings: The Politics of Korean Nationalism in the United States, 1919–1945" (Ph.D. diss., University of Southern California, 2003), and Lili M. Kim, "The Pursuit of Imperfect Justice: The Predicament of Koreans and Korean Americans on the Homefront during World War II" (Ph.D. diss., University of Rochester, 2001).

2. Notable exceptions are Gloria Chun, *Of Orphans and Warriors: Inventing Chinese American Culture and Identity* (New Brunswick: Rutgers University Press, 2000); Marjorie Lee, "Hu-Jee: The Forgotten Second Generation of Chinese America, 1930–1950" (Master's thesis, University of California, Los Angeles, 1984); Henry Yu, *Thinking Orientals: Migration, Contact, and Exoticism in Modern America* (New York: Oxford University Press, 2001); and Judy Yung, *Unbound Feet: A Social History of Chinese Women in San Francisco* (Berkeley: University of California Press, 1995).

3. Marcus Lee Hansen, "The Problem of the Third Generation Immigrant," rpt. in Peter Kivisto and Dag Blanck, eds., *American Immigrants and Their Generations: Studies and Commentaries on the Hansen Thesis after Fifty Years* (Urbana: University of Illinois Press, 1990), 195. David

Yoo, *Growing Up Nisei: Race, Generation, and Culture among Japanese Americans of California, 1924–49* (Urbana: University of Illinois Press, 2000), 5.

1. Chinese America before the War

1. On the Chinese on the East Coast, see John Kuo Wei Tchen, *New York before Chinatown: Orientalism and the Shaping of American Culture, 1776–1882* (Baltimore: Johns Hopkins University Press, 1999). The best studies of Chinese immigrants' participation in the economic development of California are Ping Chiu, *Chinese Labor in California, 1850–1880: An Economic Study* (Madison: State Historical Society of Wisconsin, 1967), and Sucheng Chan, *This Bittersweet Soil: The Chinese in California Agriculture, 1860–1910* (Berkeley: University of California Press, 1986).

2. *Report of the U.S. Congressional Joint Special Committee to Investigate Chinese Immigration,* 44th Con., 2nd. Sess. Senate Report 689, 1877, v.

3. The evolution of these laws can be traced in 22 *U.S. Statutes at Large* 58–61; 25 *U.S. Statutes at Large* 476–479; 27 *U.S. Statutes at Large* 25–26; 28 *U.S. Statutes at Large* 1210–1212; 32 *U.S. Statutes at Large* 176–177; 33 *U.S. Statutes at Large* 428; and 43 *U.S. Statutes at Large* 153–169.

4. For a history of Angel Island, see Him Mark Lai, Genny Lim, and Judy Yung, *Island: Poetry and History of Chinese Immigrants on Angel Island, 1910–1940* (1980; Seattle: University of Washington Press, 1991). Recent studies on Angel Island and the "paper son" system include Madeline Yuan-yin Hsu, *Dreaming of Gold, Dreaming of Home: Transnationalism and Migration between the United States and South China, 1882–1943* (Stanford: Stanford University Press, 2000), and Erika Lee, *At America's Gates: Chinese Immigration during the Exclusion Era, 1882–1943* (Chapel Hill: University of North Carolina Press, 2003). The most extensive memoir of a "paper son" is Tung Pok Chin, *Paper Son: One Man's Story* (Philadelphia: Temple University Press, 2000). Percentage admitted is from Lee, *At America's Gates,* 142.

5. See Ivan Light, "From Vice District to Tourist Attraction: The

Moral Career of American Chinatowns, 1880–1940," *Pacific Historical Review* 43:3 (Aug. 1974), 367–394.

6. In 1940 there were 17,782 Chinese living in San Francisco, 12,753 living in New York City, and only 4,736 living in Los Angeles. *Sixteenth Census of the United States: 1940, Population: Characteristics of the Non-white Population by Race* (Washington: U.S. Government Printing Office, 1943), 91.

7. The native-born Chinese American population of the United States in 1900 was 5,621. By 1930 it was 17,320, and by 1940 it had reached 22,880. *Sixteenth Census of the United States: 1940, Population,* vol. 2: *Characteristics of the Population* (Washington: U.S. Government Printing Office, 1943), 516.

8. Interviews with William Seam Wong and Joseph Yuu, Jan. 30, 1994.

9. Robert Dunn, "Does My Future Lie in China or America?" *Chinese Digest* (May 15, 1936), 3, 13. The Ging Hawk Club was a Chinese American women's social club based in New York. For a different analysis of these essays, see Gloria Chun, *Of Orphans and Warriors: Inventing Chinese American Culture and Identity* (New Brunswick: Rutgers University Press, 1999), 221–224.

10. Kaye Hong, "Does My Future Lie in China or America?" *Chinese Digest* (May 22, 1936), 3.

11. Chinese Students' Club, Letter to Robert Dunn in the "Firecrackers" column of the *Chinese Digest* (May 29, 1936), 11, 15.

12. Dunn, "Does My Future Lie in China or America," 3. Chinese Students' Club, "Firecrackers" column, 11. For the debate between Dunn and the students, as well as one letter written by Jane Kwong Lee, see the *Chinese Digest* of June 5, June 12, July 3, and July 17, 1936.

13. For brief accounts of these two essayists see Thomas W. Chinn, *Bridging the Pacific: San Francisco Chinatown and Its People* (San Francisco: Chinese Historical Society of America, 1989), 143–144.

14. The *Chinese News* ran from 1940 to 1942, closing when Chinn entered government service.

15. *Chinese News* (Aug. 1, 1941), 7; (Oct. 15, 1941), 7.

16. Letter from John Jan, *Chinese News* (Jan. 15, 1941), 2.

17. Grace W. Wang, "A Speech on Second-Generation Chinese in U.S.A.," *Chinese Digest* (Aug. 7, 1936), 6.

18. Ibid.

19. Ibid., 14.

20. Ibid.

21. William Hoy, "Through a Chinatown Window," *California Chinese Press* (May 9, 1941), 3.

22. Maxine Chinn, "We Who Are Without a Country!" *California Chinese Press* (May 9, 1941), 3.

23. For essays on the development of a Chinese American consciousness, see K. Scott Wong and Sucheng Chan, eds., *Claiming America: Constructing Chinese American Identities during the Exclusion Era* (Philadelphia: Temple University Press, 1998).

24. Nate R. White, "Crisis in Chinatown," *Chinese News* (April 15, 1941), 3, 7.

25. Ibid., D, 7.

26. Interviews with Dorothy Eng, June 9, 1995, and Mary Wong, Aug. 20, 2002. For a different perspective see Him Mark Lai, "Retention of the Chinese Heritage: Chinese Schools in America before World War II," *Chinese America: History and Perspectives* 14 (2000), 10–31; and "Retention of the Chinese Heritage, Part II: Chinese Schools in America, World War II to the Present," *Chinese America: History and Perspectives* 15 (2001), 1–30.

27. On Chinn's involvement with the *Chinese Digest* see Chinn, *Bridging the Pacific*, 144–147, and Thomas W. Chinn, "A Historian's Reflections on Chinese-American Life in San Francisco, 1919–1991," Regional Oral History Office, Bancroft Library, University of California, Berkeley, 1993, 98–99.

28. Chinn, *Bridging the Pacific*, 225–226. Interview with Thomas W. Chinn, June 6, 1995.

29. *Chinese Digest* (Mar. 1937), 9, 20, 23. The *Chung Sai Yat Po* was one of the most influential Chinese-language newspapers in San Francisco. See Corinne K. Hoexter, *From Canton to California: The Epic of Chinese*

Immigration (New York: Four Winds Press, 1976), and Judy Yung, "The Social Awakening of Chinese American Women as Reported in Chung Sai Yat Po, 1900–1911," *Chinese America: History and Perspectives* 2 (1988), 80–102.

30. Harold Isaacs, *Scratches on Our Minds: American Views of China and India* (1958; Armonk, NY: M. E. Sharpe, 1980), 156.

31. *Chinese Digest* (Nov. 15, 1935), 8. It is difficult to determine how "Celestial" came to be associated with Chinese. One possibility is that the term for the Chinese imperial court, "Tian chao," translates as "Heavenly Court."

32. *Chinese Digest* (Nov. 22, 1935), 8.

33. *Chinese Digest* (Nov. 22, 1935), 8; (Dec. 6, 1935), 8. In 1993 a Chinese American veteran of the Second World War informed me as we walked down Grant Avenue in San Francisco: "All these stores here were owned by Japanese. But after the war started they all had to close and Chinese were able to move back in. Hell, it's Chinatown." Interview with Harvey Wong, Aug. 25, 1993.

34. On manipulation of images of Chinatown for a variety of political agendas, see K. Scott Wong, "Chinatown: Conflicting Images, Contested Terrain," *MELUS* 20:1 (Spring 1995), 3–15; and Nayan Shah, *Contagious Divides: Epidemics and Race in San Francisco's Chinatown* (Berkeley: University of California Press, 2001).

35. Quoted in Victor G. and Brett De Bary Nee, *Longtime Californ': A Documentary Study of an American Chinatown* (New York: Pantheon, 1972), 152.

36. Karl Lo and H. M. Lai, *Chinese Newspapers Published in North America, 1854–1975* (Washington: Center for Chinese Research Materials, 1977), 14; Marjorie Lee, "Hu-Jee: The Forgotten Second Generation of Chinese America, 1930–1950" (Master's thesis, University of California, Los Angeles, 1984), 57. Lai estimates that the circulation of the *Chinese Digest* probably never exceeded 500, whereas the *Chinese Press,* published "during a period of relative prosperity," may have had a circulation of 1,000–1,500 (correspondence with Him Mark Lai, Apr. 16, 1999).

37. *California Chinese Press* (Nov. 22, 1940), 1.

38. Monica Sone, *Nisei Daughter* (Seattle: University of Washington Press, 1953), 119.

39. Judy Yung, *Unbound Feet: A Social History of Chinese Women in San Francisco* (Berkeley: University of California Press, 1995), 225.

40. Renqiu Yu, *To Save China, To Save Ourselves: The Chinese Hand Laundry Alliance of New York* (Philadelphia: Temple University Press, 1992), 78.

41. *Chinese Digest* (Sept. 1937), 9–10. The cash figures in the Chinese American periodicals are often given in Chinese currency. I have given the closest round number equivalents in American figures based on $100,000 Chinese = $30,000 US.

42. *Chinese Digest* (Dec. 1937), 14.

43. Yu, *To Save China, To Save Ourselves,* 77.

44. Immanuel Hsu, *The Rise of Modern China* (New York: Oxford University Press, 1970), 582–583.

45. *New York Times* (May 10, 1938), 14.

46. Ibid. *Chinese News* (Apr. 15, 1941), 1. Yung, *Unbound Feet,* 240.

47. *Chinese Digest* (June 1938), 13. My account of the first Rice Bowl party is based on that in Yung, *Unbound Feet,* 239–240.

48. *Chinese News* (Oct. 1, 1940), 7.

49. *Chinese Digest* (Jan. 1938), 9; (Feb. 1939), 7. Yung, *Unbound Feet,* 238.

50. *Chinese Digest* (Jan. 1939). My account of the demonstration against the SS *Spyros* is based primarily on Lim P. Lee's eyewitness report and to a lesser extent Yung's account in *Unbound Feet,* 242.

51. *Chinese Digest* (Jan. 1939), 10. Yung, *Unbound Feet,* 242. The song "March of the Volunteers" was composed in 1935 by Nie Er, a prominent leftist songwriter of revolutionary China, for a film depicting China's resistance to the Japanese. It was the Chinese version of the "Marseillaise" during the Sino-Japanese War and later became the national anthem of the People's Republic of China. I am grateful to Su Zheng for explaining the history and significance of this song to me.

52. *California Chinese Press* (Nov. 29, 1940), 1.

53. *Chinese News* (Nov. 1, 1940), 2. *California Chinese Press* (Nov. 22, 1940), 1. On Leland Kimlau and the Cathay Post of the American Legion, see Chinn, *Bridging the Pacific,* 135–136. On the Chinese American Citizens Alliance, see Sue Fawn Chung, "Fighting for Their American Rights: A History of the Chinese American Citizens Alliance," in Wong and Chan, eds., *Claiming America,* 95–126.

54. *Chinese News* (Aug. 1, 1941), cover and 2. Their promotions to captain were later reported in the *Chinese News* (June 1, 1942).

55. *Chinese News* (Jan. 1, 1942), 2.

2. *Chinatown Goes to War*

1. Rose Hum Lee, "Chinese in the United States Today: The War Has Changed Their Lives," *Survey Graphic* 31:10 (Oct. 1942), 444.

2. *Chinese Press* (May 29, 1942), 6.

3. Louise Purwin, "Chinese Daughters of Uncle Sam," *Independent Woman* 21 (Spring 1942), 336.

4. Ibid., 337.

5. Ruth Brown Reed, "Career Girl, Chinese Style," *Independent Woman* 23 (Nov. 1944), 259, 287.

6. Judy Yung, *Unbound Voices: A Documentary History of Chinese Women in San Francisco* (Berkeley: University of California Press, 1999), 473n1. The heading for this section comes from the title of a chapter in Jade Snow Wong's *Fifth Chinese Daughter* (New York: Harper, 1945) in which she describes her experiences at Marinship.

7. Judy Yung, *Unbound Feet: A Social History of Chinese Women in San Francisco* (Berkeley: University of California Press, 1995), 263; Xiaojian Zhao, *Remaking Chinese America: Immigration, Family, and Community, 1940–1960* (New Brunswick: Rutgers University Press, 2002), 55.

8. *Chinese Press* (Aug. 21, 1942), 1. Xiaojian Zhao, "Chinese American Women Defense Workers in World War II," *California History* (Summer 1996), 140–141. May Lew Gee quoted in Yung, *Unbound Voices,* 482.

9. Interview with Dorothy Eng, June 9, 1995.

10. Wong, *Fifth Chinese Daughter,* 188, 189.

11. Liberty ships were mass-produced cargo vessels, of which 2,770 were built between 1939 and 1945. They were constructed from prefabricated sections, and thus gave an important boost to U.S. shipbuilding capacity. See Elizabeth-Anne Wheal, Stephen Pope, and James Taylor, eds., *Encyclopedia of the Second World War* (Secaucus, N.J.: Castle Books, 1989), 277; I. C. B. Dear and M. R. D. Foot, eds., *The Oxford Companion to World War II* (Oxford: Oxford University Press, 1995), 689–690.

12. Constance Wong, "Marinship Chinese Workers Are Building Ships to Free Their Homeland," *Marin-er* (June 26, 1943), 3, quoted in Yung, *Unbound Voices,* 477–478.

13. *Mariner* (June 26, 1943) quoted in Yung, *Unbound Feet,* 265.

14. Yung, *Unbound Feet,* 266–267. Marilynn S. Johnson, *The Second Gold Rush: Oakland and the East Bay in World War II* (Berkeley: University of California Press, 1993), 63. *Chinese Press* (Jan. 1, 1943), 1.

15. May Lew Gee quoted in Yung, *Unbound Voices,* 484. Wong, *Fifth Chinese Daughter,* 192, 194.

16. Sandy Lydon, *Chinese Gold: The Chinese in the Monterey Bay Region* (Capitola, Calif.: Capitola Book Co., 1985), 145–149, 169–171. The fact that An Yoke Gee was a child of Jung San Choy was revealed to me in an interview with Maggie Gee, June 5, 1995.

17. Zhao, "Chinese American Women Defense Workers in World War II," 139. Interview with Maggie Gee, June 5, 1995. Maggie Gee quoted in Yung, *Unbound Feet,* 267.

18. Vera S Williams, *WASPs: Women Airforce Service Pilots of World War II* (Osceola, Wis.: Motorbooks International, 1994), 10.

19. Marianne Verges, *On Silver Wings: The Women Airforce Service Pilots of World War II, 1942–1944* (New York: Ballantine, 1991), 106, 197, 217, 227.

20. Molly Merryman, *Clipped Wings: The Rise and Fall of the Women Airforce Service Pilots (WASPs) of World War II* (New York: New York University Press, 1998). Interview with Maggie Gee, June 5, 1995.

21. Interview with Dorothy Eng, June 9, 1995.

22. Stephen Ambrose, *Citizen Soldiers: The U.S. Army from the Normandy Beaches to the Bulge to the Surrender of Germany, June 7, 1944–May 7, 1945* (New York: Simon and Schuster, 1997).

23. Rose Hum Lee, "Chinese in the United States Today," *Survey Graphic* (Oct. 1942), 444. Correspondence with Henry Joe Kim, Mar. 31, 1995. Correspondence with Ralph W. Jung, Apr. 10, 1995.

24. *Chinese Press* (Jan. 24, 1941), 3.

25. *Chinese Press* (Dec. 5, 1941), 1.

26. *Chinese Press* (Mar. 20, 1942), 1.

27. *Chinese Press* (May 29, 1942), 1.

28. *Chinese Press* (June 5, 1942), 4. Although the original AVG was dubbed the "Flying Tigers," the 14th Air Force in the China-Burma-India theater eventually adopted that name and symbol.

29. *Life* magazine (May 4, 1942).

30. King quoted in Carl Molesworth and Steve Moseley, *Wing to Wing: Air Combat in China, 1943–1945* (New York: Orion, 1990), 95.

31. Ibid., 13–14.

32. Kenneth E. Kay, "History of the 3rd Fighter Group: July through December 1943," microfilm, Department of the Air Force, Air Force Historical Research Agency, Maxwell Air Force Base, Ala., roll B0048, 6, 15. I wish to thank Geraldine Shen, granddaughter of Lieutenant Yu Wei, for providing me with a copy of this report.

33. Correspondence with Henry Joe Kim, Mar. 31, 1995.

34. Correspondence with Alfred Toy and Grace (Eng) Toy, May 6, 1995.

35. Correspondence with William Mar, Apr. 20, 1995. Correspondence with Richard M. T. Young, May 8, 1995.

36. Wong Wah Ding quoted in the *Philadelphia Inquirer* (Feb. 15, 2004), M5. Interview with Henry Wong, Aug. 30, 1990.

37. Interview with Wing Fook Jung, June 8, 1995.

38. Correspondence with William Chang, Apr. 24, 1995. Correspondence with Samuel Fong, Apr. 29, 1995. Correspondence with Sue-Chun Luke, May 24, 1995.

39. Correspondence with Wesley Ko, May 7, 1999. This account differs from that found in Tom Brokaw, *The Greatest Generation* (New York: Random House, 1998), 39. Ko informed me that the statement in the book about being "apprehensive being the only Oriental in the 82nd Airborne" was taken out of context.

40. Brokaw, *The Greatest Generation,* 40–42. Michael C. C. Adams, *The Best War Ever: America and World War II* (Baltimore: Johns Hopkins University Press, 1994), 70. Correspondence with Wesley Ko, May 7, 1999.

41. Brief profiles of the wartime activities of the Ah Tye family can be found in Lani Ah Tye Farkas, *Bury My Bones in America: The Saga of a Chinese Family in California, 1852–1996: From San Francisco to the Sierra Gold Mines* (Nevada City, Calif.: Carl Mautz Publishing, 1998), 115–121.

42. Correspondence with Harry and Ruth Jang, Feb. 19, 1996. For a profile of Ruth Jang see Yung, *Unbound Voices,* 486–495.

43. I use the phrase "Defend China and Claim America" in a way that echoes the sentiments of the Chinese laundrymen who saw China's fate to be tied to theirs in the United States. See Renqiu Yu, *To Save China, To Save Ourselves: The Chinese Hand Laundry Alliance of New York* (Philadelphia: Temple University Press, 1992).

44. *Chinese News* (May 15, 1942), 3.

45. *Chinese Press* (June 12, 1942), 5.

3. The "Good Asian" in the "Good War"

1. *Report of the U.S. Congressional Joint Special Committee to Investigate Immigration,* 44th Cong., 2nd. Sess. Senate Report 689, 1877, 27–28. "Success Story of One Minority Group in U.S.," *U.S. News and World Report* (Dec. 26, 1966), 73.

2. While there is not yet an in-depth study of these shifts in wartime images, three useful works are Harold R. Isaacs, *Scratches on Our Minds: American Views of China and India* (1958; Armonk, N.Y.: M. E. Sharpe, 1980); Patricia Neils, *China Images in the Life and Times of Henry Luce* (Savage, Md.: Rowman and Littlefield, 1990); and T. Christopher

Jespersen, *American Images of China, 1931–1949* (Stanford: Stanford University Press, 1996).

3. *Time* (Dec. 22, 1941).

4. *Life* (Dec. 22, 1941).

5. Interview with Philip Choy, Apr. 4, 2002.

6. United States Army, *A Pocket Guide to China* (Washington: War and Navy Departments, n.d.), 65–75. I wish to thank Mr. Edwin Len for providing me with a copy of this publication.

7. Ibid., 1, 12, 14, 8. On how the Chinese sought to make George Washington similar to Chinese emperors of the mythical past, see K. Scott Wong, "The Transformation of Culture: Three Chinese Views of America," *American Quarterly* 48:2 (June 1996), 201–232.

8. *Pocket Guide to China*, 2–3.

9. Ibid., 41, 45.

10. *New York Times* (Dec. 8, 1941), 5. *Life* (Dec. 22, 1941). *Chinese Press* (Dec. 19, 1941), 1. I am grateful to Dr. Albert Fong for providing me with a description of the buttons. Correspondence with Albert Fong, July 10, 2000.

11. Karl Yoneda, "A Brief History of U.S. Asian Labor," *Public Affairs* (Sept. 1976), 38. I am grateful to Gary Okihiro for bringing this article to my attention.

12. *Chinese Press* (Jan. 9, 1942), 1. *Chinese Press* (Dec. 19, 1941), 1. *Chinese News* (Dec. 15, 1941), 6.

13. *Chinese Press* (Jan. 9, 1942), 2.

14. *Chinese Press* (Oct. 30, 1942), 2.

15. Interview with Thomas Chinn, June 6, 1995. *Chinese Press* (May 1, 1942), 1.

16. *Chinese Press* (May 1, 1942), 6.

17. *Chinese Press* (Feb. 13, 1942), 14.

18. *Chinese Press* (May 1, 1942), 6.

19. *Chinese Press* (Jan. 30, 1942), 1.

20. *Chinese Press* (May 14, 1943), 5.

21. Ibid. Mayer's statement is rather ironic because this film starred Katharine Hepburn rather than an Asian actor.

22. Ibid. *Chinese Press* (Aug. 13, 1943), 1.

23. *Chinese Press* (May 14, 1943), 1.

24. Eleanor Roosevelt and Frances Cooke Macgregor, *This Is America* (New York: Putnam, 1942), n.p. I thank Greg Robinson for bringing this volume to my attention.

25. Bill Simons, "Chinatown Ready for Any Emergency for She Knows Aggressor," *Chinese News* (Jan. 15, 1942), 3. First published in the *San Francisco Chronicle* (Jan. 14, 1942).

26. *Chinese Press* (Oct. 16, 1942).

27. See Chen Yueh, *Madame Chiang Kai-shek's Trip through the United States and Canada* (San Francisco: Chinese Nationalist Daily, 1943), 11; Sterling Seagrave, *The Soong Dynasty* (New York: Harper and Row, 1985). Madame Chiang's name appears in a variety of forms. Using current pinyin romanization, it would be Song Meiling. The press coverage of her during this period varied from Soong Mayling to Soong Meiling. According to one source, she is listed in the Wellesley College records as Mayling Olive Soong and signed her name as such while in the United States.

28. Rose Hum Lee, "Madame Chiang's Children," *Survey Graphic* (Apr. 1943), 136.

29. Quoted in Jespersen, *American Images of China,* 85.

30. This account is based on Jonathan Spence, *The Search for Modern China* (New York: Norton, 1999), 406–409.

31. Chen Yueh, *Madame Chiang Kai-shek's Trip through the United States and Canada,* 14. Carnegie quoted in Jespersen, *American Images of China,* 86. *Time* (Mar. 1, 1943), 26.

32. Lee, "Madame Chiang's Children," 144.

33. *Time* (Jan. 3, 1938). Final quotation from *The First Lady of China: The Historic Wartime Visit of Mme. Chiang Kai-shek to the United States in 1943* (International Business Machines Corporation, 1943), n.p.

34. Quinn and Sandburg quoted in Barbara W. Tuchman, *Stilwell and the American Experience in China, 1911–1945* (New York: Macmillan, 1970), 349, 350.

35. Karen Janis Leong, "The China Mystique: Mayling Soong

Chiang, Pearl S. Buck and Anna May Wong in the American Imagination" (Ph.D. diss., University of California, Berkeley, 1999), xvii. Jespersen, *American Images of China,* 88.

36. *Time* (Mar. 1, 1943).

37. *The First Lady of China,* n.p. *Time* (Mar. 1, 1943).

38. *Time* (Mar. 1, 1943).

39. *The First Lady of China,* n.p.

40. Ibid.

41. *Time* (Mar. 1, 1943).

42. *Life* (Mar. 1, 1943). *Life* (Mar. 8, 1943).

43. *New York Times* (Mar. 2, 1943).

44. *New York Times* (Mar. 4, 1943).

45. L. Ling-chi Wang, "Roots and the Changing Identity of the Chinese in the United States," in *The Living Tree: The Changing Meaning of Being Chinese Today,* ed. Tu Wei-ming (Stanford: Stanford University Press, 1991), 185–186, 187.

46. Quoted in *The First Lady of China,* n.p.

47. Ibid.

48. *Chinese Press* (Mar. 26, 1943), "Welcome Madame Chiang Kai-shek" edition, 6. All the quotations from advertisements in the next few paragraphs are from this same issue, various pages.

49. Leong, "The China Mystique," 420.

50. A. T. Steele, *The American People and China* (New York: McGraw-Hill, 1966), 22–23. Neils, *China Images in the Life and Times of Henry Luce,* 94. Theodore H. White, *In Search of History: A Personal Adventure* (New York: Harper and Row, 1978), 136–137.

51. See esp. Lorraine Dong, "Song Meiling in America 1943," in *The Repeal and Its Legacy: Proceedings of the Conference on the 50th Anniversary of the Repeal of the Exclusion Acts* (San Francisco: Chinese Historical Society of America, 1994), 39–46.

52. Fred W. Riggs, *Pressures on Congress: A Study of the Repeal of Chinese Exclusion* (New York: King's Crown Press, 1950), 116.

53. Charles Nelson Spinks, "Repeal Chinese Exclusion!" *Asia* (Feb. 1942), 92–94. The account of this article's path to publication is based

on Riggs, *Pressures on Congress,* 48. On the *Ozawa* and *Thind* cases, which established Asian ineligibility for citizenship, see Ian F. Haney López, *White by Law: The Legal Construction of Race* (New York: New York University Press, 1996); and Mai Ngai, "The Architecture of Race in American Immigration Law: A Reexamination of the Immigration Act of 1924," *Journal of American History* 86:1 (June 1999), 67–92.

54. Buck: *Hearings before the Committee on Immigration and Naturalization,* House of Representatives, 78th Cong., 1943, 68. (Hereafter cited as *Hearings.*) Magnuson: ibid., 197. Curtis: *Congressional Record*—Senate, vol. 89, 78th Cong., June 11, 1943, 5745.

55. Bennett: *Congressional Record*—House, June 11, 1943, 57. Gearhart: ibid., Oct. 21, 1943, 8629.

56. Ibid., House, June 16, 1943, 5966; Senate, Nov. 26, 1943, 10014.

57. Judd: ibid., Appendix, June 11, 1943, A2928. Ford: ibid., A2950–A2951. Buck: *Hearings,* 69–70.

58. Green quoted in Riggs, *Pressures on Congress,* 67. White: *Congressional Record*—Senate, vol. 89, 78th Cong., Oct. 21, 1943, 8626–8627.

59. Wilmeth: *Hearings,* 101. Waters: *Hearings,* 184–186.

60. *Congressional Record*—House, vol. 89, 78th Cong., Oct. 11, 1943, 8193.

61. Letter appears in Riggs, *Pressures on Congress,* 210–211.

62. Riggs, *Pressures on Congress,* 113. L. Ling-chi Wang, "Politics of the Repeal of the Chinese Exclusion Laws," in *The Repeal and Its Legacy,* 66.

63. *Hearings,* 6.

64. *Chinese Press* (May 22, 1942), 2; (July 10, 1942), 1.

65. *Chinese Press* (June 11, 1943), 1; (Sept. 10, 1943), 1; (July 9, 1943), 3.

66. *Chinese Press* (July 24, 1942), 3.

67. Wang, "Politics of the Repeal of the Chinese Exclusion Laws," 80.

68. Roger Daniels, *Asian America: Chinese and Japanese in the United States since 1850* (Seattle: University of Washington Press, 1988), 198.

69. On the racial ideologies embedded in repeal see Neil Gotonda, "Towards Repeal of Asian Exclusion: The Magnuson Act of 1943, the Act of July 2, 1946, The Presidential Proclamation of July 4, 1946, the Act of August 9, 1946, and the Act of August 1, 1950," in Hyung-chan

Kim, ed., *Asian Americans and Congress: A Documentary History* (Westport, Conn.: Greenwood, 1996), 309–337.

70. Wang, "Politics of the Repeal of the Chinese Exclusion Laws," 79.

71. Letter from Donald L. Chu to Charles A. Thomson, Division of Cultural Relations, Department of State, received May 10, 1943. Walter H. Judd Congressional File, Box 71.5, National Archives.

4. *Hawai'i's Local Warriors*

1. Tin-Yuke Char, *The Sandalwood Mountains: Readings and Stories of the Early Chinese in Hawai'i* (Honolulu: University Press of Hawai'i, 1975), 37. Gavan Daws, *Shoal of Time: A History of the Hawaiian Islands* (Honolulu: University Press of Hawai'i, 1968), 50. For other histories see Clarence E. Glick, *Sojourners and Settlers: Chinese Migrants in Hawai'i* (Honolulu: Hawai'i Chinese History Center and University of Hawai'i Press, 1980); and Arlene Lum, ed., *Sailing for the Sun: The Chinese in Hawai'i, 1789–1989* (Honolulu: University of Hawai'i Center for Chinese Studies, 1988).

2. Glick, *Sojourners and Settlers,* p. 2. L. L. Torbert, "Chinese in Sugar," *The Polynesian* (Jan. 31, 1852), cited in ibid.

3. This account of the early Chinese involvement in the sugar industry is based mainly on that found in Glick, *Sojourners and Settlers,* 3.

4. Ibid., 4–5.

5. Liang Qichao, *Xiaweiyi youji* (Hawaiian Travel Notes), in *Yinbing shi he ji* (Collected Writings from an Ice-drinker's Studio), vol. 22 (Shanghai: Zhonghua shuju, 1936), 193. A detailed account of the fire can be found in Char, *The Sandalwood Mountains,* 101–110.

6. This description of the Great Mahele of 1848 is based largely on that found in Lawrence Fuchs, *Hawai'i Pono: An Ethnic and Political History* (Honolulu: Bess Press, 1961), 14–16.

7. According to Lawrence Fuchs, the native population was about 300,000 in 1778 and had been reduced to 57,000 by 1866. See Fuchs, *Hawai'i Pono,* 13.

8. The first labor strike on the plantations that involved two different ethnic groups (Japanese and Filipinos) did not take place until 1920.

See Ronald Takaki, *Pau Hana: Plantation Life and Labor in Hawaii* (Honolulu: University of Hawaii Press, 1983), 153–176.

9. Fuchs, *Hawaii Pono,* 90–91, 98, 86. See also Jonathan Y. Okamura, "Race Relations in Hawai'i during World War II: The Non-Internment of Japanese Americans," *Amerasia Journal* 26:2 (2000), 117–141.

10. Daws, *Shoal of Time,* 312. Gary Okihiro, *Cane Fires: The Anti-Japanese Movement in Hawai'i, 1865–1945* (Philadelphia: Temple University Press, 1991), 15. Interview with Mun Charn Wong, July 25, 1994.

11. Jonathan Spence, *The Search for Modern China* (New York: Norton, 1990), 227. Lum, ed., *Sailing for the Sun,* 100.

12. For the best explication of the complex relationship between American Chinatowns and the political parties during the Republican Revolution, see L. Eve Armentrout Ma, *Revolutionaries, Monarchists, and Chinatowns: Chinese Politics in the Americas and the 1911 Revolution* (Honolulu: University of Hawai'i Press, 1990). See also Glick, *Sojourners and Settlers,* 264–309.

13. Ibid., 306.

14. Ibid., 306.

15. Mainland population figures are from *Sixteenth Census of the United States: 1940 Population: Characteristics of the Nonwhite Population by Race* (Washington: U.S. Government Printing Office, 1943), 91, and vol. 11, 516; the figures for Hawai'i are from *Sixteenth Census of the United States: 1940 Population: Second Series, Characteristics of the Population, Hawai'i* (Washington: U.S. Government Printing Office, 1943), 5. Interview with Dai Hing Loo, July 25, 1994.

16. George H. Blakeslee, "Hawai'i: Racial Problem and Naval Base," *Foreign Affairs* 17:1 (Oct. 1938), 90.

17. Beth Bailey and David Farber, *The First Strange Place: The Alchemy of Race and Sex in World War II in Hawai'i* (New York: Free Press, 1992), 33.

18. Commandant's General Correspondence, Box V9375, File LL-4, 4/15–30/44, Record Group 181-PHNY, National Archives, Pacific Sierra Region (hereafter cited as "Censorship Reports"). Quoted in Bailey and Farber, *The First Strange Place,* 32, 35.

19. On the formation of the BMTCs and other "last ditch soldier" militias, see Gwenfread Allen, *Hawaii's War Years, 1941–1945* (Honolulu: University of Hawai'i Press, 1950), 94–98. This remains the best study of the overall impact of the war on Hawai'i.

20. "An Interview with Mr. Tin Yuk Char" (Mar. 8, 1943), in Romanzo Adams Social Science Research Laboratory Confidential Files, A1989:006, Box 5, Folder 5, 1 (hereafter cited as RASRL Confidential Files).

21. "An Incident on the Bus" (Aug. 5, 1944), RASRL Confidential Files, Box 18, Folder 22.

22. "Casual Report by Rose L. Chow Hoy" (Jan. 20, 1944), RASRL Confidential Files, Box 18, Folder 24.

23. "Anecdotes involving defense workers" (July 19, 1944), RASRL Confidential Files, Box 5, Folder 25.

24. The rates of intermarriage differed among Asians in Hawai'i. For example, Chinese intermarried at a greater frequency than did Japanese.

25. Dorothy Jim and Takiko Takiguchi, "Attitudes on Dating of Oriental Girls with Service Men," *Social Process in Hawai'i* 8 (Nov. 1943), 67. Cory Wilson, "Some Social Aspects of Mainland Defense Workers in Honolulu," ibid., 64.

26. Jim and Takiguchi, "Attitudes on Dating," 68, 67.

27. RASRL Confidential Files, letter dated June 1944, Box 18, Folder 23. The name of the writer has been deleted on the original letter. Jim and Takiguchi, "Attitudes on Dating," 71.

28. "Transcript of a conversation at a party" (June 1, 1944), RASRL Confidential Files, Box 18, Folder 24.

29. V. Cabell Flanagan, "Servicemen in Hawai'i—Some Impressions and Attitudes toward Hawai'i," *Social Process in Hawai'i* 9–10 (July 1945), 83.

30. "Impressions of the people of Hawai'i" (Feb. 1945), RASRL Confidential Files, Box 18, File 21. Locals in Hawai'i have informed me that even today they meet tourists who are surprised that they "don't live in grass huts."

31. Ibid. Bailey and Farber, *The First Strange Place*, 107–108.

32. *Hana Like Club* (Victory Edition) Honolulu, 1945, 4. Located in Hawai'i War Records Depository, File 58.

33. Allen, *Hawai'i's War Years,* 349.

34. Judy Kubo, "The Negro Soldier in Kahuku," *Social Process in Hawai'i* 9–10 (July 1945), 28.

35. Censorship Reports, Box V9475, III:1, 1/1–15/44, 14, and Box V9375, 4/15–30/44, 7, quoted in Bailey and Farber, *The First Strange Place,* 133, 134.

36. Ibid., Box V3977, 11, and Box V9375, II:12, 6/1–15/43, 16, quoted in Bailey and Farber, *The First Strange Place,* 134.

37. War Research Laboratory, University of Hawaii, Report no. 4 (Aug. 1, 1944), 7.

38. "J. L., Negro defense worker, 12 months, Pearl Harbor," RASRL Confidential File, Box 5, Folder 26, 3.

39. Shirley Abe, "Violations of the Racial Code in Hawai'i," *Social Process in Hawai'i* 9–10 (July 1945), 36.

40. Interview with William Lum, Aug. 10, 1994. Interview with Mun Charn Wong, July 25, 1994.

41. Interview with Marietta Chong Eng, Aug. 17, 1994.

42. Allen, *Hawai'i's War Years,* 264–265. Of the military personnel from the islands, approximately 3,392 were of Chinese descent.

43. 298th Infantry Regiment: INRG 298–0.1 (History), Washington National Records Center, National Archives (Record Group 407), 15 Oct. 1940–8 May 1944. Interview with Alfred W. C. Jay, July 28, 1994.

44. Allen, *Hawai'i's War Years,* 266.

45. Ibid.

46. Interview with Alfred Jay, July 28, 1994. Interview with Leonard Wong, Aug. 2, 1994. Allen, *Hawai'i's War Years,* 269. The number of the Hawai'i-based cadre was 9824G3. I have been unable to locate any official documentation on this group of soldiers; the account here is based on my interviews with Alfred Jay and Leonard Wong.

47. *298th Infantry Regiment: INRG 298–0.1* (History) Washington National Records Center, National Archives, Record Group 407, 15 October 1940–8 May 1944.

48. 298th Infantry Regiment: INRG 298–0.1 (History) Washington

National Records Center, National Archives, Record Group 407, 15 Oct. 1940–8 May 1944.

49. Headquarters 298th Infantry: A.P.O. #709, 5 July 1944, Washington National Records Center, National Archives, Record Group 407, 5 July 1944.

50. Interview with Ah Leong Ho, June 30, 1995. Correspondence with Warren S. Zane, Mar. 14, 1993.

51. On the treatment of Asian American service personnel during the Vietnam war, see Peter Nien-chu Kiang, "About Face: Recognizing Asian and Pacific American Vietnam Veterans in Asian American Studies," *Amerasia Journal* 17:3 (1991), 22–40; and Toshio Whelchel, *From Pearl Harbor to Saigon: Japanese American Soldiers and the Vietnam War* (London: Verso, 1999).

52. Interview with Alfred Jay, July 28, 1994.

53. Interview with Daniel Lau, Aug. 2, 1994.

54. Interview with Stanley Lau, June 23, 1995. Lau is credited with four confirmed kills, three probables, and two more destroyed on the ground. He received the Distinguished Flying Cross, the Silver Star, and the Air Medal with five clusters.

55. Interview with Arthur Shak, June 27, 1995, and correspondence with Samuel Lum, July 1, 1993. Shak remembered running into Stanley Lau in Italy one day between missions.

56. Interview with William Lum, Aug. 10, 1994.

57. For a brief account of the "Dixie Mission," see Michael Schaller, *The United States and China in the Twentieth Century* (New York: Oxford University Press, 1979), 99–103.

58. This account of Clifford Young's military career is based on an interview with him, Aug. 8, 1994, and some previously written material he shared with me.

5. The Fourteenth Air Service Group

1. "Historical Report of the 1157th Signal Company Service Group," microfilm, Department of the Air Force Historical Research Agency, roll A0466, frame 1044. The official records of these units usually refer to personnel as "Chinese" and sometimes "Americans of Chi-

nese ancestry" regardless of place of birth or citizenship status. Except where specifying country of birth is necessary, I will generally use "Chinese American" or "Americans of Chinese ancestry" when discussing the men in these units whether they were born in China or in the United States.

2. *Statutes at Large of the United States of America,* vol. 40, ch. 69, 542–548. And see James B. Jacobs and Leslie Anne Hayes, "Aliens in the U.S. Armed Forces," *Armed Forces and Society* 7:2 (Winter 1981), 187–208; Lucy E. Salyer, "The All-American Soldier: Race, Military Service and Citizenship in World War I," paper presented at Williams College, Sept. 25, 2001. I am grateful to Lucy Salyer for sharing this paper with me.

3. Interview with Joseph Yuu, Jan. 30, 1994. Yuu's brother Allen would also eventually serve in the 1157th Signal Company, while another brother, Sun K. Yuu, would serve in the Third Army under General Patton.

4. Interview with Harry Lim, June 4, 1995. Christina M. Lim, Sheldon H. Lim, and Veterans of the 407th Air Service Squadron, *In the Shadow of the Tiger: The 407th Air Service Squadron, 14th Air Service Group, 14th Air Force, World War II* (San Mateo, Calif.: JACP, Inc., 1993), 6.

5. Oliver Borlaug, ed. *History of the 14th Air Service Group and the 987th Signal Company, China-Burma-India Theatre, World War II* (Garrison, N.D.: BHG, Inc., 1994), 51, 53. P-38s and P-40s are fighters, B-25s are bombers, and C-47s are transport airplanes.

6. "987th Signal Operations Company, Unit Historical Report," declassified document 735017, 1, 2. Interview with William Ching, July 28, 1994.

7. "987th Signal Operations Company, Unit Historical Report," 6–7.

8. "555th Air Service Squadron," microfilm, Department of the Air Force Historical Research Agency, roll A0959, frame 1932. Restricted Letter, "Reassignment and Manning of Certain Army Air Forces Units with Chinese Personnel," War Department, 16 Feb. 1944. "The History of the 14th Service Group (Chinese), Venice Army Air Field, Venice, Florida," microfilm, Department of the Air Force, Air Force Historical Research Agency, roll B0804, frames 1257 and 1259.

9. Lim, Lim, and Veterans, *In the Shadow of the Tiger,* 11. Interview with Mun Charn Wong, July 25, 1994. Interview with Joseph Yuu, Jan. 30, 1994.

10. Charles Leong, "Chinese GIs Like Army Says Soldier at Buckley," *Buckley Armorer* (Feb. 4, 1944), 1, 4.

11. Interview with James Jay, Aug. 21, 1992. Interview with Richard Gee, Aug. 22, 1993.

12. Interview with Harry Lim, June 4, 1995. Interview with Mack Pong, Aug. 8, 1991. Interview with Edwin Len, Aug. 2, 1992. Pong returned to the postal service after the war. His three brothers also served in the war.

13. Interview with Henry Wong, Aug. 30, 1990.

14. Interviews with Edwin Len, Aug. 10, 1991, and Aug. 2, 1992. Interview with Harvey Wong, Aug. 26, 1993. Interview with Edwin Len, Aug. 2, 1992.

15. Interview with Lui Eng, Aug. 24, 1993; and "987th Signal Operations Company, Unit Historical Report," declassified document 735017, 1 and 3.

16. "555th Air Service Squadron," frame 1932.

17. Lim, Lim, and Veterans, *In the Shadow of the Tiger,* 10.

18. "History of the 14th Service Group (Chinese), Venice Army Air Field, Venice, Florida," roll B0804, frames 1268, 1276, and 1279.

19. "555th Air Service Squadron," frame 1933.

20. Ibid., frame 1935. "The History of the 14th Service Group (Chinese), Venice Army Air Field, Venice, Florida," microfilm, Department of the Air Force, Air Force Historical Research Agency, roll B0804, frames 1286, 1282. Interview with Harry Lim, June 4, 1995.

21. "The History of the 14th Service Group (Chinese)," roll B0804, frame 1282.

22. "555th Air Service Squadron," frame 1935. "History of the 14th Service Group (Chinese)," frames 1281–1282.

23. "History of the 14th Service Group (Chinese)," roll B0804, frames 1283, 1328.

24. Tung Pok Chin, *Paper Son: One Man's Story* (Philadelphia: Temple University Press, 2000), 45–46.

25. James B. Jacobs and Leslie Anne Hayes, "Aliens in the U.S. Armed Forces: A Historico-Legal Analysis," *Armed Forces and Society* 7:2 (Winter 1981), 194.

26. Interviews with Cecil Young, June 23, 1993, and Aug. 19, 1994. Major Harry E. Haseleu took over as the commanding officer of the 555th in July 1944. The term *paké* was originally Hawaiian slang for "Chinese," but it came to mean lower-class, miserly, and not very intelligent Chinese.

27. Interview with William Ching, July 28, 1994. Ching informed me that it was fairly common for students from Hawai'i to attend either Yenjing University in Beijing or St. John's University in Shanghai.

28. Interview with Hon Chung Chee, Aug. 1, 1994; Borlaug, ed., *History of the 14th Air Service Group and the 987th Signal Company,* 17. Interview with Mun Charn Wong, July 25, 1994.

29. Interview with Cecil Young, Aug. 19, 1994. Interviews with Howard Chang, Aug. 4, 1994, Mun Charn Wong, July 25, 1994, and Cecil Young, Aug. 19, 1994.

30. *Gung Ho,* Dec. 25, 1943, 1. All of the citations to *Gung Ho* are to the reproductions found in Lim, Lim, and Veterans, *In the Shadow of the Tiger.*

31. *Gung Ho,* Dec. 31, 1943, 2.

32. *Gung Ho,* Jan. 21, 1944, 2.

33. "Unit History of the 407th Service Squadron," microfilm, Department of the Air Force, Air Force Historical Research Agency, roll A0954, frames 1354 and 1360. Lim, Lim, and Veterans, *In the Shadow of the Tiger,* 76.

34. The general details of the units' movements are based on the accounts provided in Borlaug, ed. *History of the 14th Air Service Group and the 987th Signal Company.*

35. For an illustrated account of the building of the road, see Don Mosser, *China-Burma-India: World War II* (Alexandria, Va.: Time-Life Books, 1978), 195–203. Despite the contribution made by thousands of African American soldiers in building the road, Chiang Kai-shek made it clear that they were not to enter China. All of the men I interviewed agree that they did not see black soldiers in China.

36. Malcolm Rosholt, *Flight in the China Space, 1910–1950* (Amherst, Wis.: Palmer Publications, 1984), 54. Interview with Hon Chung Chee, Aug. 1, 1994. Interviews with Edwin Len, Aug. 10, 1991, and Aug. 2, 1992. For brief accounts of the experiences of the 1544th Ordnance Supply and Maintenance Company and the 2122nd Quartermaster Trucking Company driving the Ledo-Burma Road, see Borlaug, ed., *History of the 14th Air Service Group and the 987th Signal Company,* 19–26, 66–69.

37. Wanda Cornelius and Thayne Short, *Ding Hao: America's Air War in China, 1937–1945* (Gretna, La.: Pelican Publishing, 1980), 256.

38. Edward Fisher, *The Chancy War: Winning in China, Burma, and India in World War II* (New York: Orion Books, 1991), 83. Rosholt, *Flight in the China Space,* 143; Mosser, *China-Burma-India,* 80.

39. "Night Flight over Hump," Charles Leong Papers, University of California, Berkeley, Asian American Studies Library, Box 2, Folder 3.

40. "555th Air Service Squadron," frame 1950. Borlaug, ed., *History of the 14th Air Service Group and the 987th Signal Company,* 48, 39.

41. Interview with Hon Chung Chee, Aug. 1, 1994. Interview with Howard Chang, Aug. 4, 1994.

42. "Unit History of the 407th Service Squadron," frame 1453.

43. Charles Leong, "Kunming V-J Day," Charles Leong Papers, Box 2, Folder 3.

44. Lim, Lim, and Veterans, *In the Shadow of the Tiger,* 61. Interview with James Jay, Aug. 21, 1992.

45. Hong quoted in Borlaug, ed., *History of the 14th Air Service Group and the 987th Signal Company,* 6.

46. This quotation brings together two statements by Richard Gee and Mack Pong, Aug. 22, 1993, in response to the following question: "When you were stationed in China, did you see yourself as an overseas Chinese going to defend China, or as an American to go where sent?" Richard Gee answered: "A sense of duty. Because I am an American in the American service as a citizen, native born, a sense of duty." Mack Pong replied: "We are Americans first."

47. "555th Air Service Squadron," frame 1967.

48. "History of the 14th Service Group (Chinese)," frame 1387. "555th Air Service Squadron," frame 1967.

49. Nancy Gentile Ford, *Americans All! Foreign-born Soldiers in World War I* (College Station: Texas A&M University Press, 2001).

50. "555th Air Service Squadron," frame 2012.

51. Interview with Lui Eng, Aug. 24, 1993. Interview with Woody Moy, Aug. 24, 1993. "555th Air Service Squadron," frame 2012.

52. Interview with Harry Lim, June 4, 1995.

6. *Into the Mainstream*

1. Interview with Dorothy Eng, June 9, 1995.

2. The documentary evolution of these acts can be found in the *United States Statutes at Large,* vol. 59, pt. 1, 659; vol. 60, pt. 1, 399–400, 975; and vol. 61, pt. 1, 401. The best study of the impact of these laws on Chinese American families is Xiaojian Zhao, *Remaking Chinese America: Immigration, Family, and Community, 1940–1965* (New Brunswick: Rutgers University Press, 2002).

3. "555th Air Service Squadron," microfilm, Department of the Air Force Historical Research Agency, roll A0959, frames 2059–2060.

4. This was the case in Louis Chu's famous novel *Eat a Bowl of Tea* (Secaucus, N.J.: Lyle Stuart, 1961). The central character, Ben Loy, is a veteran who served in the China-Burma-India Theater. He returned to his home village to marry a woman who had been selected by his parents.

5. Zhao, *Remaking Chinese America,* 82.

6. Wing quoted in Elfrieda Berthiaume Shukert and Barbara Smith Scibetta, *War Brides of World War II* (Novato, Calif.: Presidio, 1988), 198–199.

7. Zhao, *Remaking Chinese America,* 80. See also Xiaolan Bao, "When Women Arrived: The Transformation of New York's Chinatown," in Joanne Meyerwitz, ed., *Not June Cleaver: Women and Gender in Postwar America, 1945–1960* (Philadelphia: Temple University Press, 1994), 19–36.

8. Rose Hum Lee, "The Recent Immigrant Chinese Families of the San Francisco-Oakland Area," *Marriage and Family Living* (Feb. 1956), 15–16.

9. On the reasons behind the building of the Ping Yuen East Housing Project, see Nayan Shah, *Contagious Divides: Epidemics and Race in San Francisco's Chinatown* (Berkeley: University of California Press, 2001), 239–245.

10. All employment statistics in this section are taken from U.S. Department of Commerce, Bureau of the Census, *Sixteenth Census of the United States: 1940,* vol. 2: *Population: Characteristics of the Nonwhite Population by Race* (Washington: U.S. Government Printing Office, 1943), 5, 47, 97; and *Seventeenth Census of the United States: 1950, Special Reports: Nonwhite Population by Race* (Washington: U.S. Government Printing Office, 1952), 3B-19, 42, 80.

11. All employment statistics for Hawai'i are taken from *Sixteenth Census of the United States: 1940, Population: Second Series: Characteristics of the Population: Hawaii* (Washington: U.S. Government Printing Office, 1943), 5, 19–20; and *Seventeenth Census of the United States: 1950,* vol. 2, *Characteristics of the Population,* parts 51–54, *Territories and Possessions* (Washington: U.S. Government Printing Office, 1953), 52–13, 52–115–118.

12. Lawrence H. Fuchs, *Hawaii Pono: An Ethnic and Political History* (Honolulu: Bess Press, 1961), 377.

13. Lizabeth Cohen, *A Consumers' Republic: The Politics of Mass Consumption in Postwar America* (New York: Knopf, 2003), 137. This study provides an insightful critique of the GI Bill and how it served to discriminate against African Americans, women, and homosexuals.

14. Interview with Clifford Young, Aug. 8, 1994.

15. Charles Leong, "The Fighting Forties," 1, Charles Leong Papers, University of California, Berkeley, Asian American Studies Library, Box 5, Folder 27. Portions of this essay appeared in Victor G. and Brett De Bary Nee, *Longtime Californ': A Documentary Study of an American Chinatown* (New York: Pantheon, 1972).

16. Leong, "The Fighting Forties," 6–7.

17. Ibid., 3–4.

18. Ibid., 9.

19. Lui quoted in Diane Mei Lin Mark and Ginger Chih, *A Place Called Chinese America* (Dubuque, Ia.: Kendall/Hunt Publishing, 1982), 97–98. Interview with Woody Moy, Aug. 24, 1993.

20. Interview with Maggie Gee, June 5, 1995. For a study which documents the postwar struggle of the WASPs to gain veteran status and benefits, see Molly Merryman, *Clipped Wings: The Rise and Fall of the Women Airforce Service Pilots (WASPs) of World War II* (New York: New York University Press, 1998).

21. Interview with Marietta Chong Eng, Aug. 17, 1994.

22. Interview with Dorothy Eng, June 9, 1995.

23. Linda K. Kerber, "'History Can Do It No Justice': Women and the Reinterpretation of the American Revolution," in Kerber, *Toward an Intellectual History of Women* (Chapel Hill: University of North Carolina Press, 1997), 92. I am grateful to Patricia Hill for suggesting this collection of essays to me.

24. *Chinese News* (Nov. 15, 1940), 7.

25. Reed Ueda, "The Changing Path to Citizenship: Ethnicity and Naturalization during World War II," in Lewis A. Erenberg and Susan E. Hirsh, eds., *The War in American Culture: Society and Consciousness during World War II* (Chicago: University of Chicago Press, 1996), 202.

26. The information on Thomas Lew is taken from a series of interviews and correspondence with Lew from July 29, 1991, to March 3, 1996.

27. Interview with Yin Yee, Aug. 10, 1991.

28. Rose Hum Lee quoted in Harold R. Isaacs, *Scratches on Our Minds: American Views of China and India* (1958; Armonk, N.Y.: M. E. Sharpe, 1980), 120.

29. Rose Hum Lee, "Chinese in the United States Today: The War Has Changed Their Lives," *Survey Graphic* 31:10 (Oct. 1942), 444.

Acknowledgments

In 1991 I attended a reunion of Chinese American veterans of the Fourteenth Air Service Group. Having grown up on air force bases in the United States and abroad, and having played with my father's Flying Tigers patches, medals, and other war memorabilia as a child, I was curious about whether other Chinese Americans had a similar background. It had always seemed that we were the only Chinese American family on base, so the idea of a reunion of Chinese American veterans intrigued me. I spoke to Retired Colonel Thomas Lew, who assured me that I would be welcome. I quickly put together an information sheet and a brief questionnaire. When I arrived at the reunion I met Edwin Len of New Jersey, who quickly introduced me to other veterans, and thanks to their warm hospitality and eagerness to talk, I lined up a number of interviews. Cecil Young of Honolulu was especially receptive, and when he returned to Hawai'i he encouraged other veterans there to get in touch with me.

In the next several years I traveled to other reunions and to interview sessions in San Francisco, New York, Honolulu, and points between, conducting more than fifty interviews and corresponding with another fifty men and women. Many commented that no one, not even their own children, had ever asked about their wartime experiences. These men and women form the core of my oral history base.

Working on this book has deepened my conviction that history is fundamentally about individuals—people with desires, dreams, disappointments, and memories—and the social conditions that shape their circumstances. While the veterans and their families have been willing and generous "informants," they have also shown me great kindness and affection. I have spent time in their homes, been treated to wonderful lunches and dinners, received gifts for my new daughter, and been saddened to read their obituaries. I owe them all a great deal. The Chinese once had a saying: "Do not use good iron to make nails; do not use good men to make soldiers." Nothing could be further from a description of the men and women who contributed to this book. I have tried to present their stories with the same candor with which they were told to me, and in the same spirit of respect and reflection.

Among those who agreed to be interviewed or who corresponded with me, I would especially like to thank Mr. and Mrs. Hon Chung Chee, William Ching, Thomas Chinn, Dorothy Eng, Lui Eng, Marietta Chong Eng, Maggie Gee, Richard Gee, Ah Leong Ho, Alfred Jay, James Jay, Ralph Jung, Mr. and Mrs. Wing Fook Jung, Wesley Ko, Daniel Lau, Stanley Lau, Mr. and Mrs. Edwin Len, Mr. and Mrs. Thomas Lew, Christina Lim, Mr. and Mrs. Harry Lim, Dai Hing Loo, Samuel Lum, William Lum, Woody Moy, Mack Pong, Arthur Shak, Harvey Wong, Leonard Wong, Mun Charn Wong, William Seam Wong, Mr. and Mrs. Cecil Young, Clifford Young, Joseph Yuu, and Warren Zane.

Over the years of conducting research and presenting portions of this work at conferences, I have had the good fortune to receive advice, criticism, suggestions, and materials from a number of colleagues. Among them are Roger Daniels, Chris

Friday, Patricia Hill, Madeline Hsu, J. Kehaulani Kauanui, Lili Kim, Him Mark Lai, Bob Lee, Erika Lee, Karen Leong, Roger Lotchin, Gary Mormino, Franklin Odo, Gary Okihiro, Claire Potter, David Reimers, Lucy Salyer, Jack Tchen, Geoffrey White, Judy Wu, David Yoo, Henry Yu, Judy Yung, and Su Zheng. In addition to their scholarly insights, I value their friendship, companionship, and mentorship. I am also indebted to William Strobridge, Ralph Waara, and Henry Wong for answering questions about military institutions and regulations.

I am very fortunate to have found a home at Williams College, where teaching and scholarship are valued equally. I could not ask for better friends and colleagues than those I have here. Working with Robert Dalzell, Charles Dew, Cathy Johnson, Tom Kohut, Regina Kunzel, Karen Merrill, Kenda Mutongi, Bill Wagner, Chris Waters, Jim Wood, and my other colleagues in the history department has brought me much joy and the appreciation of professional friendship and collegiality. Williams College is also a place where undergraduates can be involved in our work in ways that benefit us both. Jessica Coffin, Cordelia Dickenson, Rebecca Krause, Osterman Perez, Geraldine Shen, and Alison Swain helped track down sources and provided insights while we discussed and practiced the craft of history. I am especially thankful to Rebecca Brassard, Margaret Bryant, Shirley Bushika, Donna Chenail, Cynthia Davis, and Lori Tolle, who spent many weeks transcribing hours of tapes of oral histories.

I am grateful for research grants from Williams College and the National Endowment for the Humanities, which enabled me to travel to archives and interview sessions during teaching sabbaticals. I am indebted to librarians and archivists, especially Wei Chi Poon of the Asian American Studies Library at the University of California, Berkeley, the staff of the Air Force Historical Research Library at Maxwell Air Force Base, Alabama, James F. Cartwright and Michaelyn Chou of the University of Hawai'i

Library, and the staff at the Williams College Libraries. I also appreciate permission from the University of Illinois Press to use material that appeared in my article "War Comes to Chinatown: Social Transformation and the Chinese of California," in Roger Lotchin, ed., *The Way We Really Were: The Golden State in the Second Great War* (2000).

At Harvard University Press, I am eternally grateful to Joyce Seltzer and Camille Smith for their incisive editing, patience, and encouragement. Together, they helped me think beyond the classroom and write a book our folks would read. I am also indebted to Annamarie Why for designing a cover that has brought my parents great joy, giving their images a place in the American public that their generation never thought possible. And I wish to thank Rachel Weinstein for her assistance in shepherding the manuscript through the publication process.

It is a pleasure to have the opportunity to thank in print those who shaped my development as a scholar and teacher. Peter Li of Rutgers University was the first to show me "one corner of the argument," while Chun-shu Chang, James Crump, and Ernie Young of the University of Michigan and Sucheng Chan of the University of California, Santa Barbara, taught me how to bring back the "other three." Their friendship and academic standards have been the models by which I have measured my own career. I can only repay them by extending myself to my colleagues and students as they did to me.

No one has sustained me more than my family. My parents, Henry and Mary Wong, have consistently encouraged and supported my personal and professional efforts, as have my brothers Keith and Christopher. I only wish our brother Kenny had lived to read this book. My deepest love and gratitude are reserved for my wife, Carrie, and our daughter, Sarah. The joy of their companionship reminds me daily of what is truly important in life.

Index

WITHDRAWN
U. C. BERKELEY LIBRARIES
C079622104